PRAISE FOR

How Queer Bookshops Changed the World

'I have savoured every chapter, practically every sentence... a testament to the small, unsung acts of love and perseverance that have allowed gay bookshops to flourish in different times and places, and to change lives.'

James Cahill, author of *Tiepolo Blue*

'A terrific read! Widely researched and full of fascinating information... Queer bookshops are places of refuge and resistance, groundbreaking then and necessary now – just as much. We must know our history and this is a vital contribution told with passion and panache.'

Jane Cholmeley, author of *A Bookshop of One's Own*

'A crucial history of love, struggle, solidarity and liberation, vividly brought to life and written from the heart.'

Jake Arnott, author of *The Long Firm*

'What a vital, life-affirming book this is. A.J. West is the perfect guide to a history of the most important queer space of them all: the bookstore. Without self-knowledge and without community, we're screwed – and West shows just how vital queer bookshops have been to both.'

Will Tosh, author of *Straight Acting*

'This is a unique and important book. A fascinating history – both expansive and intimate – told with the novelist's flair. I'm overwhelmed by the many stories of determined heroism and personal sacrifice... This is a really brilliant work which any queer person (or ally) ought to read.'

Christopher Stephens, author of *The Light of Day*

PRAISE FOR

The Betrayal of Thomas True

A *Sunday Times* Bestseller

'A vivid exploration of a largely forgotten aspect of London's past… compelling.'

The Times

'Plunges readers into the dark, treacherous streets of Georgian London in this epic adventure of love in a time of danger – a must-read for lovers of gritty, thrilling, historical fiction. An absolute page-turner!'

Hallie Rubenhold, author of *The Five*

'Very, very good.'

Stephen Fry

'A.J. West has a rare ability to bring voices from the past so vividly to life, they whisper in your ear and send shivers down your spine… heartfelt and meticulously researched.'

Janice Hallett, author of *The Appeal*

'Quite simply divine. Genre-defying, it is historical, a thriller, comedic, fantastical and above all a love story that had me in all sorts of tears.'

Jennie Godfrey, author of *The List of Suspicious Things*

'I've rarely been so transported, moved and gripped by a story from the first page… Heartbreaking, beautiful, lyrical. I was captivated… you won't want to put it down.'

Catriona Ward, author of *The Last House on Needless Street*

'A rare gem of a novel. Gorgeously gritty and compelling constructed with the pungent, evocative vernacular of the era, it's a darkly thrilling romp in eighteenth-century London that simmers with sinister menace and illicit temptation.'

Susan Stokes-Chapman, author of *Pandora*

HOW QUEER BOOKSHOPS CHANGED THE WORLD

A.J. WEST

A Oneworld Book

First published by Oneworld Publications Ltd in 2026

Copyright © A.J. West, 2026

The moral right of A.J. West to be identified as the Author of this work has been asserted by him in accordance with the Copyright, Designs, and Patents Act 1988

All rights reserved
Copyright under Berne Convention
A CIP record for this title is available from the British Library

ISBN 978-1-83643-169-5
eISBN 978-1-83643-170-1

Typeset by Tetragon, London
Printed and bound in Great Britain by Clays Ltd, Elcograf S.p.A.

No part of this publication may be reproduced, stored in a retrieval system, or transmitted, in any form or by any means, electronic, mechanical, photocopying, recording or otherwise, or used in any manner for the purpose of training artificial intelligence technologies or systems, without the prior permission of the publishers.

The authorised representative in the EEA is eucomply OU,
Pärnu mnt 139b–14, 11317 Tallinn, Estonia
(email: hello@eucompliancepartner.com / phone: +33757690241)

Oneworld Publications Ltd
10 Bloomsbury Street
London WC1B 3SR
England

Stay up to date with the latest books,
special offers, and exclusive content from
Oneworld with our newsletter

Sign up on our website
oneworld.co.uk

Contents

INTRODUCTION 1

Part One: First Editions

In the Beginning… 5
The Highlander & Dove, Cecil Court, London, 1749–unknown 7
La Librairie Parisienne, London, 1889–1898 14
Shakespeare and Company, Paris, 1919–1941 26

Part Two: A Cottage Industry

City Lights Bookstore, San Francisco, 1953–still open 41
The London Underground: Secrets in Cecil Court 56
The Adonis Bookstore, San Francisco, 1967–it's complicated 72

Part Three: Gay Power

The Oscar Wilde Memorial Bookshop, New York, 1967–2009 81
Glad Day Bookshop, Toronto, 1970–still open 102
Lambda Rising, Washington and Beyond, 1974–2010 111
Giovanni's Room, Philadelphia, 1973–still open 120
A Different Light, Los Angeles, 1979–2011 130

Part Four: A Bookshelf of One's Own

Amazon Bookstore Cooperative, Minneapolis, 1970–2012 141
A Woman's Place, Oakland, 1970–1989 149
Womanbooks, New York, 1975–1987 156
Sisterwrite, London, 1979–1993 160

Part Five: Rough Trade

Gay's the Word, London, 1979–still open	**173**
AIDS and the Queer Bookstore: Refuge and Resource, 1981–present day	**200**
Prinz Eisenherz, Berlin, 1978–still open	**209**
Vrolijk, Amsterdam, 1983–2017	**214**
Lavender Menace and West & Wilde, Edinburgh, 1982–still open as archive	**218**
Silver Moon, London, 1984–2001	**224**
Section 28: Pride and Prejudice, 1988–2003	**234**

Part Six: Pride Before a Fall

O Canada: The Trials of Glad Day Bookshop and Little Sister's, 1982–still open	**245**
A Different Light, San Francisco, 1987–2011	**256**
The Bookshop Darlinghurst, Sydney, 1982–2025, and Hares & Hyenas, Melbourne, 1991–still open	**262**
Genderqueer	**269**
Requiem	**274**
Revival	**287**
Queerly Beloved	**304**
Fanfare	**311**
ACKNOWLEDGEMENTS	**323**

Introduction

SO MUCH HAS BEEN WRITTEN ABOUT THE RICH AND varied history of LGBTQ+ literature, from books on the questionable queers of Ancient Greece, to the hidden homosexuals in Victorian novels, to modernism's revolutionary lesbians. We've got books about queer pirates, homosexual folklore and vampires who like to suck more than blood. But who is selling these books? And who inspired and supported authors throughout those censorious centuries to put pen to paper? Well, if you leaf carefully through dense thickets of venerable tomes, you might discover the humble queer bookshop lurking in the undergrowth, rather embarrassed, unassuming, quite probably asking to be left alone. It is this book's intention to study them in their own right, for the first time. Modest they may be, but deserving nonetheless of our adulation.

In the following chapters, we'll come across *Teleny*, a mysterious erotic novel published in 1893 about a Hungarian musician who makes an admirer climax with his piano. You may have heard of it, but did you know that a London bookshop played a titillating central role in its origin? Doubtless you have heard of James Joyce's *Ulysses*, but did you know it was first published by a pair of indefatigable lesbian booksellers who outwitted the Nazis? Meanwhile, when gay activists and British coal miners formed an unlikely union, it was a lesbian and gay bookshop in London that gave them refuge, while battling for its own existence. And how many of us know that the Pride movement itself was invented by the owner of the world's very first lesbian and gay bookshop?

Queer bookshops were never an afterthought for those who stood amongst their shelves and wept to find, for the first time, their own feelings reflected in books; to read truths denied them by parents, teachers, priests and politicians. Nor were they peripheral when they hosted meetings, which became marches, which became historic milestones, or offered sanctuary to men with nowhere to go when a likely death sentence was handed down by stony-faced doctors, nor when queer women gathered to fight misogyny, nor when trans people stood their ground in a hostile world. They are certainly not a sideshow today. In spite of book banning and a resurgence in queerphobia, they remain as vital as ever.

The generation that opened those first fully-fledged lesbian and gay bookshops are either retired or looking down from the great library in the sky. Many received little if any recognition in their own lifetimes. Now, therefore, is our chance to bring their stories to light, often for the first time, and to say a heartfelt 'thank you' to some overlooked heroes who never asked to be thanked, to give credit where it is long overdue, to tell the untold story of how queer bookshops changed the world.

Part One

FIRST EDITIONS

In the Beginning...

WHERE, PRECISELY, TO BEGIN? THE TRUTH IS, WE CAN'T possibly be sure where or when the first LGBTQ+ bookshop opened. Perhaps the question we ought to be asking is: what makes a queer bookshop in the first place? Does it need to have bookshelves, displaying queer books for all to see? What about a counter with a till? What if it stocks a mix of straight as well as queer books? Must it out itself publicly as a 'queer bookshop', or might it sell queer literature under the counter?

The temptation for the queer community is to loosen things up and reject such rigid rules, allowing the LGBTQ+ bookshop to live its own truth and identify however it likes. The problem with this approach, is that while some might find a certain elegance in egalitarianism, others will consider it a dereliction of historical duty. After all, if a queer bookstore can be qualified as 'any space offering access to any form of documented queer experience', then we can happily speculate that the first queer bookstore was a cave in Palaeolithic times where Og, the *Homo erectus*, and his Neanderthal companion, Jasper, allowed their fellow hominids to barter acorns for palm leaves daubed with lurid finger paintings. To be less glib, but equally inclusive, we could reasonably roll forward to Ancient Greece and wonder if Athenian philosophical schools acted as proto-queer bookshops, by allowing the likes of Herodotus, Plato or Xenophon to explore homosexuality while eating grapes in steam baths, if so they did. Their ideas were only written down on papyrus scrolls for reference and preservation (the Ancient Greeks preferred to share their notions orally) but if we're to be truly unbridled by a modern understanding of a bookshop's constitution, those scrolls and that forum *might* bear some of the key characteristics that signify queer bookselling today.

The point is, without a time machine and a very generous tenure, it's unlikely anyone will ever discover the true and absolute origin of the queer bookshop. Like a river, modern queer bookselling is a confluence born of many tributaries, some of them dried up and dammed, some running far underground.

So, for our purposes, let's agree that the first queer bookshop was:

a) a shop;
b) a purveyor of the printed word which …
c) touched meaningfully and substantively on homosexuality or queerness.

Which might as well lead us to a snuff shop in Georgian London…

The Highlander & Dove
CECIL COURT, LONDON
1749–unknown

A *'new sort of sin'*.

UNKNOWN

CECIL COURT REMAINS AN ICONIC BOOKSELLING LOCAtion in the West End of London. A Victorian gaslit street with a fine assortment of antiquarian bookshops nestled between purveyors of silverware, antique maps, costume jewellery and eccentric curiosities. With its looming butterscotch tiles marching five storeys high in an attractive boulevard, it seduces many a strolling tourist.* It was built in the early 1600s on land bought by Robert Cecil, First Earl of Salisbury, chief spymaster and *éminence grise* of the Elizabethan and Stuart courts respectively. Notable past residents include the poet T. S. Eliot, the legendary theatre actress Ellen Terry, and a child prodigy named Wolfgang Amadeus Mozart. Later patrons of the shops below included the writer and journalist Graham Greene and the mercurial occultist Aleister Crowley. Situated a short walk from the cinemas of Leicester Square, it was well known in the early 1900s as 'Flicker Alley', home to early British cinema.

---

* A few too many of them, some might say, and for all the wrong reasons. In 2023, when the sheer volume of wizard hats, loudhailers and speculative nonsense threatened to choke the life out of local businesses, Cecil Court shopkeepers successfully enlisted council backing to tackle the blight of wizarding tour guides making spurious connections between the Court and a certain franchise. Cecil Court remains Westminster's most picturesque Anti-Social Behaviour Focus Area.

Back in the 1700s, Cecil Court was less a court than an insalubrious passageway of rookeries, home to highwaymen, harlots and one rascally character named Elizabeth Calloway. Lizzie regularly annoyed her neighbours with rowdy late-night boozing, and in 1735 she stood accused of deliberately burning down her own brandy shop for the insurance money. Evidence was incriminating, if not damning. A plume of smoke was spotted mere minutes after Lizzie left the premises and she had recently purchased kindling. Perhaps most suspiciously of all, she had over-insured her stock and emptied her brandy barrels. She was calmly smoking her pipe and drinking good Sussex beer when she heard about the fire. 'I wish it may not be in our Court', she said, or, depending on the witness, 'I hope it's not in our house'. All circumstantial of course, but however it started, the fire spread at a furious pace to St Martin's Court, destroying fifteen houses. Lizzie was acquitted in spite of the evidence against her, but what's all this got to do with queer bookshops?

Well, in the year 1749 that very fire caused the gutted buildings to be knocked down and rebuilt. Come, let us step onto the fresh cobblestones of the new street and wander in by the light of our flaming torches. Here, we discover a frowsy crowd of old Londoners fighting and arguing to gain entry to an unassuming snuff shop. The Highlander & Dove specialised in a popular form of ground tobacco imported from the Americas which could be snorted up one's Georgian nose or stuffed inside one's rosy cheeks for an instant nicotine hit. A filthy but fashionable drug habit predating rolled cigarettes, snuff spawned all sorts of accoutrements, including filigreed snuff boxes and even miniature silver shovels to aid in the snorting. *Imagine*. But the Highlander & Dove was offering more besides tobacco. Records show that it was also selling a line of salacious pamphlets, guaranteed to make Londoners' wigs pop off. And one such pamphlet was proving as popular as it was provocative.

Satan's Harvest Home is a breathless rant about the sinfulness of Georgian London, the city having been overrun by whores, adulterators, fornicators, pimps and – not to be left out – homosexuals. After lambasting harlots for debasing their bodies and souls, and wealthy women for employing strapping young men as sex slaves, the pamphlet goes on to lament the new fashion for *Flats*. The 'game of flats' was a card game, but the women in the pamphlet had no interest in playing piquet. The full name for their 'ungodly' activity was: *Flats with a swinging clitoris* – vernacular for lesbian sex. According to our anonymous guide, this 'new sort of sin' was being practised 'in Turkey, as well as at Twickenham'. The pamphlet does not limit itself to lesbians, however, promptly swelling with turgid outrage as it exposes the perils of male masturbation, where a man may make 'this copulative science his whole study', exhausting his 'animal spirits' and causing injury, for 'those parts which suffer the violence of this exercise are liable to many accidents'. The author seems *very* well versed on the subject and it's hard to escape the impression that he was writing with one hand on his quill and the other banging the underside of his escritoire…

Though the titillating tome is written with all the necessary piety and disapproval one might expect from an upstanding author, many readers of *Satan's Harvest Home* would undoubtedly have bought the pamphlet for their own arousal. The final pages are populated with rampant homophobia and thumping accounts of sodomy and effeminacy. One chapter, catchily titled 'Reasons for the Growth of Sodomy', begins with a diatribe against overweening mothers and nurses who, in raising their boys 'in all respects like a girl' by feeding them tea and teaching them to dance and read along with 'other fiddle faddles', were unwittingly turning their boys into sodomites. What did they expect? These mollified lads were playing with *dolls* instead of soldiers! And taking carriages rather than dashing about the streets. This 'effeminate animal', the author warns, will struggle to pleasure his wife, while his own child – if he manages to sire one – will be a 'feeble, unhealthy infant, scarce worth the rearing'. Ultimately, this poor wretch becomes 'unfit to serve his King, his Country or his Family' and 'this man of clouts [nappies or diapers] dwindles into nothing.' Unable to please women, our unfortunate cove has sex with men instead – supposedly an easier option.* On the author goes, spitting about the new fashion for foppish wigs and hats and, worst of all, the 'hateful, predominant, and pernicious' fashion for men kissing each other instead of shaking hands: this being the fault of the immigrant Italians who were the 'mother and nurse of sodomy'. No need to repeat the worst the pamphlet has to offer; suffice it to say, the author goes on to celebrate the arrest and pillorying of 'sodomites' but suggests they really ought to be burned at the stake.

Satan's Harvest Home was published at a time of moral panic around 'molly' culture.† A collective calling itself the Society for the Reformation of Manners had appeared in the latter part of the 1600s, funded by the highest echelons of society. Its mission was to purge London of whores, homosexuals, and all forms of vice, all in the name of Christian morality. Effectively a self-governing religious vigilante force, it sent spies into secret gay meeting places called molly houses, entrapped denizens, accused them of sodomy, often with false testimony, then privately funded trials in which men were either fined, imprisoned, pilloried, transported or hanged. The most significant raids took place in

---

* It was understood at the time that homosexuals were either in the grip of misogyny or impotency. Likely some of them were, but that wasn't the reason they liked a bit of cudgel.

† The term 'molly' is thought by some to come from the Latin *mollis*, meaning 'soft', and will be familiar to the modern reader as the likely derivation of the term 'mollycoddling', whereby a mother – it is always the mother, isn't it? – turns her sons into spoiled weaklings by being overly indulgent.

1724, when Mother Clap's Molly House on Field Lane in High Holborn was raided, with more than forty men marched off to Newgate Prison. Transportation was itself often a death sentence at the time, with squalid, disease-ridden ships ferrying convicts through stormy waters to the colonies in North America or the West Indies. Pillorying, meanwhile, would often lead to the poor souls being choked or beaten to death by the baying mob as their wrists and neck were locked into the crossbeam. Indeed, the owner of Clap's, a straight ally named Mrs Margaret Clap (her real name) is thought to have collapsed and died after being violently pilloried for aiding and abetting her mollies. The author of *Robinson Crusoe*, political journalist, spy and satirist Daniel Defoe* proposed that mollies should be pilloried away from public scrutiny, not out of sympathy for the convicts, but because it was widely believed that buggery must be a form of contagion, leading the impressionable crowds to immoral and disorderly behaviour. Here he is, writing in his daily journal in 1707:

> Again, the publick Prosecution and Punishment of these hellish Creatures makes it but too publick, that there are such Monsters among us; O tell it not in Gath, nor publish it in Ascalon; smother the Crime and the Criminals too in the dark, and let the World hear no more of it.

Satan's Harvest Home was written at a time of fanatical ignorance, but in an era when lesbians, bisexuals and gay men were risking their necks to find companionship, friendship and sex.

---

* Defoe was himself pilloried in 1703 for publishing a satirical pamphlet. Found guilty of seditious libel, his experience was rather tame compared to the unfortunate mollies, with fans of his writing throwing him flowers while friends sold copies of his pamphlets to spectators who cheered him on. It's been suggested Defoe was himself homosexual, based on quasi-Freudian speculation about his various works, but there's no rigid evidence to support the theory.

The Highlander & Dove does not deserve to be counted as a queer bookshop *per se*. It was a purveyor of salacious, populist, violently homophobic, misogynistic bigotry. And snuff. Still, there is undoubtedly a double purpose to this sort of material. Similar to another literary hit of the day – a tongue-in-cheek guide to London's outrageous tourist spots titled *The London Spy* – it presents an intoxicating, sensual portrait of the City's underbelly which is likely why it sold so many copies. We can't know whether the owner of the Highlander & Dove was a homophobe or a secret molly themselves. All we *can* say with confidence is that the shop was selling published material about lesbian women and gay men which would most certainly have been bought and pored over by molly Londoners, as well as their heterosexual counterparts. And that's enough to qualify its place in the very early stages of this chronicle. It may not be the proudest starting point for the history of queer bookshops, but it does evidence an important point for any scholar standing knee-deep in the primordial soup of early Western bookselling. Centuries before the bookstores that make up the better part of this history opened their doors, queer lives were already forming an indelible part of our shared culture. In fact, the very same year that *Satan's Harvest Home* went on sale, one of the first pornographic novels in English was published and it too featured gay sex.

Memoirs of a Woman of Pleasure, better known as *Fanny Hill*, was written by John Cleland while he was being held in the Fleet Prison as a debtor. It was then published in two parts in 1748 and 1749, framed as a middle-aged woman's epistolic tale of her own misadventures. Cleland himself was thought by his associates to be a 'sodomite' and was duly imprisoned again following the publication of his story. Fanny, his heroine, falls on hard times and finds herself engaging in a bit of frisky flat-play with Phoebe, a bisexual prostitute, before going on to indulge in various outrageous encounters. Near the end of the second instalment, she witnesses two men having anal sex, which proves too much even for Fanny, and she duly trips over and knocks herself out. The novel caused outrage, and this last encounter was redacted from subsequent publications, some critics claiming it had never existed. They were proved wrong when it was found in the first edition.

Condemned, ridiculed and criminalised, homosexuals and gender nonconformists were scorned by publishers from the earliest days of the printing press, but crucially, they were not invisible. Those early references to queer communities set the foundation for the bricks-and-mortar lesbian and gay bookshops to come. But there could be no such bookshops without lesbian and gay *books* and it would be more than a century before the first outwardly homosexual novel was published; entering into existence thanks to a peculiar bookseller and his even more peculiar customer, thus giving rise to perhaps the greatest mystery in the history of queer publishing.

La Librairie Parisienne
LONDON
1889–1898

'Tell me your story from its very beginning ...'

THESE ARE THE OPENING WORDS OF A NOVEL, FIRST published in 1893, which has puzzled readers, collectors and academics for over a century. *Teleny* is a tale as old as time: boy meets boy, boy falls in love with boy, boys fall out of love, boy shares visions of the past resulting in debt, blackmail, disastrous affairs, rape and suicide. We meet our hero, the young Frenchman Camille Des Grieux,* as he remembers the first time he met René Teleny, a Hungarian musician. They proceed to fall in love so fervently they share a hands-free telepathic orgasm during a piano recital at a charity benefit. We've all been there. Set in *fin de siècle* Paris, it stands as one of English literature's earliest gay novels. There are works that might predate it – namely Jack Saul's *The Sins of the Cities of the Plain* (1881) and Alan Dale's *A Marriage Below Zero* (1889) – but it is argued that no previous work boasts *Teleny*'s richness of plot, textured characters and novelistic sensibility; nor its exploration of gay sex and sexual attraction; nor, for that matter, its lyrical depictions of male sexual arousal:

---

* Perhaps inspired by, but not to be confused with, Antoine François Prévost's *Manon Lescaut*'s Chevalier des Grieux. Full marks to any reader capable of such confusion.

my nerves quivered from head to foot with delight, then it sank downwards into my reins, and Priapus, reawakened, uplifted his head.

Priapus, for context, is a minor Greek god, dedicated to male genitalia,* and there is quite a lot of semantic priaping throughout the story, as the plot strains and elevates through a curly mass of metaphors:

> My blood began to boil and bubble like a burning fluid, so that I felt my – (what the Italians call a 'birdie,' and what they have portrayed as a winged cherub) struggle within its prison, lift up its head, open its tiny lips, and again spout one or two drops of that creamy, life-giving fluid.

Well, quite.

It's a wonderfully absurd novel in its own right, but our principal concern is with *Teleny*'s unique link to a Victorian ancestor of the queer bookstore.

La Librairie Parisienne was notorious to those 'in the know' for its illicit stock, mostly imported from Paris and Amsterdam by its French owner, Charles Hirsch. Monsieur Hirsch was careful to hide his stock from the authorities and was regularly visited by the police. Only thirty years prior, Lord John Campbell and the Society for the Suppression of Vice had introduced the world's first law criminalising pornography, the Obscene Publications Act 1857, and Hirsch was certainly skirting beyond the rim. His bookshop is hard to pin down but may have been located within one of the glass-fronted street-level premises of the Prince's Building, perched on the corner of Coventry Street and Whitcomb Street at the upper west corner of Leicester Square.

---

* Nice work if you can get it.

Fin de siècle London was proof that the Society for the Reformation of Manners had, in its molly house raids two centuries earlier, failed to rid the city of sodomy. The gay male subculture was still very much alive and frolicking. Young *flâneurs* cruised St James's Park hoping to pick up off-duty soldiers, while the shadowy nooks, dimly lit lanes and cloistered arcades of the West End writhed with the silhouettes of 'Mary-Anns' hoping to 'make a bargain'. The historic Alhambra Theatre was one such haunt, sitting at the eastern end of Leicester Square. Hidden within the murky hindquarters of the theatre, there lurked a gathering of often wealthy homosexual men seeking trysts with male prostitutes. The Strand Theatre had a similar reputation, and in April 1870, a national scandal erupted when a pair of ladies named Fanny Graham and Miss Stella Boulton emerged from a show, only to be arrested and charged with conspiring 'to induce and incite other persons feloniously with them to commit said crime', and 'disguis[ing] themselves as women and frequent[ing] places of public resort, so disguised, and to thereby openly and scandalously outrage public decency and corrupt public morals'. Quite a mouthful. You see, Fanny and Stella were not your average ladies enjoying a show; they were in fact Frederick William Park and Thomas Ernest Boulton. There remains some debate as to whether they would have identified as gay or trans in contemporary society, but regardless of their motivations, they shocked Victorian England to its core. They were subjected to physical examinations at Charing Cross Hospital, searching for evidence of sodomy, but in spite of all that probing, a jury found them not guilty following a sensational six-day trial. On hearing the verdict, Stella (Thomas) fell into a well-deserved swoon.

Still, homophobes can be terribly sore losers and the case is thought to have partly inspired the Labouchère Amendment in 1885, which stated:

Any male person who, in public or private, commits, or is a party to the commission of or procures (a) or attempts (b) to procure the commission by any male person of, any act of gross indecency (c) with another male person, shall be guilty of a misdemeanour, and being convicted thereof shall be liable at the discretion of the court to be imprisoned for any term not exceeding two years, with or without hard labour.

In law, there is often a direct correlation between absurdity and verbosity. The Criminal Law Amendment Act was originally intended to counter the sexual exploitation, abduction and detention of women and girls, raising the age of consent from thirteen to sixteen, and strengthening legislation against prostitution, including specific measures relating to brothels. It followed a series of disturbing articles by crusading editor W. T. Stead in his newspaper, the *Pall Mall Gazette*, in which scandalised readers were taken on a tour of London's 'flesh trade' which operated in the depths of the city's labyrinthine streets. However, the eleventh-hour addition of the Labouchère Amendment ensured that consenting homosexual adults were demonised alongside abusers of women and children. Now an individual could be charged with gross indecency even in instances where 'sodomy' could not be proven.

Victorian moralists knew that homosexual men were in their midst* and they found themselves on a particularly sticky wicket some four years after the Amendment was passed, when the Metropolitan Police uncovered a male brothel in no. 19 Cleveland Street, near Tottenham Court Road. In spite of the usual media frenzy, the case was hushed up when it was discovered that many of the brothel's patrons were not the sort of men Victorian

---

* And, in many cases, their underwear no doubt.

society liked to arrest. They included Lord Arthur Somerset, the Earl of Euston, and Prince Albert Victor, second in line to the throne.

Oscar Wilde, however, would be less fortunate, and it was the Labouchère Amendment that secured his conviction for gross indecency in 1895. More on that to follow, but for now, back to *Teleny*.

It was around 1889–90, and Charles Hirsch had only just moved to London from France, taking over management of La Librairie Parisienne. According to Hirsch in his *avant propos* (preface) to the 1934 translation, he was working in the shop one day when a peculiar man entered:

> I had noticed, because of his very particular bearing, his physique, and his slightly eccentric dress, a gentleman about forty years old, tall, rather podgy, a pale olive face without a trace of beard and slightly puffy, wearing a series of thin gold bracelets studded with coloured stones on his wrists.

This, unmistakably, was Oscar Wilde. Hirsch's telling of events some forty years later is clearly intended to tease and ultimately convince the reader that Wilde was co-author or at least the primary mover behind the book. By then, Wilde's name had been trashed and posthumously resurrected, adding considerable value to a lost work. Hirsch goes on to recall how the mystery gentleman 'hardly ever came alone' and was regularly accompanied by young men who 'accorded him familiar deference', giving him the air 'of a Master surrounded by his disciples'. Another of the French bookseller's regulars discreetly identified Wilde and after a few visits, the ostentatiously anonymous customer 'ventured to order certain licentious works of a special genre, which he euphemistically referred to as "socratic"'. Wilde was duly provided with a copy of *Alcibiade enfant à l'école* ('Alcibiade the Schoolboy'), a rather pungent fifteenth-century account of a male schoolteacher seducing a young boy, supposedly as a means of imparting wisdom:

> I will introduce into the receptacle of your intelligence seeds of fertile and agreeable doctrine which will seem supernatural to you.

In addition to this stinky little volume, a copy of the aforementioned *The Sins of the Cities of the Plain* was pressed into Wilde's hands; a short work of pornographic literature published in 1881, it follows a male sex worker – 'Mary-Ann' – as he recounts his likely embroidered exploits. The book also boasts additional material titled: *Short Essays on Sodomy and Tribadism* – the latter being the lesbian sexual practice better known today as 'scissoring'. We get a glimpse of what Wilde supposedly made of these books; he promptly returned them, along with other 'ribald titles, printed in Amsterdam, whose vulgarity displeased him'.

Over time, bookseller and customer seem to have established a certain understanding and in 1890 Wilde entered the shop with: 'a thin notebook, tied up and carefully stamped with a wax seal'. One can imagine the famous raconteur leaning in with a confidential air, whispering the words recounted by Hirsch many years later: 'One of my friends will come round to fetch the manuscript. He will show you my calling card.'

After a few days, a young man appeared, keeping the package for a while before returning it – larger now with added pages – saying another 'friend' would fetch it soon after. This curious ceremony took place three more times, only for the last gentleman to prove 'less discreet and less conscientious than the others', according to Hirsch, depositing the package with no wax seal, tied with no more than a simple ribbon. Hirsch could not resist:

It was a very strong temptation. I confess that I succumbed to it. I opened the package and on the grayish paper cover which held the bundle of handwritten pages I read the simple title written in large capital letters: *TELENY.*

Hirsch devoured the entire manuscript that same night, remarking on the:

> odd mixture of different handwritings ... by various hands! It was obvious to me that several unequally talented writers had collaborated on this anonymous but extremely interesting work.

Though expressed with due discretion, the Frenchman was clearly unconvinced by the quality of the writing, as we shall see, implying that the whole was somewhat smaller than the sum of its parts. He recounts handing the manuscript back to its owner (Wilde) and hearing nothing more about it.

If the novel itself, and the supposed literary legend propagating it, were extraordinary, the process by which it was written was relatively ordinary for its day. In the latter part of the nineteenth century, when erotic novels of any kind were banned from sale in bookshops, it was quite common for intimate circles of sexually frustrated male aristocrats to tickle their carnal lusts by writing pornographic novels together. It is notionally familiar to the 'soggy biscuit game',* only with literary prose in the middle of the circle rather than a digestive. Thus, when these young men weren't attending their clubs, extravagant parties, or Parliament, they were hunkered over their desks by the dim flicker of their gas lamps and candles, bashing out torrid 'round-robin' erotica with urgent industry.

---

* If you don't know, ask a male friend who attended boarding school, but be warned: the digestive biscuit will lose all innocence ... and crunch.

Richard Monckton Milnes – aka Lord Houghton – for instance, ran a '*salon érotique*' with his closest confidantes. Milnes was a renowned parliamentarian, women's rights campaigner, rejected suitor of Florence Nightingale and parapsychologist; a friend to the most celebrated society figures of the Victorian age, famed for his legendary breakfasts in his London town house and family seat in Yorkshire, Fryston Hall. As well as co-founding the London Library, he held one of the most extraordinary collections of erotica in Britain. Meanwhile his friend, the famed adventurer Sir Richard Burton, proved the perfect collaborator, travelling the world as a diplomat while bringing home books including *The Kama Sutra* (1883) – which he translated into English – and *The Ananga-Ranga* (1885), going on to author *The Book of the Thousand Nights and a Night* (1885–88), an erotic adventure more commonly known as *The Arabian Nights*.

Together, Milnes and Burton would publish their round-robin novels under pseudonyms, distributing a strictly limited number to their most intimate friends, 'for private circulation only'.

Milnes died in 1885, but Burton soon found a protégé in Leonard Smithers, a lawyer from Sheffield who was secretly translating and publishing erotica with his friend, a bookseller named H. S. Nichols. Together, the three men collaborated on several erotic works under a false imprint known as the 'Kama Shastra Society'. Around 1892, with support from their wealthy underground clientele, Smithers and Nichols moved from Sheffield to London. Nichols relocated his bookshop to Wardour Street and in 1893, he and his chum Smithers published a precious 200 copies of the best-known and finest example of all round-robin novels: *Teleny, or The Reverse of the Medal: A Physiological Romance of To-day*.

You see? We made it back again. And so, we return to Monsieur Hirsch.

Our bookseller had heard nothing of the manuscript for three years, not since it last left his shop in 1890, wrapped and beribboned, supposedly tucked under Oscar Wilde's arm. He got quite a surprise when it turned up on his counter, edited, typeset and beautifully bound by a fictional publisher, Cosmopoli.

Perhaps it's important to note here that Hirsch was not, as far as we know, homosexual. Nor, it seems, was Mr H. S. Nichols for that matter, nor Smithers who is described in a letter written by Nichols in 1937 as 'a lustful, lascivious and shameful satyr'.

Smithers, dubbed in his day the 'publisher of the decadents', was considered a monster of depravity by his mainstream counterparts and, while this might be a little dramatic, he was certainly an unsavoury man. A known womaniser, an unfaithful husband, a neglectful father and a boozer. Quoting Wilde: 'He never touches water: it goes to his head at once', and in a considerably more troubling tone: 'He loves first editions, especially of women: little girls are his passion.'

Thankfully, our French bookseller on the Strand, Monsieur Hirsch, proves less repulsive. But straight.

Apparent heterosexuals are often found at the vanguard of the underground gay and lesbian bookselling scene and we can only speculate as to why this might be. Some were running respectable bookshops while profiting from homosexual clientele — simply following demand — while others might have been bisexual or closeted themselves, hiding their lusts from a hostile world.

Teleny was indeed a beautiful book, bound in olive cloth with morocco labels and 'salmon pink wrappers'. However, Mr Hirsch, exhibiting a certain parental instinct, was not impressed when he encountered the finished product. He had no idea how the work had fallen into Smithers' hands, and by his own account, he wished it hadn't. 'The prologue had been omitted, which meant that the dialogue began abruptly without the reader being acquainted with the characters.' It was one of a few unforgivable transgressions and Hirsch branded Smithers 'a clumsy editor'.

As intimated earlier, modern scholars and enthusiasts continue to debate the origins of *Teleny*. In fact, some of those who contributed to the research for this book have stated with fervent indifference that Wilde simply couldn't have written any part of something so *dreadful*. Others, meanwhile, find Wildean beauty in the book's stylistic schizophrenia. Amongst the possible readers and contributors to the novel are Wilde's devoted first love and truest friend, the critic and art dealer Robert 'Robbie' Ross, also the novelist and Catholic priest Reggie Turner, along with poet John Gray, not forgetting Oscar's lover and eventual ruin, the unprincipled and bone-hearted Lord Alfred 'Bosie' Douglas, who, incidentally, paid for Leonard Smithers's burial in an unmarked grave. Did one of them hand the manuscript to Smithers after removing it from Hirsch's bookshop, or was it Wilde himself? If Oscar Wilde *had* approached Smithers to publish the novel, it seems unlikely he would have allowed it to be edited so clumsily; the author was exacting when it came to the publication of his work. Or is the entire tale nothing but a fantastic illusion? Perhaps the legend of the novel's origin was nothing more than a promotional enterprise, a stunt, designed to profit from Wilde's posthumous notoriety. What proof is there that Wilde walked into Hirsch's shop at all? For his part, Hirsch remained unyielding on the matter and though he fails to identify which specific passages were written by Wilde, he did meet the writer during his final months in France.*

Once the darling of Victorian society, Oscar's reputation was utterly destroyed by his conviction and incarceration for gross indecency in 1895 under the Labouchère Amendment. He had served two years' hard labour under the so-called 'Separate

---

* France had removed sodomy from the French penal code in 1791, and it was rumoured a number of British aristocrats had fled there in the immediate aftermath of Wilde's incarceration, fearing a similar fate.

System' which aimed to reform offenders by forcing them into a life of silence and crushing isolation, a torturous existence for one of literature's greatest minds. Intended to invoke remorseful contemplation, it caused extraordinary psychological distress, not least for Wilde, who left prison a broken man.

As we shall see, Oscar would later – *much* later – become a direct inspiration for the world's first fully-fledged lesbian and gay bookshop, but in his own time he supported other writers who would seed the ground from which queer bookselling grew. He wrote the obituary for the young, queer, Jewish poet and novelist Amy Levy, the first Jewish woman to study at Newnham College, Cambridge, before taking her own life in 1889 having endured a lifetime of misogyny and antisemitism. Meanwhile, following his death, Wilde's unfailing champion and literary executor Robbie Ross found a new role as a mentor to young 'musical' men (as gay men were then known) including the heroic war poets Siegfried Sassoon (with whom he had an affair) and Wilfred Owen (with whom he did not). In fact, the night before Ross died of heart failure, he and Sassoon had their evening ruined in a club when a pair of 'screaming queens' crashed the venue. Those queens were Scott Moncrieff, translator of Proust, and a boy actor and sometime bookshop thief, Noël Coward.*

Ultimately, whether or not Wilde himself committed his own writing to *Teleny*, the role Hirsch and Smithers played in its ever-growing renown reflects the fact that booksellers, even in Victorian London, have done far more than simply *sell* queer books; they have incubated, inspired and championed those literary figures who brought them into being.

---

* It's said that Coward stole comics from WHSmith and once walked into Hatchards in Piccadilly and filled an entire suitcase – itself stolen from Fortnum & Mason – with books before marching out unchallenged.

There is, alas, a sorry end to Hirsch and his bookshop on Coventry Street. In November 1898, five years after the publication of *Teleny*, he was arrested and charged on a warrant with 'selling obscene photographs'. When constables searched the basement, they discovered two cupboards fitted with false bottoms. Inside these secret compartments were several hundred illicit books in French and English. Hirsch was charged with distributing indecent material and was sentenced to nine months in Wormwood Scrubs. He returned to Paris shortly after his release, where he opened a similar shop at 24 Rue de Rivoli, before moving to 2 Rue des Pyramides, and then Galeries du Palais Royal, where he remained until his death in the mid-1940s.

Inadvertently, La Libraire Parisienne had become a crucible for a moment in time, an inadvertent gay space and a glimpse of the future. The new century would see those possibilities burst into life with a groundbreaking new bookshop in Paris, all thanks to the lesbian daughter of a Baltimore clergyman.

Shakespeare and Company
PARIS
1919–1941

'Paris was where the twentieth century was.'

GERTRUDE STEIN

PARIS, 1944. AFTER FOUR YEARS OF OCCUPATION, THE Nazi war machine was at last collapsing to the rattle of gunfire and the boom of distant shells. Allied planes swaggered freely across the sky, while below, the city held its breath. For too long, hope had been torture, and the citizens peeped through their shutters, all too aware that they mustn't wish, mustn't speak, mustn't even *think* the word 'Freedom'.

About halfway along the shaded Rue de l'Odéon lay a boarded-up shopfront and, above the walls of flaking cream paint, shutters which trembled to the noise of street fighting. Behind them, a pair of eyes peeped out, ever dark and alert. At the far end of the street, a vehicle crossed beneath the swastika-draped portico of the Odéon Theatre. It stopped suddenly with a squeak, then rolled backwards. Only the previous day, these streets had been the stronghold of the Nazis; now, the shrapnel-pocked walls looked down on a snaking convoy of green jeeps with white stars painted on their bonnets. A man stood tall, shielding his eyes, and bellowed an order, the dark eyes behind the window flicking wide. In a second, the shop doors flew open, and Sylvia Beach was out, waving her arms, followed by Adrienne Monnier. Their liberator had come, and when he pulled up outside, they knew the nightmare was over.

Sylvia Beach and Adrienne Monnier's liberation from the Nazis is a truly extraordinary tale, but how did these two indomitable lesbian booksellers meet, and what led to them becoming such towering booksellers? Their story begins across the Atlantic…

Sylvia Beach was born in Baltimore on 14 March 1887 and was educated at home, the middle daughter of Presbyterian pastor Sylvester Beach and Eleanor Thomazine Orbison. Aged fourteen, she moved with her family to Paris where her father served as an associate pastor in an American church, staying there for three years. In 1906, they moved back to the United States, settling on a street appropriately named Library Place in Princeton, New Jersey. Sylvester Beach's congregation was notable to say the least, with former president Grover Cleveland and future president Woodrow Wilson amongst the congregation. In spite of her return to America, Sylvia simply couldn't forget Paris, and she returned to France as a volunteer relief worker in 1916 at the height of the First World War.

It was in October 1917, browsing poetry at the Bibliothèque nationale, that she was directed to a bookshop called La Maison des Amis des Livres. Off she went, never suspecting she was about to meet a woman who would change her life.

That woman's name was Adrienne Monnier. Born in Paris in 1892, she'd graduated secondary school in 1909, aged seventeen, with qualifications to become a schoolteacher. She'd lived in England for a brief period and then returned to Paris, where she'd found work as a secretary at a mainstream publisher – a true achievement for a woman at the time. She held a burning ambition: to own a bookshop. There was little hope she could afford such a thing, until fate stepped in when her father was involved in a train crash. Monsieur Monnier – a railway postal worker – was seriously injured in the disaster, but his subsequent compensation allowed Adrienne to bring her ambition to life.

Still in her early twenties, she opened La Maison des Amis des Livres – 'The House of Friends of Books'.

The shop welcomed its first customers in 1915, quickly attracting some of France's best-known writers, critics, journalists and, as luck would have it, a young American woman named Sylvia Beach.

Sylvia had picked her way through the city, dressed in a stylish Spanish cloak and hat, with her dark hair cut in waves to her jaw. Photographs from the time reveal a striking face peeping from a bob with large, curious eyes and high cheekbones. There she stood at the shop doorway, astute and curious. Adrienne spotted her instantly. She went to welcome the visitor inside, but just as she did so, a sudden gust of wind blew the young woman's hat straight into the bookseller's hand. Adrienne passed it back to the American with a smile and they shared a brief exchange. '*J'aime beaucoup l'Amérique*', declared Adrienne, to which Sylvia replied, '*J'aime beaucoup la France.*' They dipped inside and talked. 'That was the beginning of much laughter and love', Sylvia would later recount in her memoirs. 'And of a lifetime together.'

In interviews, Sylvia would only ever describe Adrienne as her *friend*. The anodyne word obscured a passionate relationship built on love and mutual admiration, world-altering friendships, epoch-defining literary contributions and feats of death-defying bravery.

In 1919, with Adrienne's encouragement, some savings and borrowed money, Sylvia opened her own bookshop: Shakespeare and Company. 'A warm cheerful place with a big stove in winter', recalled one of their visitors, a solid, all-American man by the name of Ernest Hemingway. 'Tables and shelves of books, new books in the window, and photographs on the wall of famous writers.' Prominent amongst these were twin portraits of Oscar Wilde, signifying the owners' sensibilities. Poor, lamented Oscar had been redeemed and beatified in the twenty or so years following his death; his image an unspoken calling card to lesbian women and gay men alike. In the hedonism of '*les Années folles*', the relationship between Sylvia and Adrienne imbued Shakespeare and Company with its free spirit, encouraging the interchange of avant-garde ideas, philosophies and acts of social rebellion at the precise time a new form and character of literature was being born.

An instinctive bookseller, Sylvia saw an untapped market for books published in Great Britain and the United States, catering to Paris's large American and British expatriate community. Parisian customers, too, enjoyed reading books in English, long before they were translated.

The likes of F. Scott Fitzgerald and Gertrude Stein loitered about the shop, buying, borrowing and – no doubt – dreaming up books while discussing literary matters with their peers. In fact, Sylvia's store was so established amongst the literati she began loaning French francs to recently arrived writers who were stuck waiting for their dollars to come in.

André Gide was the first subscriber to the bookshop's lending library. The resident genius of the influential French literary review magazine *La Nouvelle Revue française*, Gide would go on to win the Nobel Prize for Literature in 1947. At the time he visited, he was busy outing himself as a homosexual by publishing *Corydon* (serialised privately in 1911–20; published in full in 1924), a series of 'Socratic' dialogues arguing that same-sex love is more authentic and natural than heterosexuality. His wife was horrified. It was, in its day, a revolutionary act, yet for Gide, speaking out about homosexuality wasn't so much courageous as it was vital. He had witnessed, first hand, Oscar Wilde's descent into ignominy and death. Though it was not a criminal offence in France to be homosexual, Gide was aware he'd stepped from the warmth of respectability into the cold climate of honesty. The Catholic right was already busily vilifying him, but Gide seemed to welcome the gathering frost as a form of creative enervation, stating defiantly:

'I must, absolutely *must* lift this cloak of lies that has sheltered me since my youth … I'm stifling under it!'

Alongside Shakespeare and Company's literary gods – Hemingway, F. Scott Fitzgerald, Paul Bowles, T. S. Eliot and many others – the shop provided a salon where new and controversial writing which risked censorship in Britain or America was both nurtured and protected. Yet it was one author and one book which carved the Shakespeare and Company name into the loftiest voussoirs of the queer bookselling acropolis.

The story goes that Sylvia crashed a party with Adrienne on a summer's day in 1920. The atmosphere was buzzing with excitement that a mercurial literary prodigy was in their midst.

James Joyce had been invited by the American poet, critic and incubating antisemite, Ezra Pound. After lunch, Sylvia encountered Joyce standing alone in a little library off the side of the dining room. She recalled the encounter in an interview with the Irish broadcaster RTÉ some forty years later.

> I was so frightened and so scared, and I imagined Joyce up in the clouds somewhere with the gods you see, I never thought I could meet him in the flesh, and it seemed terribly frightening, and I thought at first I would run home, but I didn't, I stayed.

Joyce was sober, having taken a characteristically sombre vow not to drink… until nighttime. He was 'drooping', remembered Sylvia. Joyce had shown little interest in his fellow luminaries, but when a young, female bookseller approached him, he lifted his long face and listened.

> We had a conversation together and he seemed very much interested in my bookshop. He said, 'What do you do?' and I said, 'I have a bookshop'. He said, 'give me the address' …

He took this all down peering very close at it because his eyes were not good and I was very much impressed with Joyce. I thought I'd never seen anyone so interesting and so fine.

Typically forlorn, Joyce went on to lament that his beloved masterpiece, *Ulysses*, was being suppressed in the United States and –

In fact, here, we might dash across the Atlantic for a little context. *Ulysses* had been serialised before its full publication in *The Little Review*, an avant-garde magazine founded by Margaret C. Anderson in 1914. Two years later, Anderson met the socialite Jane Heap – whom she called 'the world's greatest talker' – and the two wildly influential figures in the transatlantic literary scene became lovers as well as business partners. The magazine was soon publishing the greatest artists and philosophers of the time, from Gertrude Stein and Jean Cocteau to Max Ernst and Pablo Picasso, and had begun serialising *Ulysses* in 1918. Gasp-inducingly frank about bodily functions, things really hit the wall when the novel's main character, Leopold Bloom, masturbates on a beach while gazing at a seventeen-year-old girl called Gerty.

It was this particular episode that outraged the daughter of a lawyer, who referred it to the New York Society for the Suppression of Vice. A prosecution was launched and both Margaret C. Anderson and Jane Heap were convicted of obscenity charges, fingerprinted and fined. The US Post Office seized and burned four issues of the magazine, leaving US publishers unable and unwilling to publish *Ulysses*. Other countries, including the UK, followed suit.

Sylvia Beach, however, did not. We return to Paris and a gloomy James Joyce. Sylvia had a thought:

> I said to him: 'would you like me to publish *Ulysses*?' He said, 'I would.' He seemed very much relieved, in fact. Why, I don't know, because it wouldn't inspire confidence in anyone who

had such a book that he'd taken seven years to write, to give it into the hands of someone so inexperienced and young and with just a little bookshop not a publishing house at all … This *Ulysses* might have been in a great publishing house, you know, the great star of it, but Joyce was not afraid of that at all … so that's the way I started publishing *Ulysses*.

It was a formidable task. While Joyce used the bookshop as his office and study, Sylvia acted as his agent, publisher and publicist, dealing with his daily correspondence and helping to arrange his financial support, sometimes from the shop's meagre turnover. It was painstaking work preparing the manuscript, especially since Joyce preferred to write with coloured pencils. A true original.

In 1922, the Shakespeare and Company shop moved to Rue de l'Odéon and published its limited edition of *Ulysses*. It was assumed that Sylvia Beach had made a fortune from it. On the contrary, it left her out of pocket. There was no proper distribution system for books at the time and pirated copies began popping up in territories all over the world, cashing in on the novel's newfound fame and notoriety. Then, in 1932, James Joyce committed an act of betrayal that hurt Sylvia very deeply. A mainstream publisher offered him a considerable sum for world rights and he cut Sylvia out of the deal. In the preface to the new edition, Joyce belittled her involvement in the original publication, giving more credit to Ezra Pound, who had by then blossomed into an inveterate fascist. 'He [Joyce] has not only robbed me', Sylvia wrote to her sister, 'but taken away my character.'

What Joyce couldn't take away from Sylvia, however, was the pivotal role a lesbian bookseller and bookshop had played in bringing an acclaimed novel to the world when all others turned their backs. Her place in the pantheon of the most influential booksellers of the twentieth century was sealed, but there was more adventure to come, involving another complex male author.

Ernest Hemingway's reputation is today somewhat tarnished by the modern world's vigilance regarding misogyny, racism and vainglory, but in Sylvia's own personal recollections, he was – quite literally – a liberator. The bluff American had first visited the shop on his travels back from Italy in 1918, where he'd been an ambulance driver in the First World War. He'd proudly removed his shoe and pulled up his trouser leg to show Sylvia the still-fresh leg wound following an explosion. He was privately struggling with the post-war shakes, but to the young bookseller he was a returning hero, a part he would revive some two decades later.

By 1940, the skies above Paris were darkening to the promise of a second world war. Soon, Sylvia found herself looking on in horror as her once happy customers fled the city in panic.

> [The Nazis] were getting nearer and nearer and Paris was emptied of the Parisians, none were left hardly, and packs of dogs were running through the streets, wild hungry dogs, and the Parisians fled, I saw them passing Shakespeare and Company on foot, they didn't know where they were going, retreating, and the Germans were coming in.

Adrienne and Sylvia stood together, watching, as tears streamed down their cheeks. In their terror, they decided to keep their respective shops open. They knew the threat the Germans posed to books and citizens who didn't fit with Nazi ideology. After all, Hitler's thugs had begun their tempest of literary immolation on 6 May 1933 with the ransacking and burning of the Institut für Sexualwissenschaft (Institute for Sexual Science) in Berlin, led by an openly homosexual Jewish scientist named Magnus Hirschfeld, a world-leading expert in the emerging discipline of 'sexology'. He'd pioneered research into the lives of thousands of patients, including those he referred to as – antiquated now, but considered inclusive then – 'total transvestites' or 'extreme transvestites'. In the case of homosexuals, they were people born with male bodies but the sexual drive of women – and vice versa – positing that 'inverts' represented an intermediate sex, reflecting both male and female qualities. Through his published papers and outspoken advocacy, he argued that some people had 'characteristics that did not fit into heterosexual or binary categories', while demanding equality for homosexuals, transgender people and women. The Sturmabteilung could hardly get there quickly enough. It systematically confiscated thousands of books and documents from the Institute's library and archive, burning them four days later in a huge pyre. As many as 25,000 of the Institute's books, many containing unmatched insights into transgender history and medicine, were immolated in the Bebelplatz. Hirschfeld had already fled to France before the attack and died there in 1935.

Shakespeare and Company's days were numbered in Hitler's Paris, but Sylvia kept going for as long as she could:

> The Germans, of course, didn't like me, but I kept myself open for a while until a German officer came in and said 'I want that copy of *Finnegans Wake* you've got in the window.' I said 'That's the only copy left in Paris and you can't have it, you don't understand it anyhow, you don't know Joyce,' and he said 'Oh, but we admire James Joyce very much in Germany.'

The officer marched out to his military car and drove off. Sylvia hoped she'd seen the last of him, but he returned about ten days later, demanding to know where the book had gone. Sylvia had only hardened in her resolve.

> I said, 'I've put it away, it's for me,' and he was so furious, he said, 'Well, you know we're coming this afternoon to confiscate all your goods,' and I said, 'Very well do so,' and

he said, 'Now will you sell me *Finnegans Wake*?' and I said, 'Not at all, come along.'

Off went the officer again, booming that he would be back in two hours. Immediately, with help from Adrienne and their friends, Sylvia cleared out the shop, piling every single book into clothes baskets and carrying them upstairs to be hidden. When the Germans returned, the windows were shuttered, the shelves removed, even the name 'Shakespeare and Company' had been painted over above the door. In one sense, it was a victory, but hardly a triumph, as Sylvia retired upstairs to hide in the shadows amidst her baskets of books.

In the years that followed, the Gestapo kept track of Sylvia, visiting the little rooms above the shop, accusing her of having employed a Jewish girl, threatening: 'We have a black mark against you. We'll come for you, you know.' And they did. She was forced to leave the shell of her bookshop and was hustled into the back of a truck which transported her to a zoo-cum-makeshift prison and from there by train to a prison camp. She was locked up for months before being let out on sick leave. Back in Paris, she absconded and went underground until liberation finally came at the end of the war.

> They were shooting at us in the streets and my friend and I, Adrienne Monnier, went out one day because we heard the enemy was leaving us, and everybody was cheering and the Germans were retiring with all their mechanised forces down the street and they got so angry because people were so happy and waving WC brushes that they began to shoot their machine guns along the sidewalk and my friend and I had to lie on our stomachs and stay there until it was over and when we raised our heads, we saw the stretchers taking away wounded people.

It was, indeed, Hemingway who gave Sylvia and Adrienne their first sighting of an American face since the beginning of the war.

> I heard a noise out in the street, and I saw a string of jeeps with these men in them, and then I heard this big voice calling 'Sylvia, Sylvia.' I rushed down the stairs and he [Ernest Hemingway] picked me up and swung me around and then everybody was looking out of the windows so pleased and they cheered and then I took him up to Adrienne Monnier's apartment and he sat down there with his clanking machine gun and he was all bloody with a bloody battle dress and we asked him what he would like us to do for him and he said, 'soap, soap.'

The enemy were still firing their guns from the roof above their heads, so Hemingway took his men up for a shoot-out and, after several minutes of cracks and booms, Sylvia and Adrienne were saved. Their war was over.

Sadly, so was Shakespeare and Company. It never reopened; at least, not in a literal sense. It had altered bookselling forever, bringing to the world some of the most celebrated prose ever written. Between two cataclysmic world wars, a pair of fearless lesbian women had nurtured some of the greatest figures in twentieth-century literature.

Sadly, it must be recorded that Adrienne Monnier took her own life in 1955, while her companion and fellow bookseller, Sylvia Beach, died in 1962, a still sprightly seventy-five-year-old. Her legacy would endure.

Following Sylvia's death, the American bookseller George Whitman renamed his Parisian bookshop Shakespeare and Company in her honour. It had been called Le Mistral in the 1950s, hosting 'Beat Generation' icons including Allen Ginsberg, William S. Burroughs, Gregory Corso and a young American who – radicalised by the horrors of war – now takes us back across the Atlantic.

Inspired by Sylvia Beach and Adrienne Monnier, this bookseller would revolutionise American publishing and help to unleash a poem that thundered across the continents with queer rage.

His name was Lawrence Ferlinghetti – and he was straight.

Part Two

A COTTAGE INDUSTRY

City Lights Bookstore
SAN FRANCISCO
1953–still open

'I greet you at the beginning of a great career.'

LAWRENCE FERLINGHETTI

ON 11 JANUARY 1943, A RADICAL ITALIAN-AMERICAN publisher named Carlo Tresca was shot dead in New York. The incident was proof that such things can be equally shocking and entirely predictable. The sixty-four-year-old elder statesman of the socialist movement had long been using his newspaper, *Il Martello*, to hammer Italy's fascist dictator, Benito Mussolini.*

---

* Il Duce was a violent fascist dictator but also an avid reader and, little-known fact, a romantic novelist. In 1910, he published *The Cardinal's Mistress*, in which a seventeenth-century cardinal has an illicit affair with a woman named Claudia. His competency as a novelist matched Hitler's perspective-bending flair for painting, and perhaps it was Mussolini's artistic frustration that led, in part, to the establishment of the National Committee for Public Morality, a dark force tasked with censoring the Italian publishing industry.

One of its victims was a beloved (fascist-sympathising) Jewish novelist named Guido da Verona, who made the mistake of publishing a sardonic parody of Catholic Italy's favourite nineteenth-century novel, Alessandro Manzoni's *I promessi sposi* (The Betrothed). In his satirical version, da Verona's nun of Monza manifests lesbian tendencies, which caused such a stink in the Vatican everyone thought the myrrh had gone off. Da Verona was beaten up by thugs and, worse still, accused publicly of being a homosexual, while bookshops were attacked by packs of fascist students, just for displaying the book in their windows. Mussolini seems to have sympathised with the author initially but in 1939, at the rise of Italian antisemitism, da Verona was found dead, supposedly having shot himself in the head. His death remains a mystery.

Tresca exhibited a reckless political sensibility. Along with the Mob and worldwide fascism, he'd also managed – over years of doughty socialist campaigning – to make an enemy of the unions, the communists and, perhaps most dangerously of all, the NYPD. He was a walking ghost, complete with a barrel stomach, a bushel of hair like a pan of capellini, a pointed beard and a full, flowing moustache. He was one of those peculiar men whose head looks too small and too handsome for his body and the two were almost separated when an attacker narrowly failed to cut his throat. It was one of many close shaves, including a string of bomb attacks and death threats. He survived them all. Until, that is, 11 January 1943.

Most nights, Tresca would have been flanked by a pair of bodyguards, but on this particular evening, he'd changed his routine and stepped out with friends unprotected. A fatal mistake. At just before ten o'clock, while waiting to cross Fifth Avenue, he lingered beneath the glow of a streetlamp, illuminated in the murky depths of a wartime blackout, when suddenly there was a *crack* and the night lit up with a series of rapid blue flashes. Tresca turned to see a gunman stalking towards him, but it was too late to escape. He was shot multiple times in the head and body, raising his hands and stepping back into the road with a bewildered expression before stiffening like a board and toppling to the ground with a dead *thump*. His murderer was never found, the case left unsolved.

It was a violent end to the life of a true socialist hero, but we're not here for him; it's his son we're interested in – one Peter D. Martin.

Peter's mother was Bina Gurley Flynn, who'd had a fleeting relationship with Tresca after the ill-fated rabble-rouser dumped her sister, Elizabeth Gurley Flynn, herself a labour leader, feminist and pioneering civil liberties campaigner. Peter seemed destined to follow in his family's footsteps as a revolutionary of some sort, and in a way he did. In 1952, he created the pop culture magazine *City Lights*, named after the 1931 Charlie Chaplin film. It was one of the earliest pop culture magazines in the US and came at just the right time.

San Francisco in the early 1950s was a city of contrasts, marked by post-war prosperity, a booming population and urban renewal that led to both enrichment and displacement; brilliance beneath the palm trees and deprivation in the slums. Still, to the young at least, the city was experiencing a neon wave of optimism and expansion following the end of the war, sloughing off the mud-soaked serge of military life. The revolution was directly fuelled by the GI Bill, which gave returning veterans financial support for education and training, as well as low-interest mortgages and loans. The influx of young, demobbed men led to a vibrant nightlife, charged with blood-pumping possibilities. For Peter D. Martin too, the city offered the chance to fulfil a burning ambition.

His magazine opened above a florist at the edge of Chinatown on Columbus Avenue, a broad strip where elderly women still wore cloche hats and fur-trimmed coats, and Chinese elders sported the traditional *changshan*. In contrast, young men dashed across the climbing streets in their broad-shouldered jackets and fat, colourful ties, girls in swinging skirts and tailored blouses. In those very early days, Peter worked alone in his office to the clatter and ring of the trams, while, beneath his feet, the budding florist wilted and died. Peter took over the lease and opened a bookstore in its place. The extra income supported the magazine and paid the rent, but it was the side hustle that became the main event.

The shop was tiny, triangular and revolutionary: the first in the United States to sell only paperback copies of vaunted titles: an outlandish proposition at the time. Invented by the British founder of Penguin Books, Allen Lane, as late as

1935,* paperbacks were still seen as the hardback's runtish sibling: a little cheap, a little basic. They were not for *serious* readers, let alone serious bookshops.

But, sitting in his tiny store on Columbus Avenue, Peter knew – as all entrepreneurs do – that there's no greater mark of a fine idea than a snob's disapproval. He could see the demand for lightweight books by heavyweight authors, allowing readers to stow their latest read in their pockets as they hurried about the city. These paperbacks weren't just more *portable*, they were more *affordable* too, costing around twenty-five cents, while hardback books from traditional bookstores tended to cost anything between a dollar fifty and three dollars – the same as a nice shirt.

Peter sensed he was on to something. Soon after, he was hanging a 'Pocket Book Store' sign above his shop door when a familiar man walked up to him and lifted his hat.

Lawrence Ferlinghetti's poems had been published in *City Lights* but the two had never met. Like Peter, he was born in New York, the son of an Italian father and Jewish mother. His early years were marked by terrible loss; his father died shortly before he was born, and his mother was subsequently institutionalised in a psychiatric hospital. Tragedy and insanity, the perfect start for a bookseller. He was then raised largely by his aunt, before serving in the US Navy during the Second World War, arriving in Japan seven weeks after America dropped the second atomic bomb. The devastation he witnessed in Nagasaki filled him with

---

* The inspiration to bring high-quality paperbacks to the mass market came to Lane (according to company legend) while standing at a railway station in Devon with crime writer Agatha Christie. Frustrated at not being able to find anything to read, he wondered if there wasn't a way to put books on wire racks in public spaces rather than bookshops. So, contrary to general understanding, it was more the method of distribution, *not* the format of the covers themselves, that led to a sea change in publishing. People who would never have ventured into a bookstore could now browse titles at the chemist's or local bus station, paying no more than the price of a pack of cigarettes for their latest read.

a searing rage that guided his principles for the rest of his life. He became a radical, an anarchist, a poet and a passionate booklover. He moved to Paris in 1948 to study poetry at the Sorbonne and there, he became close friends with George Whitman, who – if you'll recall – went on to open the second Shakespeare and Company bookshop in Paris, following the death of Sylvia Beach.

Returning to America in 1951, Ferlinghetti headed to California, sensing something new and exciting was happening on the West Coast. Two years later, he was passing City Lights bookstore and stopped to talk to the owner, watching as the gentleman fixed a sign above the door. Nostalgic for his beloved Shakespeare and Company, he told Peter that he'd always wanted to run his own bookstore. They decided to run the shop on Columbus Avenue together and each put in $500. By the following year, however, Peter decided to sell his share and move to New York with his wife.

Thus, our story passes from Peter D. Martin to Lawrence Ferlinghetti, the sole proprietor of his own little pocket-bookselling business on the corner of 261 Columbus Avenue. From there, he launched City Lights Publishing, inspired by Sylvia Beach and Adrienne Monnier's Parisian model. Now, all he needed was his very own James Joyce to put the business on the map.

The Pocket Poets Series were cheap editions of poetry, priced at a few cents, packaged and marketed like popular contemporary books. Thanks to City Lights, poetry was becoming fashionable, portable and affordable. The bookshop quickly became a hub for a new movement, selling accessible classic and contemporary literature and radical and progressive journals. It remained open until midnight on weekdays, 2 a.m. on weekends, offering a place for the new 'Beat Generation' to hang out. The 'Beats' prided themselves on nonconformity but they could be as prone to racism, misogyny and homophobia as any other cohort of 1950s society. Ferlinghetti had no time for discrimination, and his shop was an established refuge for lesbian, gay, bisexual and 'transexual' visitors. Meanwhile, North Beach was fast becoming a queer neighbourhood. Just a block from City Lights was the legendary Black Cat jazz bar, which became a gathering place for alternatives, and is obliquely referenced in Jack Kerouac's *On the Road*,* while Mona's legendary lesbian bar, the first in San Francisco, was tucked around the corner on Broadway Street, close to Finocchio's drag club. Mona's 440 – later Mona's Candlelight after moving to 473 Broadway – gave cabaret performances by drag kings, carrying the club's slogan: *'Where girls will be boys!'*, while a portly drag queen named Jan Jensen sang popular jazz music in gowns dripping with sequins, her lips crimson.

The City Lights bookstore was sitting right at the intersection between Beat and queer subculture, an advantageous position for a radical bookseller.

In fact, despite his politics, Ferlinghetti was self-effacing and modest in person. And, as we have come to expect in these heady days before the advent of queer bookselling, he was straight – both sexually and by the standards of the Beats. A clean-cut family man, he hardly ever took drugs and projected a professional image. None of this dampened his rebellious impulses, however, nor his willingness to stand up to oppression and censorship. By 1954, he was well on the road to becoming a fabled LGBTQ+ ally.

* * *

The leading literary lights of the Beat movement are commonly cited as Jack Kerouac, Allen Ginsberg and William S. Burroughs, but there was a fourth member of that fated group, a striking young beau who allegedly exhibited greater talent than the rest of them put together. His name has the instant ring of celebrity

---

* *On the Road*: 'That's not writing, that's typing' – Truman Capote.

about it, as though dreamed up by Oscar Wilde himself, but in fact, he's almost entirely forgotten.

Lucien Carr attracted admirers wherever he went. Pretty and blond with a pixie face, charismatic and intellectual, he was the binding force that drew the literary Beats together. Burroughs was an old friend; he bonded with Ginsberg over Brahms, and befriended Kerouac through his girlfriend at a nighttime painting class. He was at the epicentre of a literary salon that would alter modern American literature forever and effectively give birth to queer publishing. Ironic, then, that homophobia would soon spare him the charge of murder.

It was just after midnight on 14 August 1944 that Kerouac rose from his table at the West End Bar. He'd been drinking with Carr but decided to leave alone and was walking towards Amsterdam Avenue on his way to his girlfriend's apartment, when he saw a tall, bearded man approaching him through the darkness. It was David Kammerer, asking where Lucien was.

Thirty-three-year-old Kammerer had been Carr's scoutmaster and mentor, nurturing the boy's literary talent. But Carr was more than Kammerer's protégé, he was his obsession. For years, Kammerer had trailed the boy from school to school, and now in a sinister escalation, he had followed the nineteen-year-old to Columbia University, New York.

Kammerer longed for a sexual relationship, but whether Carr had interest in men or not, he was dating a female student at the time, arousing the older man's anger and jealousy. Kerouac told Kammerer where to find Carr, and both Carr and Kammerer drank together until the early hours. At around 2 a.m., they left and headed down to Riverside Park, then lounged on the grass at the foot of West 115th Street. Kammerer made a pass, but Carr rejected it and they grappled. As the younger man struggled, he pulled out a penknife and jabbed it twice into Kammerer's chest. As Kammerer bled out in panic, Carr quickly rolled him to the edge of the river, trussed him up by the limbs, weighted him down with rocks and pushed him quietly into the black depths of the Hudson.

Doubtless, Carr's evening had taken a somewhat unexpected turn so he headed straight to Burroughs's apartment, then Kerouac's lodgings, confessing his crime. The three headed out, buried Kammerer's spectacles in Morningside Park, then ditched the knife down a grate in Harlem. With the vision of the electric chair before them, they wandered to Midtown. Finally, Lucien Carr handed himself in to the district attorney's office, ready to face the music. The next day, both Kerouac and Burroughs were arrested as witnesses.

Ginsberg escaped arrest, but he suffered nonetheless. Struggling with his homosexuality, he was in love with Carr and deeply fond of Kammerer and in the lonely weeks following the murder, he twice drafted suicide notes in his journal. Not only had the object of his infatuation been arrested for the murder of his friend, but Ginsberg felt, somehow, that the particular magic between the four creatives had died that night. In Carr, their leader – their beautiful, clever, inspiring, gathering bond – was gone.

Carr stood accused of second-degree murder, but the defence was strong. He was, after all, a young, white, middle-class student, forced to fight off the unwanted advances of a lascivious and predatory homosexual. The judge took pity on him, and the charges were commuted to manslaughter. He was committed to the Elmira Reformatory rather than the dreaded Sing Sing jail in New York and spent just eighteen months behind bars. Upon release, he embarked on a rather unassuming existence as a respected, though hardly vaunted, newspaper journalist.

To the modern eye, Kammerer's reported actions are deeply problematic to say the least, but there's no doubting that his homosexuality made his life less valuable in the eyes of the law, his gruesome murder somehow excusable, precisely because he was gay.

It was a fact that did not go unnoticed by Ginsberg, whose heart was howling. Ginsberg was born in New Jersey in 1926 to Jewish parents. Like Ferlinghetti, his mother struggled with mental illness and he grew up in an unstable environment, ever conscious of social stigma. He started writing poetry as a teenager, before attending Columbia University in New York to study literature. There he met Jack Kerouac and William Burroughs and became part of a bohemian group of students, hustlers, drug addicts and small-time criminals. In 1949, around five years after the murder of his friend, Ginsberg was arrested for possession of stolen property and – as part of a plea bargain – agreed to undergo treatment in the Columbia Presbyterian Psychiatric Institute to avoid jail time.

There, Ginsberg's homosexuality was treated as one of various psychiatric problems, an aspect of a warped and criminal mind. He blamed his homosexuality at the time on his mother, whose delusional, 'inappropriately seductive' behaviour had supposedly turned him off women. To the psychiatrists, this was proof he had suffered something they called 'genital shock', an archaic term referring to a child who has been exposed to adult sexuality. Indeed, Ginsberg's mother was herself placed in confinement and lobotomised before she died. He was subjected to psychological conversion therapy, believing his homosexuality could be cured, but avoided more drastic treatments such as electroshock therapy and chemical procedures, where subjects were encouraged to associate their sexual urges with fear and pain. His friend, Carl Solomon, was not so lucky. He was electrocuted in a failed attempt to turn him straight; another source of anguish that would come to inspire a poem yet incubating in Ginsberg's consciousness.

Allen moved to San Francisco in 1954, thinking (or kidding) himself cured, living with a woman in an elegant apartment with a good job at an advertising agency. Deep down, however, he knew it was a performance. At the house of an artist, he found himself transfixed by a full-length portrait of a young, naked man. This was cash-strapped bisexual model Peter Orlovsky, whom he met in the flesh soon after. They fell in love and became lifelong partners. Finally shirking off all pretence of middle-class propriety, he quit his steady job and devoted his life to poetry.

So, Ginsberg is standing at the door of the City Lights bookstore, where he would find a common cause with Lawrence Ferlinghetti who was still searching for a startling poet to bring his bookstore to fame and fortune.

One afternoon in August 1955, a year after arriving in San Francisco, Ginsberg sat at his typewriter and raked through his pain. The murder of Kammerer, the tragedy of his young infatuation, the torment of his mother, his own psychological anguish, the supposedly curative electrocution of his friend. The typewriter clicked, *tap, tap, tap*, then set to a beating rhythm...

On 7 October 1955, he stood before a small crowd in a converted auto-repair shop and performed his poem *Howl*. He was possessed by it, swaying to the musicality of the words, the chanting rhythm, like a cantor in a synagogue, savouring the outrageous language. As he drove on, so the crowd grew wild, Jack Kerouac encouraging his friend with cries of 'Go! Go! Go!'

Howl spoke of misfits struggling in the world, tortured minds and buttock-gripping lust, and in a *cri de cœur* against alienation and repression, it celebrated, at last, gay men in all their rampant, homosexual glory, not peeping furtively at their sexuality through a literary glory hole, but facing it full-frontal, turgid and dripping.

One can only imagine the gaping mouths and ringing silence once his recital was spent, Ginsberg panting for breath, hair dangling in cords as the makeshift gallery swung in the visions he'd created. Blond and naked angels had come from on high to pierce Turkish bathers with their swords. Semen had been scattered by seraphim, motorcyclists had been satisfied. The love that dared not speak its name had now been spoken, chanted, shouted out loud to the world, defiant as any pulpit-bellowed sermon. With it, a new kind of poetry was born.

Ferlinghetti, who had been in the audience that night, buzzed. He sent Ginsberg a telegram: 'I GREET YOU AT THE BEGINNING OF A GREAT CAREER', echoing the message Ralph Waldo Emerson had sent to Walt Whitman after reading *Leaves of Grass* a century before. 'WHEN DO I GET THE MANUSCRIPT?'

He got it promptly, and *Howl and Other Poems* was published in November 1956 to countercultural acclaim and mainstream horror.

On 21 May 1957, two officers of the San Francisco Police Department snuck into City Lights and purchased a pocket-sized copy. They obtained two warrants: one for Ferlinghetti, as the publisher of 'obscene and indecent' material; the other for the bookstore's Japanese-American manager, Shigeyoshi 'Shig' Murao, for selling it. The trial began on 16 August and, though the case against Murao was soon dropped, there was a real risk that Ferlinghetti would be convicted and *Howl* banned. The First Amendment of the US Constitution protected free expression, but 'obscenity' was traditionally seen as exempt, lacking cultural value and upsetting traditional order and morality. But things were changing.

An unrelated Supreme Court case – argued on 22 April 1957 and decided on 24 June the same year – reshaped the meaning of obscenity in American law and thus helped spare Ferlinghetti from prison.

As a bookseller, Samuel Roth was cut from the same cloth as Charles Hirsch of Victorian London's La Librairie Parisienne. His racy titles came wrapped in brown paper, sold in the sordid sanctum of Times Square, that red-lit flush of peep show doorways and bright flashing signs illuminating the faces of lascivious men with visions of parting legs and kissing lips; all the lowest temptations were alluded to. *Nude girls now! Strip show! Pepsi!* Like

Hirsch, and, before him, the owners of that snuff shop on Cecil Court, Roth knew what people wanted, and he was determined to give it to them, damn the censors.

The son of Ukrainian Jewish immigrants, Roth was born in 1897 and spent his early years in a small town by the Strypa River in the shade of the Carpathian Mountains. His family emigrated to the United States, hurling their four-year-old son into New York's Lower East Side: a pell-mell of clashing cultures, but also home to Yiddish newspapers, theatrical shows and strident rabbis. At eight, he was subjected to an exorcism after he brushed against a girl and saw a demon. He was a working 'man' by then, mind you, earning money for his keep as an 'egg chandler', holding thousands of the things up to the flame of a candle to peer inside and tell which were fertilised. By ten, he was a newsboy, selling papers on the street and by sixteen he was the *New York Globe*'s correspondent for the Lower East Side. He was also harbouring a deep resentment for his family's obsession with sexual restraint, leading to a teenage rebellion against his father and teachers. The die was cast.

After the First World War, Roth opened a bookstore, the Poetry Shop in New York's West Village, having a run-in with James Joyce and his publisher, a certain Sylvia Beach from Shakespeare and Company in Paris. He'd founded a selection of magazines including one titled *Beau*, a forerunner of *Esquire* and quite possibly the first American men's magazine. In another, *Two World Monthly*, he chanced his luck and published, without permission and in contravention of censorship, the most electrifying segments of James Joyce's *Ulysses*. In 1927, at Joyce's insistence, Sylvia Beach whipped up an international protest against Roth, with 167 authors coming out against him. Roth was now a very impressive thing: a bona fide international literary pariah.

The following year, embracing scandal, thirty-five-year-old Roth published a gay novel titled *The Strange Confession of*

Monsieur Mountcairn by Benjamin Francis Musser. Undaunted by outrage, he also published pirated editions of *Lady Chatterley's Lover*, likely the first American to do so. The outcome of all this was inevitable. In 1929, the New York Society for the Suppression of Vice raided his Fifth Avenue warehouse and found themselves unacceptably aroused. Roth was flung into prison for over a year for distributing pornography.

The Wall Street Crash bankrupted him the same year, but he bounced back in the 1930s with his William Faro imprint, publishing an expurgated version of *Lady Chatterley's Lover*, as popular as it was outrageous. As was another title, *A Scarlet Pansy** (1932) by Robert Scully, a picaresque account of a gender-defying adventurer.

Come 1940, Roth was running a mail-order business, allowing him to distribute queer and straight erotica to every corner of America. The Post Office was proving itself just as sensitive as the police, with inspectors regularly declaring his publications 'unmailable'. Perhaps the stamps wouldn't stick. He changed the name of his presses more than sixty times to dodge the authorities, branding his censors 'Dame Post Office'. The excitement around Roth's shameless behaviour climaxed when inspectors set up a special unit solely to hunt down his deliveries.

In 1957, they nabbed him. Roth was up in court as fast as a popped button, this time for publishing his erotic quarterly magazine *American Aphrodite*. Justices ruled that obscenity was *not* protected by the First Amendment, and the vile pornographer was locked up in Lewisburg Penitentiary for four years. All was not lost, however, at least not for other booksellers facing charges

---

* One of the most remarkable novels about queer identity published in the first part of the twentieth century, *A Scarlet Pansy* is a portrayal of turn-of-the-century queer life in New York but, more importantly, an early account of the sexual adventures of a triumphant transgender protagonist, Fay Etrange, referred to throughout, with ease and unconcerned savoir faire, as 'she'.

of obscenity. *Roth v. United States* had set in motion a series of cases that would incrementally redefine the legal understanding of the term 'obscenity'. The ruling jettisoned the so-called 'Hicklin test' which inspected specific passages, judging what impact they might have on vulnerable individuals. Instead, in Roth's trial, it was declared that obscene works should instead be judged on the whole, while their impact was measured not on an imaginary vulnerable waif, but on an 'average person'. So, regardless of Roth's* conviction, the trial significantly impacted the regulation of sexually explicit publications and set new legal precedents for future cases. The first of which would involve a Mr Ferlinghetti who had been found publishing a poem called *Howl*.

Back to San Francisco. Leading academics appeared as expert witnesses in court to testify to the literary merit of Ginsberg's poem and the judge ruled in the defence's favour thanks to Roth's recent trial, stating that *Howl* was of 'redeeming social importance' and that while some homosexual acts might be illegal, simply writing about them was not.

Allen Ginsberg became an international star, though he would later spoil his reputation by signing up to support the American paedophile organisation NAMBLA† (to howls of derision, he claimed his membership stemmed from his support for free speech rather than his being a proponent of paedophilia). Even so, his literary contribution and the changes it brought to US law remain significant. Besides, it is the bookseller we are concerned with, not the poet.

---

* For those still waiting for a gay male bookseller to arrive, Roth does not provide relief. He married his long-suffering and not unsatisfied wife Pauline in 1917. They had three children together. It has been claimed Roth might have been bisexual, but, unlike every other case surrounding this most fascinating man, the jury is still out.

† In the interest of historic detail and with a shiver: NAMBLA was the North American Man/Boy Love Association.

Ferlinghetti: the married father, the straight ally, the benefactor. Just as Sylvia Beach had proved with *Ulysses*, he recognised not only the literary genius of *Howl*, but also the potential for his bookshop to be a safe haven for a radical new voice. City Lights heralded the beginning of a tradition that would span generations. From a lesbian-owned bookstore in Paris to a queer-friendly bookstore in San Francisco, the germ of an idea had been carried across the ocean. Yes, Ferlinghetti might have been a married father of two, and he might not have described himself as a queer ally at the time, but his place in the pre-history of queer bookshops is indisputable.

It is almost time then. Queer books and poems were being written by celebrated writers who were claiming their own voice, now straight bookstores were selling them to an increasingly curious, if not entirely accepting, mass audience. Very soon, the first openly queer bookstore would arrive… though it would not be selling Ginsberg.

The London Underground: Secrets in Cecil Court

'SIR – We are homosexuals...'

ROGER BUTLER

AND SO, WE RETURN TO CECIL COURT IN LONDON. BY the late Victorian period, the thoroughfare had degraded into a slum, the area owned by shame-faced Prime Minister, Lord Robert Gascoyne-Cecil, Marquess of Salisbury. He was already under some pressure in the press after it came out that police officers were being stationed at either end of the court to prevent pedestrians being hit by falling masonry. Not a popular use of police time when officers were sorely needed in Whitechapel to catch a phantom serial killer named 'Jack'. Thus, Salisbury resolved to clean up his properties and his own reputation, conceiving of a smart and pleasant new street of respectable shops with flats above them where theatrical performers might be spared the perils of travelling home at ungodly hours amidst the hoi polloi. Residents were forced to move out and the dwellings and shops were promptly demolished. Gone, the crooked roofs and blackened brickwork, gone the Georgian bowed windows and gap-toothed cobbles, gone the snuff shop, remembered little better than the mollies hanged at Tyburn. As the sun dipped below the eaves of the 1800s, the little lane by Charing Cross was rebuilt in regimented elevations of red brick, clad with glazed faience tiling.

It's a funny thing, though, the way certain streets revert to form, as though the very earth below their flagstones is soaked with something flavoursome and intoxicating, and no amount of gable nor any weight of brick can conceal their true nature. So it was for Cecil Court which, by the 1950s, had shucked Salisbury's scheme for seemliness and snuck back to scandal. Various booksellers came and went, selling queer fiction under their counters, the surrounding snickets and lanes drawing gay men to their shadowy recesses. Police constables in plain clothes patrolled the Court, knowing the nearby urinals were popular with ardent cottagers. In fact, the open urinals on nearby Brydges Place were removed in 1953 to deter 'the behaviour of perverts' for the coronation of Elizabeth II, cleansing the processional route of superfluous queens.

The queer men of post-war Charing Cross were not so easily deterred, and try as the authorities might, the booksellers on Cecil Court continued to benefit from a steady flock of homosexual customers. After all, the surrounding West End theatres offered shops a perfectly respectable excuse to place photographs of dashing actors in their windows next to illustrations of sinewy male dancers, complete with muscly calves and bulging tights. If a police officer stepped inside, his beady little eyes would spy nothing more than an innocent collection of photographic muses for the figurative sculptor or illustrated sheet music for musicians. All the while, queer books were hidden from his view, wrapped in brown paper for good measure, and stowed beneath the counter. In that sense, not much had changed since Oscar Wilde patronised La Librairie Parisienne half a century earlier. The main difference was that homosexuality was being openly *written* about in traditionally published books.

Fritz Peters's much-admired story *Finistère* was published in 1951 by the then up-and-coming American publisher Farrar, Straus and Company (Robert Giroux had yet to join the party). They had previously published *Corydon* by André Gide in 1950. Gide, you will remember, was the first of Sylvia Beach's subscribers to the Shakespeare and Company lending library and *Corydon* was his most candid work yet: a series of dialogues on themes of homosexuality. First published anonymously in France, it was a courageous decision to name the author in the United States, but name him they did, and sales were strong. *Finistère* was a less literary venture, but it too exhibited brave candour, depicting gay men, their relationships and subcultures, while telling the story of young Matthew Cameron and his dashing tennis teacher, Michel Garnier. All is pleasantly gymnastic until family tensions lead to poor Matthew taking his own life. Meanwhile, Radclyffe Hall – who preferred to be called John by friends – penned the archetypal lesbian tragedy *The Well of Loneliness* at the height of their career. Published by Jonathan Cape in 1928, it stubbornly cast its gloom over the prospect of lesbian love, until it was banned for obscenity. James Barr's popular novel of the time, *Quatrefoil* (1950), weaves an uplifting story about empowerment and acceptance when a young naval officer Phillip Froelich is taken below deck by his older lover and fellow seaman, Tim Danelaw. All is shipshape until the author torpedoes their relationship by killing Tim off in an accident.

The enduring criticism faced by so many mid-century books about queer life is that, while they explored the thrill of homosexual sex, sexual awakening and the authenticity of queer love, they often paid a toll for their existence, ending in tragedy or beginning in tragedy or being characterised by the all-pervasive sense that the characters have been, or at some point really ought to become, tragic.

We may turn briefly to Claude J. Summers's exhaustive and utterly brilliant encyclopaedia, *The Gay and Lesbian Literary Heritage: A Reader's Companion to the Writers and Their Works, from Antiquity to the Present* (1995),* which reflects on the character of gay literature at the time.

---

* A title guaranteed to cause conjunctivitis.

In their association of homosexuality with violence, suicide, murder, or other kinds of pathetic death or at best with lives of freakishness or isolation, many works in the post-World-War-2 outpouring of published gay male writing seemed to confirm Mart Crowley's famous line in *The Boys in the Band*:* 'Show me a happy homosexual, and I'll show you a gay corpse.'

After stating the above, Professor Summers goes on to carefully unpick the claim that queer books of the mid-century were effectively forced by the publishing industry to present gay lives as endemically cursed. The genuflection of gay literature to such a demand wasn't total, he explains. There were – as we have seen – some happy gay stories, though they tended to be considered of less artistic merit. Secondly, Summers writes that while gay authors were trained to be tragic, their work should still be seen as an act of empowerment. If the authors who wrote those books had been drummed into misery against their will, they wouldn't have picked up the pen in the first place. And besides, there *was* misery, wasn't there? These novelists were not wimps. The fact they wrote their books at all in the face of such manipulative gaslighting and discrimination remains an act of defiance, regardless of whether publishers whipped them to write this way or that way or any other way that gave them the muse. As Summers states in a welcome burst of effusion after a breathless list of tragic gay books: 'during years when homosexuality was still largely invisible in society and chiefly vilified when it was spoken of at all, these writers persisted in writing about the subject and in mounting numbers.'

---

* Mart Crowley wrote the stage play *The Boys in the Band*, an instant hit off-Broadway, debuting in 1968 – a theatrical precursor to the Stonewall riots the following year. Incidentally, the father of queer bookstores, Craig Rodwell – whom we'll meet shortly – claimed in *QQ Magazine* in 1971 that a ubiquitous cola brand refused to have one of its signs on stage in the play to avoid giving the impression that 'queers drank their soda'.

Not all of those pioneers were men writing about men, mind you. The lesbian writer Mary Renault's bestselling hit *The Charioteer* was published in the UK in 1953. A romantic war story with a generally positive portrayal of its homosexual lead character, it was the first traditionally published novel in England to feature a gay romance with a happy ending.

A Room in Chelsea Square by Michael Nelson also sold well in mainstream bookshops, it being an overtly camp story about a wealthy gentleman luring an attractive young man to London. Nelson had published it anonymously, partly because of its homosexual content, partly because it was based on famous gay literary figures of the day. I shall name them in a footnote, at the risk of being haunted by waspish phantoms.* Following on from his review above, the sexually ambiguous poet John Betjeman praised *Chelsea Square* in the *Daily Telegraph*, complimenting the various male characters as 'not merely types, but flesh and blood'. At the more literary end, Christopher Isherwood's *The World in the Evening* allowed gay male characters a sympathetic send-off, and Truman Capote's debut novel, *Other Voices, Other Rooms*, published in 1948, catapulted the twenty-three-year-old to international fame, partly for its sensitive and ultimately optimistic depiction of a homosexual thirteen-year-old boy coming to terms with himself in strange surroundings, partly due to the author slapping an outrageous portrait of himself across the back of the first edition. The black-and-white photograph reveals the young author lounging on a sofa with golden hair, his right hand resting suggestively on his groin like a portrait of a Tudor monarch, only with his zipper where a globe should be. Staring out from the image with wide, innocent eyes and soft, indulgent lips, he begs the reader: *touch me*. Capote claimed he was taken by surprise

---

* Namely poet and critic Sir Stephen Spender, arts benefactor Peter Watson and literary critic and writer Cyril Connolly. A fascinating and attractive trio, geniuses all.

in the photograph – a preposterous lie – and the subsequent uproar made him the public personality (as well as the notorious author) he aspired to be. And good for him. Bold, unapologetic, sexual... society found itself arrested by a gay writer rather than the other way round.

Still, so many queer books of the time felt ephemeral in their depiction of gay men's lives, or found their depth by reflecting injustice, sadness, shame, a sense of isolation. Then, in 1956, James Baldwin's second novel, the defiant *Giovanni's Room*, was published, offering a substantial and candid homosexual romance, initially outraging the literary world before securing the author a hallowed throne amongst the pantheon of literary deities. A quite extraordinary achievement for a black writer at the time, though the cast of his book was entirely white. A lyrical novel of remembrance, loss and atonement, and that familiar sense that homosexual stories earn significance through pain.

Then there's Angus Wilson, a compelling reflection of the literary establishment's tentative acceptance of homosexuals. A flamboyant and emotionally volatile Oxford graduate and Bletchley Park codebreaker, he was remembered for his brightly coloured bow ties and a habit of throwing ink pots at people. The great codebreaker of the Second World War, Alan Turing was there at the same time and both seem to have taken advantage of the relatively permissive atmosphere at Bletchley, with Wilson particularly open about his homosexuality. It's a little-known fact that Turing wrote an unfinished short story of his own at the end of his short life, a sci-fi mystery set in outer space. The near-autobiographical 'Pryce's Buoy' is about an interplanetary travel scientist, Alec Pryce, who 'always liked to parade his homosexuality'. The two pages of scribbled prose show scant literary merit, but Turing's writing seems to have been influenced by that of Wilson, emulating the author's cynical, socially aware style. It's thought the story was penned by Turing when he was undergoing therapy following his prosecution in 1952 for 'homosexual acts' under the aforementioned Labouchère Amendment.* Turing accepted chemical castration as an alternative to prison and died in 1954, aged forty-one.†

Angus Wilson's first novel, *The Wrong Set* (1949), was a collection of short stories about gay life, followed soon after by a second novel, *Hemlock and After* (1952). Both earned favourable reviews and are notable here because the sexuality of certain characters was secondary to the narrative and perfectly natural rather than a tumorous growth of existential crisis. The fact that Wilson went on to become a Knight Bachelor and President of the Royal Society of Literature proves that the right people, of the correct pedigree, could live and write openly as homosexuals without necessarily wrecking their careers. However, gay men do have a taste for tragedy, foisted or otherwise, and by the end of his life, Wilson managed to do a good job of wrecking his own plinth. Poor and isolated, lashing out in public flounces, he was seemingly consumed by a bitter grudge against those he felt were better respected and better paid than an internationally celebrated knight of the realm. Nevertheless, he deserves praise and recognition for his bold books and for speaking out publicly and passionately in 1984 on behalf of the Royal Society when

---

* We might imagine Oscar welcoming Alan to the pearly gates in a white smoking jacket, remarking with languorous indifference: 'Darling man, welcome to Heaven, a sinfully delicious place. I should like to introduce you to Mr Labouchère, but, alas, he is beneath us.'

† Contrary to popular belief, Turing almost certainly did *not* commit suicide. He was far too intelligent, witty and pragmatic to recreate a Snow White pantomime with a poisoned apple. In actual fact, he'd been experimenting with cyanide in his home laboratory for some time and likely poisoned himself by not washing his hands properly before taking a bite. Hardly riven with self-hatred, his contemporaries remembered him as a jovial, energetic man with much to do and many plans for the future. Even modern society prefers to pity homosexuals before celebrating them.

the Gay's the Word bookshop was raided by Customs. More on that to come.

Following in the footsteps of Wilde and Turing, the respected journalist Peter Wildeblood was imprisoned in 1954 under the now depressingly familiar Labouchère Amendment for gross indecency and 'conspiracy to incite certain male persons to commit serious offences with male persons'. The *Daily Mail* newspaper's diplomatic correspondent was convicted along with Lord Montagu of Beaulieu and Michael Pitt-Rivers, their scandal having been splashed across the newspapers. The silver lining of this darkening cloud was a book that changed society's view of homosexuality and inspired many queer people to speak out. *Against the Law* was Peter Wildeblood's memoir, published in hardback in 1955 by Weidenfeld & Nicolson, then in paperback by Penguin two years later, reaching a far wider audience. It gave a fluent and highly charged account of events surrounding the trial and spoke eloquently about life from the homosexual perspective:

> The truth is that an adult man who has chosen a homosexual way of life has done so because he knows that no other course is open to him. It is easy to preach chastity when you are not obliged to practise it yourself, and it must be remembered that, to a homosexual, there is nothing intrinsically shameful or sinful in his condition. Everywhere he goes, he sees other men like himself, forbidden by the law to give any physical expression to their desires. It is not surprising that he should seek a partner among them, so that together they may build a shelter against the hostile world.

The book won sympathy from the public and stirred a hidden audience of queer readers with its calm yet insistent rallying cry.

We find one such reader sitting on a bench in Leicester Square one sunny Saturday afternoon in the spring of 1957.

Twenty-two-year-old estate agent Roger Butler had been roving around the 'seedy little bookshops' of Soho and Charing Cross – including Cecil Court no doubt – searching for something he couldn't quite identify. The new Penguin edition of Peter Wildeblood's book had caught Roger's eye through his milk bottle glasses and 'Prompted by no precise impulse except an unaccountable curiosity', he'd bought a copy for three shillings and sixpence, then taken it to one of the seats in the square. He tore through the pages, oblivious to the traffic and bustling crowds around him.

> It suddenly dawned on me that everything Wildeblood was saying about himself and homosexuality fitted my situation exactly. It seems extraordinary that I could have reached the age of 22 without recognising this, but so it was. Or perhaps it was – and this is more likely the case – that an awareness of my true nature had been growing inside me for some time but it took Wildeblood's book and his defiant exposition to make me face up to the same reality and spell out unequivocally to myself the uncomfortable truth, 'I am a homosexual.' I remember feeling no sense of shock, no surprise even, more a sense of relief at knowing exactly where I stood. I simply had never looked at myself so starkly.

Within a few months, thanks in part to the Peter Wildeblood case, *The Wolfenden Report* was published, recommending the decriminalisation of homosexuality.

> WOLFENDEN REPORT RECOMMENDATIONS, 4th September, 1957
> The following is a summary of our Recommendations:–
> Homosexual Offences
> We recommend:–

(i) That homosexual behaviour between consenting adults in private be no longer a criminal offence (paragraph 62).

(ii) That questions relating to 'consent' and 'in private' be decided by the same criteria as apply in the case of heterosexual acts between adults (paragraphs 63, 64).

(iii) That the age of 'adulthood' for the purposes of the proposed change in the law be fixed at twenty-one (paragraph 71).

(iv) That no proceedings be taken in respect of any homosexual act (other than an indecent assault) committed in private by a person under twenty-one, except by the Director of Public Prosecutions or with the sanction of the Attorney General (paragraph 72).

Parliament was minded to ignore its own advice, however, and Roger became one of the first volunteers at the newly formed Homosexual Law Reform Society, set up to pressure the government into taking action. Then, on 3 June 1960, three years after buying his book in a Charing Cross bookshop, Roger Butler did something nobody had ever done before. He wrote a letter to the *Spectator*, publicly stating that he was a homosexual, signing off with his own name, thus telling the entire country that he was an unashamed member of this reviled, criminal group.

> SIR – We are homosexuals and we are writing because we feel strongly that insufficient is being done to enlighten public opinion on a topic which has for too long been shunned …
> Yours faithfully,
>
> ROGER BUTLER

Nobody had ever outed themselves like that in the press before, at least not by choice. Previously, letters were signed anonymously or with invented names. The secretary of the Homosexual Law Reform Society, Anthony Wright, had himself written a powerful campaigning letter to *The Sunday Times* in 1954, emphasising his own sexuality, but signing it, 'Yours faithfully, HOMOSEXUAL'.

Roger's voluntary act of defiance inspired more to follow, helping to demystify homosexuality in the public consciousness. It was the inevitable next step on the road to equality, inspired by Roger's purchase of a humble paperback.*

Queer books were changing the world, but they lacked a native home. The idea of an openly queer bookshop remained a phantom notion, lurking behind camouflaged shop fronts, many of which were in and around the familiar setting of Cecil Court.

It is difficult for the historian to piece together precisely which units these shops inhabited mid-century, or to pin down when they opened or closed, or even to identify the owners. Many were, after all, breaking the law, so no detailed inventories were kept, no ledgers, no advertisements. To add to the researcher's incredulity and frustration, the tenancy records for the entire Court going back generations were seemingly destroyed in the 1990s. The following details then are recorded here for posterity from those who were running shops on Cecil Court in the middle of the 1900s, or frequenting the street as customers themselves, a compilation of memories, a collective folklore pieced together with scraps of detail drawn from various witnesses.

There was the Adelaide Bookshop (not to be confused with the Adelaide Bookshop at no. 9 Adelaide Street around the corner which sold books on fine art, which can only have led to excruciating confusion and embarrassment). The Adelaide Bookshop on Cecil Court was at no. 14, its large, square window

---

* His diary and many private letters would become a book in their own right, *The Light of Day: The First Man to Come Out at the Dawn of Gay Liberation*, by Christopher Stephens and Louise Radnofsky. A touching and expertly written biography.

displaying a scant few photographs of semi-naked men. It had virtually no stock, some of the Fortune Press* novels such as the *Diary of the Teens* books† and a couple of US cartoon magazines. Maybe there was more behind the counter. That would have been in the early 70s. It was considered the most scandalous shop on the street, certainly the most openly queer of them. None of the other booksellers – those who knew – spoke to the owner or went anywhere near the place. The current owners of the shop, Robert Mace and Christopher St James (a fabulous gay couple, as sparkly as their handmade designer jewellery, often seen in films, television and on the stage) recall moving in to find various nude postcards slipped under the floorboards and hidden underneath the woodwork surrounding the front window. 'Sporty pictures, muscle model sort of things,' says Christopher, 'not full-on sex porn, but we also found various cards to various gay establishments.' His discovery serves as proof that these nascent queer bookshops acted as signposting services for a hidden queer world. Alongside the posing pictures, they also found calling cards for secret gay bars. One was for the Festival Club on Brydges Place, where members were trusted with their own keys, leading to a rickety staircase up to three secret rooms, one for bopping, two for taking tea.

A man named Fred Sterling had an eponymous shop on the opposite side of St Martin's Lane. He and his Hungarian

---

* The Fortune Press, founded in London in 1924 by Reginald Ashley Caton, was a small but influential publishing house at the margins of the literary avant-garde, known for its finely printed poetry. In its early years, the press played a daring role in queer literary history, issuing homoerotic verse and works with openly gay themes at a time of strict censorship.

† Marketed as diaries of adolescent self-discovery, the writing was heavily coded with homoerotic undertones: idealised descriptions of boys' bodies, same-sex attachments and an emphasis on youthful intimacy. They were: *Fifteen: A Diary of the Teens by a Boy* (1938), *Sixteen and a Half: A Diary of the Teens by a Boy* (1940) and *Seventeen: A Diary of the Teens by a Boy* (1950).

assistant Steve sold 'vanilla'* gay books, studies of the male body, that sort of thing, and if you ever accused Fred of selling queer books, he'd have been utterly scandalised by the very suggestion – 'How dare you, darling!' he might say. 'We simply celebrate the beauty of the male body.' Still, the author and eminent profiler of the 'Uranian' poets,† Tim D'Arch Smith, recalls asking Steve if they had anything cheap, to which the Hungarian chirpily answered: 'me'.

Back in Cecil Court, Pocket Books at no. 9 was an undercover queer bookshop, later called Ballet Bookshop and finally, Dance Books. It was originally owned by Ted Mason, a young, scruffy, charmingly cheerful bookseller who did a good line in under-the-counter bookselling until his sudden death aged thirty-nine. It was taken over by his grieving partner, the Ballet Rambert dancer John O'Brien, who then met his enduring love David Leonard, who was roped into organising the bookshop's finances for the next twenty years. As with many queer bookshops to follow, book*keeping* was less appealing than book*selling*. They were the UK agents for an American publication, *Dance Magazine* – which boasted an ardent following of petite ballerinas and gay men alike, all showing appreciation of Rudolf Nureyev – as well as *After Dark*, which was ostensibly about theatre but actually featured topless American actors. Such stock attracted a regular flow of customers, including the thespian Sir John Gielgud,‡ who wouldn't have risked entering

---

* 'Tame' – for the vanilla reader.

† Uranian was a term coined before the widespread use of 'homosexual', meaning an intermediate sex, adopted by a coterie of English poets including Oscar Wilde's lover Lord Alfred Douglas. Wilde is recorded using the term once in a letter to his confidant Robbie Ross, describing it as a 'noble' love.

‡ Christopher St James of no.14 grew up in a theatrical family and well remembers Sir John knocking on the doors of younger male dancers to ask whether they were decent. Only if they replied in the negative did he pop in for a chat, feigning surprise and remorse: 'Oh my darlings you are *déshabillé*; I'll only stay for a few minutes.'

the grubby Adelaide Bookshop in a month of matinées, but was comfortable frequenting an establishment specialising in the theatrical arts. This was, after all, only a few years after he was arrested in a public lavatory for giving an undercover policeman a wink. David Leonard remembers him requesting a copy of the performing arts magazine *Plays and Players*, adding with a nonchalant flick of the hand towards something saucy, 'Oh, and one of those as well.'

'We had many gay customers', David recalls, 'but we were a dance bookshop, a serious bookshop not a *gay* bookshop. We were a community though, that's true, and gay-owned, with dancers and gay customers dropping in for a chat. They would stay a while and share their lives, and many customers became friends. There was the odd romantic pick-up, but we weren't a major dating site, they'd go to The Salisbury (the theatrical pub) on the corner for that.'

Though David is at pains to reiterate that his shop was 'never a gay bookshop', there were the early signs of what lesbian and gay bookshops were destined to *become*: discreet places for like minds, social venues for making new friends, somewhere to share local tips on the best – and safest – drinking holes, trusted spaces for the celebrity and the everyman alike to commune and explore.

Cecil Court then was known in creative circles as a place to go for queer books, but as we learned at the beginning of our history, it was also known as 'Flicker Alley', the home of the early British film trade. In 1961, the thoroughfare's booksellers, filmmakers and underground queer community came together in a controversial new film, itself heralding a less closeted Britain.

Victim was released in 1961, the first British film to actually name homosexuality. The word 'homosexual' isn't spoken until twenty-seven minutes into the film and there's no kissing or handholding, let alone sex, leaving much of the premise to be hinted at through sideways glances and suggestive language. But explicit or implied, the film was about queer men and their hidden lives. It's telling, therefore, that the screenwriters Janet Green and John McCormick chose a bookshop for some of the film's most important scenes, not least the climax. And where is the fictional bookshop located? Cecil Court.

The filmmakers used the interior of a bookshop owned by former Lancaster bomber engineer and married father, Bill Fletcher. His son Keith confirms the legend, remembering the ramshackle crew turning up with a tiny budget and filming for a short time before disappearing again: 'There was a screening', Keith remembers only vaguely, 'and a bit of a hoo-ha about it, but everything died down soon enough.' A hoo-ha is an understatement. Cecil Court found itself at the centre of a scandal, not least because the matinée idol Dirk Bogarde effectively outed himself by starring as a closeted gay barrister trying to unmask a blackmail ring. In an opening scene, amidst the gloom of tightly stacked bookshelves, a young man, Jack 'Boy' Barrett, attempts to find sanctuary with Mr Doe, a closeted bookshop owner, only to be turned away before hanging himself in a police cell. The film is replete with damning statements on the treatment of gay men, turning its glare on the Labouchère Amendment.

'Nature played me a dirty trick', complains one character in the film, while another says: 'Why should I live outside the law because I found love the only way I can?'

In the penultimate scenes of the film, before the traitor is revealed, Bogarde's character returns to Cecil Court to exchange a ransom for the negatives of an incriminating photograph. He presses his way to the back of the bookshop and finds what he's looking for in the 'Minor Classics' section, before being arrested. It is another deft reference to the character of books being sold in such shops and how they might have been euphemistically classified, the writers confident that such details would chime with worldly cinemagoers of the day.

Mentions of bookshops in novels and films about the queer underground might be fleeting, but the fact they're mentioned at all is significant. They are simultaneously conspicuous and elusive, significant yet peripheral, a setting for a scene, the backdrop for a knowing glance, but never quite in focus. At some point those shadowed, liminal bookshops would transform into something less furtive. The ingredients were all there, the authors and readers were waiting for them. The world's first certified queer bookshop would soon open its doors in New York City and we'll get there, right after a couple of riots, a pornographer and a poet.

The Adonis Bookstore
SAN FRANCISCO
1967–it's complicated

*'Fifteen million adults in the US today
are predominantly homosexual …'*

HAL CALL

THE WORLD'S FIRST RECORDED LESBIAN AND GAY BOOKstore appeared amidst the smoke of an LGBTQ+ uprising that's been overshadowed, until recently, by the subsequent Stonewall riots in New York. In similar fashion, the bookstore itself has been overshadowed, not by anyone's design particularly, merely by the human habit of remembering the most interesting story rather than the most accurate fact.

The stage for this historic milestone is set by an unlikely group of irrepressible sex workers in the burning heat of a San Francisco summer. It was 1966, in the beatdown 'Tenderloin' district,* a few blocks south-west and a world away from City Lights bookstore.

The Tenderloin was – and remains – a hub for sex workers, and many at that time were trans women. It was dangerous work and at the end of a long night they would gather to check

---

* The term 'Tenderloin district' has no definite origin. It has been accredited to a New York City police captain named Alexander S. Williams, in 1876, who apparently stated that he could afford to eat 'tenderloin' (filet mignon) instead of 'chuck steak' after being transferred to a more corrupt area because of the potential for bribing crooks. The alternative theory: that the area was seen as the juiciest 'meat' for cops to get their crooked teeth into, hungry for a feast of extortion and intimidation.

on each other, laugh, argue, console and exchange knowledge. Compton's Cafeteria at the crossroads of Turk and Taylor was their favourite haunt, better for talking than eating and their only option since the local gay bars kicked them out. Not that Compton's was accommodating. In an effort to deter their trans diners, staff frequently called the cops who would arrest the trans sex workers for the crime of female impersonation. This law, repealed in 1974, allowed people to be arrested simply for wearing makeup and 'women's clothing'. The legislation dated back to 1848, when residents of Columbus, Ohio were subject to an ordinance forbidding them from appearing in public 'in a dress not belonging to his or her sex'. By determining which clothes citizens *belonged* in, the state was effectively banishing people for wearing skirts or buttoning their shirts 'the wrong way'. In the decades that followed, more than forty US cities, including San Francisco, created similar laws limiting the clothing people were allowed to wear.

Officers had all the power they needed to harass those trans women at Compton's. There were often bust-ups, giving cops an excuse to raid the cafeteria on spec and shut it down whenever they pleased.

In '66, the community fought back. It was the first known queer uprising against police oppression in the United States, predating the better-known Stonewall uprising by almost three years, though hardly diminishing its relevance. There's no exact date for the riots because the media didn't cover it and police records are lost, but historians and activists believe it began when an officer attempted to arrest a trans woman who responded by flinging a cup of coffee in his face. The cafeteria erupted, patrons throwing sugar shakers, tables and dinnerware at the police, shattering the Plexiglas windows. The police retreated to the streets under assault from a barrage of purses and high heels. They called for backup, but the fighting continued outside the cafeteria. More protesters joined the fray, damaging a police car and burning down a newsstand.

Protests followed, then dwindled as the days became weeks and months, but while Compton's Cafeteria declined, the Tenderloin district developed an increasingly self-assured queer population.

The next summer, in 1967, a small shop opened its doors just three minutes' walk from Compton's Cafeteria at 350 Ellis Street. It didn't look like much and purposefully so, because the owner sought to avoid the attention of the police. It wasn't classy and it wasn't literary, and it sold more than books, but regardless of all that, arguably the world's very first openly gay bookshop was born. It was owned by a man named Hal Call.

Hal is a difficult guy to pin down, at once sanctimonious and dubious. The decorated Second World War veteran and journalist had arrived in San Francisco having lost his job at a Chicago newspaper. He'd been arrested for 'lewd conduct' at one of his favourite underground gay bars. He evaded charges with an $800 bribe and fled to the West Coast. Amidst the closeted anti-communist mania of McCarthyism, he joined the Mattachine Society: the country's first 'homophile' or gay activist organisation. The leaders of the society had just stepped down in fear and Call took their place. A shrewd businessman with a keen eye for an opportunity, he established Pan-Graphic Press, a gay publisher and magazine. His political goal wasn't so much to engineer revolution as to assimilate gay people politely into American society. His magazine, he stated, was intended to serve two audiences: 'the general public, educating Mom and Dad about the realities of homosexuality' and 'the homosexual, helping him raise his self-esteem and to fit in'. Articles discouraged gay men from trying to create a subculture, a position that led to friction within the Mattachine Society, causing members to leave and set up their own splinter groups.

Undeterred, in 1956, Pan-Graphic printed first editions of the lesbian magazine *The Ladder*, and in 1957, it published the first of its full-length gay novels, *The Gay Bar*. Pan-Graphic was now the number one gay publishing service in North America, distributing booklets on everything from 'transvestism' to West Coast bars and sexual philosophy.

From their offices in San Francisco's South of Market (SoMa) neighbourhood, Call printed and sold mail-order books via the Dorian Book Service to people in isolated towns across the country. Titles were advertised through Call's own *Dorian Book Quarterly*, a short circular that included order forms for subscribers. Its first issue, from January 1960, laid out its purpose:

> Fifteen million adults in the US today are predominantly homosexual, according to sexological research experts. Here is one of the nation's largest 'minority groups' not yet widely served with books explaining their situation and providing answers to the dilemma in which most of these people find themselves … *Dorian Book Quarterly* is a new and unique venture which will attempt to make known to an ever-expanding readership the availability of most of the books on sex variation and related themes.

Unfortunately, Pan-Graphic only published ten issues before Hal found himself searching for his true calling once again.

Thus, in March 1967, he joined forces with three friends – Bob Damron, Robert Trollop and Jack Tennyson – and opened the Adonis Bookstore. He knew better than anyone the growing and largely unsatisfied demand for gay novels and erotica.

The Adonis Bookstore catered to both. Inside, Hal sold his own pulp paperbacks along with nude male magazines, paintings, physique art, gay greetings cards, records, sculptures, novelties and gifts. It was an instant hit, with hundreds of visitors a day. Before the city's gay population migrated further south to the Castro, the Adonis Bookstore was a gathering place for activists, a safe space for the nascent queer radical movement, not to mention a recruiting ground for male models. Books, activism and pornography made for a heady cocktail and within a year of the store's opening Hal was busily collaborating with erotic photographers and adult film producers under his own production house: Grand Prix Photo Arts.

Police raided the shop in 1970, seizing his in-house films, but the charges were dismissed by a judge and the book and erotica store continued to operate. His victory set a legal precedent for similar businesses to come.

Some might question the Adonis's place in our historical timeline, considering its focus on erotica instead of literature, but it represents a defining moment in the evolution of queer bookshops. Perhaps this is a good moment to return to our required characteristics. A queer bookshop must be:

a) a shop; (Check)
b) a purveyor of the printed word (Check) which …
c) touches meaningfully and substantively on homosexuality or queerness. (Check)

It was an openly gay shop describing itself as a bookstore, owned and run by an openly gay man, publishing and distributing gay books to gay people, uncowed by conservative society and the law. Okay, so it probably didn't stock James Baldwin, Christopher Isherwood, Allen Ginsberg or Fritz Peters, and its customers were more disposed to *prowl* than *Howl*, and yes, the erotic novels were surrounded by sex toys and explicit cinefilm, but that would be the business model for a plethora of bookstores around the world right up to the present day, many of which couldn't have survived without mating literature with erotica.

Thus, the wait is over. We have been on quite a journey but, at last, the first approximation of a gay bookshop has opened its doors.

Now, we follow a guiding star to New York, where the first true queer bookstore is about to be born.

Part Three

GAY POWER

The Oscar Wilde Memorial Bookshop
NEW YORK
1967–2009

*'It was ... one of those moments in history
that if you were there, you knew, this
was what we've been waiting for.'*

CRAIG RODWELL

'WHEN I WAS YOUR AGE, WE WERE GOING OUT AND FINDing queers and beating them up!' Former prize fighter Henry Hank Castman towered over his fourteen-year-old stepson, Craig Rodwell. Slight and elegant, Craig had been arrested for juvenile delinquency after hooking up with a thirty-year-old man in the local park. He peered up at his stepfather and squared his narrow shoulders. 'You *big, brave* man,' he replied, his voice dripping with disdain. From an early age, Craig was undaunted by bullies.

His account of the incident can be heard in a crackly interview recorded in 1970 with Kay Tobin Lahusen, the first openly lesbian American photojournalist. 'That was my stepfather', he says with a deep sigh. 'Ugh, I hated him.'

Craig Rodwell was born on 31 October 1940, in Chicago, Illinois. His biological father had walked out when he was just a baby, leaving his mom, Marion, to raise the family alone. She struggled, and at six years old he was sent to a tiny Christian Science boarding school for 'problem boys'. In all, forty-five children bunked together in a trio of cabin-style dormitories in the middle of the woods. It was an intensely religious education, but hardly a chaste one. There were Bible readings every morning and prayers before lights out, but in the darkness of the dormitory, Craig found a boyfriend and, every day, they held hands on the way to the lunch hall, regularly sneaking into the woods to 'play'. Aged thirteen, he returned home to his mom and her new husband. By this point he was better educated in boys than maths but his thirst for romance was frustrated. He was enrolled in a mixed public high school with 600 boys and 600 girls – and scant opportunity to find a boyfriend – so he skipped class to go cruising in downtown Chicago. That's when he was arrested in the park for going home with a man seventeen years his senior, beginning a long and troubled relationship with the authorities.

Leaving high school, he eventually relocated to New York on a ballet scholarship, moving to Greenwich Village around 1959. He'd heard rumours of a growing queer community there and he was keen to get involved with the Mattachine Society. At eighteen he was too young to join, however, but he threw himself into the gay scene nonetheless, making friends, learning about gay culture, experimenting briefly with cross-dressing in underground drag bars on 42nd Street and generally finding his way around NYC's arcane map of hidden bars and cruising spots. One night in 1961, he was cruising Central Park when he found himself looking into the eyes of an attractive thirty-year-old stranger named Harvey Milk. Milk was closeted then, unlike Craig, but they made each other laugh and must have felt that tingle of electricity because, in a short time, they started dating. Craig, still only twenty, was impressed by his new boyfriend's apartment and grown-up job on Wall Street. Harvey would call him in the mornings to wake him up in time for ballet class and at Christmas he walked to Craig's digs laden with sentimental gifts. It was Craig's first grown-up romance but, alas, it wouldn't last. Less than a year later, while out for supper, Harvey brought up an awkward subject. He had contracted gonorrhoea and there was only one explanation.

He'd been monogamous you see, so... The conversation went as expected, with Craig admitting he'd been seeing other guys and the romance began to cool. Then, in 1962, Craig was arrested for resisting a police crackdown on inappropriate swimwear during a drag night at the popular gay cruising spot, Jacob Riis Park. He was treated violently by the prison guard and when he met up with Harvey after his release, it was clear things had changed. Harvey wasn't ready to come out, and Craig's lifestyle felt dangerous and messy. Over the following weeks, phone calls grew less and less frequent until they stopped talking completely. With no boyfriend, few prospects and a lifetime of displacement, injustice and heartbreak, Craig managed to get his hands on a bottle of sleeping pills and swallowed the lot. He'd left a note asking his flatmate, Collin, to break the news to his aunt who would then tell his mother. Many millions of queer people the world over can be grateful Collin came home early, discovered Craig on the floor with a faint pulse and rushed him to Harlem hospital. Craig's stomach was pumped and he was given a shot of adrenaline, coming back to life just in time.

It was a long path to recovery, and Craig didn't return to New York until 1964. Then, aged twenty-four, he was officially old enough to join the Mattachine Society, finding focus with the movement and instantly infusing it with his restless energy. He volunteered full time as vice-president and quickly formed the Mattachine Young Adults support group. He campaigned furiously and in 1966 took on the Mob and the government by staging a 'sip-in' demonstration at Julius' Bar in Greenwich Village. The State Liquor Authority's regulations prohibited bars from serving gay clientele, leaving gay bars in the clutches of the Mafia. The intention of the sip-in was for a bunch of lesbian and gay activists to sit at the bar and demand to be served, but unfortunately, someone had tipped the owners off and when the demonstrators arrived, the venue was closed.

More protests would follow, but Craig was growing frustrated by the cautious approach of the Mattachines. Under the influence of Hal Call,* their strategy was to present a 'respectable' front, with restrained behaviour and equally restrained attire. Homosexuals should wear sensible suits, they advised, and have sensible haircuts. This, in theory, would show the rest of the world that they were decent citizens, worthy of equality.

Aside from the fact that this strategy threw trans people and cross-dressing gay men and lesbians under the bus, along with anybody else incapable of, or unwilling to, assimilate with mainstream society, it simply didn't work. Diligently camouflaged gay people were still being hounded out, ostracised, sacked, pilloried, mocked, arrested, raped, ruined and murdered by people who didn't seem to notice their sensible clothing. Radical action was required.

Many members of the Mattachine Society were still using pseudonyms to protect themselves from the law, but Craig never did. His determination to campaign for lesbian and gay rights in his own name came around two years after Roger Butler's defining letter to the *Spectator* in the UK, and when viewed from afar, it's striking that these two young men – who knew nothing of each other – living very different lives on separate continents, nonetheless came to the same conclusion: the best antidote to homophobia was to be out and unashamed.

But something was missing. The movement needed to understand its history, share its philosophies, arm itself with facts and publish its ideas. There were no lesbian and gay community centres in New York, and, to Craig's frustration, it was impossible to find a serious selection of gay books in mainstream shops. Homosexuality was systemically catalogued as a deviance or

---

* Of the Adonis Bookstore, San Francisco. Hal espoused respectability before going on to become a pornographer.

disorder. Known as 'sickness theory', this was a broadly unchallenged doctrine tolerated by many within the gay community itself. Back in 1952, the newly created *Diagnostic and Statistical Manual of Mental Disorders* had listed homosexuality as a sociopathic personality disturbance, along with substance abuse and sexual disorders. It was used as the basis for laws and regulations denying lesbian and gay people employment. Many states also passed sexual psychopath laws that put homosexuals in the same category as rapists, paedophiles and sadomasochists. As we saw with Ginsberg, psychiatrists were practising conversion therapies including hormone treatments, aversive conditioning with nausea-inducing drugs, lobotomies, electroshock 'therapy' and even castration. Such terrifying cruelty might explain why the Mattachine 'old guard' chose assimilation over rebellion, but Rodwell petitioned the society to adopt a defiant new statement:

> In the absence of valid evidence to the contrary, homosexuality is not a sickness, disturbance, or other pathology in any sense, but is merely a preference, orientation, or propensity, on par with and not different in kind from heterosexuality.

If such intelligent discourse was to flourish, it would require a steady diet of serious literature, but all New York could offer at the time was a collection of grubby smut stores around Times Square carrying pulp erotic fiction and out-and-out pornography. Libraries and mainstream bookstores did carry homosexual books, but they'd be jumbled up with mainstream fiction, meaning they had to be rooted out or requested at the counter, risking exposure.

So, Craig set up a literature table at the Mattachine meetings, tucked away in a little office on Broadway and 26th Street, too closeted for Craig's vision. He wanted Mattachine to open a storefront. '[I] actually got them to let us look around at a few storefronts, the board of directors, but they chickened out.'

Jaded by the Mattachine's lack of affirmative action, he confirmed his resignation by letter in January 1967. If they wouldn't invest in a storefront, he would go it alone. He'd already anticipated their lack of support, so – starting in 1966 – he spent two summers as a house boy and assistant manager at a gay resort on Fire Island, working the bar, making beds and cleaning toilets, scrimping money for his project. The homophobic harassment of gay guests left him feeling grubbier than the toilet pans, however, with strict rules forcing men to face a woman while dancing to avoid homosexual contact. It was Craig's job to climb a ladder and shine a flashlight around the room, monitoring the dancefloor for 'violators'. The risk of arrest was ever-present. The Suffolk County police were raiding gay venues at the time, chaining men to each other or a pole before marching them to a makeshift 'court' set up in the back room of a drugstore, where fines were extorted. Craig worked during the height of the raids which were finally terminated by a series of trials in 1968.

By the end of the second season, Craig had scraped together $1,000 for his new shop and it didn't take long to find the right premises. A one-room, brick-fronted store was available at 291 Mercer Street, with a single plate-glass window. It was a classic side-street address with foot traffic, a deli on the corner, a pet grooming shop, a high-rise opposite and an art gallery nearby. All for just $115 a month. He told the landlord he was planning to open a bookshop named after the famous Irish playwright Oscar Wilde and – failing to appreciate the significance of the name – the owner agreed.

His proud mom Marion flew to New York from Chicago the day before opening, and Craig collected her from the airport, whisking her directly to the shop. After so many trials and such a difficult childhood, mother and son worked together overnight, putting together ten shelves and filling them with a modest selection of just twenty-five titles, three copies of each.

They had pamphlets and buttons (badges) too, promoting the homophile movement. Taking inspiration from his school and Christian Science upbringing, the shop would be modelled on the church's idiosyncratic reading rooms, offering a welcoming, quiet space for study and interaction with resources to learn from and discover 'the way'. He simply replaced God with gay rights. A queer thing to contemplate in hindsight ... the innate character of queer bookshops, first established on Mercer Street, was born of the Christian Science movement. Praise be.

By daybreak, the shop was ready to open, but would anybody turn up? There was already some buzz in the community thanks to a mysterious notice he'd placed in the *Village Voice* (New York's alternative newspaper) the previous week. 'Curious?' it teased. 'You should be.'

At 11 a.m. on Saturday 18 November 1967, Craig took a deep breath and unlocked the door to the world's first bookshop dedicated solely to gay and lesbian literature. A sign in the window declared: 'GAY IS GOOD.'

A pot of complimentary coffee was standing ready, along with pastries and the offer of a ten per cent discount for students and members of homophile organisations. All visitors would receive a free copy of the American Civil Liberties Union's statement on homosexual law reform.

In a press release for the opening, Craig announced his pioneering new venture, justifying the store's name.

> The example of his [Oscar Wilde's] life was a moving force in the recent passage by the English Parliament of the Wolfenden proposals which, in effect, legalized homosexuality in England.

The opening was a grand success. The windows were soon steamed up with customers' breath and steaming coffee cups. Even in those first few hours, patrons could sense they were witnessing something revolutionary. Nobody had ever seen such a liberated literary space for homosexuals before. There were no drawn blinds or 'adult only' signs or 'peep shows' or shuttered windows with suggestive neon signs. The building's landlord, mind you, was not impressed. On realising the nature of Craig's store, he threatened to challenge the lease but was thwarted by the terms of his own contract and all he could do was watch as his premises became a beloved hub for homosexuals. Some of whom were dealing with their own demons, struggling to find the courage to step inside.

It would become an established custom for all queer bookshops to have an invisible portal on their threshold, at once alluring and terrifying, but Craig and his new staff had never witnessed the phenomenon before. Nobody had. Customers were pacing back and forth outside, making a beeline for the door, then veering away at the last moment. Most would eventually plunge inside but some were overcome by the sense of exposure once they did, covering their faces with their hands. One of them would later recall his sense of fear approaching the shop door: 'I walked around the corner twice before going in the first time.' This was Jonathan Ned Katz whose book *Gay American History* would help create the field of lesbian, gay, bisexual and transgender history. Another early visitor was twenty-two-year-old Ora McCreary.

> On my first visit I approached it from the opposite side of the street, glancing into the shop with pretended nonchalance, my nervousness barely hidden. I walked back and forth probably ten times before I went in.

Ora would later become friends with Craig and his new boyfriend and shop manager, Fred Sargeant, enjoying dinners and impassioned debates in their new apartment on Bleecker Street.

By 1968, Fred was opening the shop in the mornings, with Craig taking over in the afternoons.

The couple wanted to make everyone feel at home with a warm greeting, hot coffee and a selection of doughnuts, not to mention a fluffy welcoming committee, 'Michael' and 'Albert', a pair of happy schnauzers. Albert the pooch was, by Craig's account, 'gay'. In that same interview with his lifelong friend and fellow activist Kay Tobin Lahusen, he laughs as he describes the dog's very promiscuous temperament, with a habit of sniffing and mounting male dogs on the street. 'Well, he tries to mount them', says Rodwell, 'but he's never actually managed to consummate it.' Poor Albert.

Meanwhile, the shop's new mail-order catalogue explained their mission to:

> provide young homosexual men and women with literature and counselling to help them gain a sense of pride and dignity as young Homosexuals. In our first year, we counselled more than 1,000 young people along these lines.

The Oscar Wilde was already changing lives, but not necessarily attitudes. Printing the mail-order catalogue was a trial in itself. The periodical contained nothing pornographic, yet Rodwell still had difficulty finding a printer willing to produce it. 'When I do manage to get someone who is willing,' Craig wrote in 1970, 'I am overcharged – a consequence of existing prejudice which puts the printer in a position to demand more, and myself in a position to pay up or give up.' In 1968, when Craig placed an ad in the *Village Voice*, he was told by a female clerk that he couldn't use the word 'gay' because she found the word 'morose', adding that she thought homosexuals were 'sick and perverted'. Craig protested to the editor but was ignored and had to switch the word 'gay' for 'homophile' until a series of protests forced the supposedly liberal newspaper to change its policy. A later Christmas advert for the Oscar Wilde included the call for customers to 'Buy Gay', the slogan morphing into the now legendary proclamation 'Gay and Proud'.

Meanwhile, there were ominous rumblings from within the lesbian community. Craig caught word that a picket was being considered to protest his perceived bias towards gay men, He responded in a letter to Barbara Grier – editor of lesbian publication *The Ladder* – stating that around twenty-five per cent of his customers were women and lamenting that he was finding it difficult to source books written by and for lesbians. He was stocking the study *Sex Variant Women in Literature* (1956) by Jeanette Foster and French novel *The Mesh* (1951) by Lucie Marchal, not to mention the Daughters of Bilitis newsletter – distributed by the first lesbian political organisation of the same name. Until the shop came along, the publication had been circulating through underground networks, accessible only to those who knew the right women. Craig also stated that he paid women booksellers the same as men. Grier replied immediately, reassuring him she'd heard nothing about a picket and wouldn't support one. But Craig didn't rest. As the shop grew, so did the diversity of its offering. Lesbian pulp fiction and poetry had their own sections, while leading lights of the scene such as Rita Mae Brown would later stand beside Christopher Isherwood and Tennessee Williams.

The criticism from the lesbian community must have cut deep. Craig took great pride in his philosophy as a bookseller. He would later satirise himself as a puritan, refusing to sell any material he considered 'sexploitation': things that made sex look dirty and furtive with 'a ten-dollar cover', and any books, pulp, porn or literary that – to Rodwell's personal judgement – used homosexuality to exploit people 'as a gimmick and a play on guilt, fear and prejudices'.

Rodwell devoted a section of the store to gay liberation periodicals, including the *New York Hymnal*, Rodwell's new periodical for the Homophile Youth Movement in Neighborhoods, HYMN.*

Word travelled fast across the States, then around the world, with lesbian and gay supporters writing letters from far-flung towns and cities asking for book suggestions. Tourists arrived by plane and sea, and American soldiers fighting in Vietnam ordered books and subscriptions to the *New York Hymnal*. There were more personal letters too, young men asking Craig how to come out and requesting reading lists to learn about gay culture. The Oscar Wilde was like a wireless receiver, turning the dial through the gabble of the mainstream to discover, amidst the static, a previously untapped wavelength of hidden voices expressing pain, sadness and rage.

* * *

Friday night, 27 June 1969. Craig and Fred closed up their bookshop after a long, sweltering day and were ready for some dinner and drinks. They wandered down to Washington Square Village to see friends – including their once-nervous customer Ora McCreary – then decided to make sure the bookshop door was secure before heading home to their flat on Bleecker Street. Reassured the shop was safe for the night, they meandered back via Waverly Place and caught sight of a crowd stirring outside the Stonewall Inn. They drew closer, wondering what was going on. The bar had only been raided three days earlier; surely it wasn't being raided again? They stood on the opposite side of the street as the crowd grew in size and anger. Officers in uniform and plain

---

* In praise of that rarest lexical polyptych, baptised here as a *punironymophone*: pun – irony – acronym – homophone: Him, Hymn, HYMN, Him + Hymn (+ blasphemy) = X.

clothes were seizing alcohol and arresting Mafia staff,* herding some 200 patrons into groups. Something was different; there was an indefinable electricity in the air. As patrons were identified and released, they hung around rather than scurrying home as they usually did. A paddy wagon (police transport) had been called and as people were loaded inside, the crowd grew volatile. Police took shelter in the bar and called for backup as bottles, rocks, pennies and cans were flung at the door and windows. Just then, a bellowing cry rang out, bounding across the street and racketing from the walls.

'GAY POWER!'

It was Craig. The response was tepid at first, but he shouted it again, Fred cautioning him to 'watch it' as officers turned towards them.

'GAY POWER!'

Now the crowd responded, cheering and taking up the slogan. Just then, a lesbian was bundled into the wagon, catching Fred's eye before facing the crowd in a fit of desperation and rage. 'Why don't you *do* something?'† she called.

The crowd exploded, rocking the wagon and hurling trash cans. A parking meter was used as a battering ram and the windows to the bar were smashed. Under siege, the officers realised things were getting out of hand.

This was the outcry Craig had sensed for years; the trampled rage and misery he'd been hearing in his shop for the past eighteen months; the injustice he'd battled since childhood. He and

---

* The raids were led by NYPD Deputy Inspector Seymour Pine, then aged fifty, who would later claim that while the police were biased against homosexuals, yes, the actual purpose of the raids was to tackle the Mafia. On a panel of the New York Historical Society in 2004, aged eighty-four, he was challenged to apologise for his part in the uprising, to which he dutifully said, 'I'm sorry!'

† She was later identified as the lesbian drag king Stormé DeLarverie, who would later claim – unchallenged – to have thrown the first punch at Stonewall.

Fred raced to the nearby subway station to call the newspapers on public phones. People *had* to know what was happening. Meanwhile, one of the officers had managed to squeeze through a back window or vent and raise the alarm. Reinforcements arrived with helmets and batons as the riot intensified.

By now, there were hundreds of protestors running circles around the enforcers who tried to repel them. Craig and Fred were in the 'mob', shouting chants until the fighting finally fizzled out some time before dawn.

There was no time for sleep and as the sun came up Craig got straight to work on his typewriter, bashing out a leaflet telling the story of the previous night's events. By the next day, Craig was pressing it into the hands of the Saturday crowd.

That evening, following Craig's report from the scene, the *New York Post* ran a disapproving story on the previous night's 'melee', recording Craig's now historic cry of 'Gay Power!'

It was an equally thrilling and anxious moment for the community, some of whom – including the Mattachines – feared such violence would set the movement back. Craig was uncowed and, thanks in large part to his leaflet, the second night saw an even larger crowd. Traffic was blocked, fires were lit and the police were out in force. The rioting continued until 3.30 a.m., when Craig returned to write a second, excoriating leaflet.

GET THE MAFIA AND THE COPS OUT OF GAY BARS.

The nights of Friday, June 27, 1969 and Saturday, June 28, 1969 will go down in history as the first time that thousands of Homosexual men and women* went out into the streets to protest the intolerable situation which has existed in NYC

---

* Transgender people, including Marsha P. Johnson and Sylvia Rivera, were present during the Stonewall uprising in June 1969. While accounts differ on specific actions, many historians agree that trans people played a visible and active role in resisting police harassment. More on Marsha and Sylvia to come.

for many years – namely, the Mafia (or syndicate) control of this city's Gay bars in collusion with certain elements in the Police Dept. of the City of New York ... The only way this monopoly can be broken is through the action of Homosexual men and women themselves.

As the journalist and scholar John Van Hoesen writes in *Insist that They Love You* (2025), there was now, thanks to Craig and the Oscar Wilde Memorial Bookshop, 'a documented political anchor to the Stonewall uprising'.

Today, the riots are often referred to as the genesis of the gay rights movement, but those involved at the time understood it was more of a lightning flash and thunderclap after years of building energy, a furious moment that transformed existing campaigns into direct action. And the Oscar Wilde Memorial Bookshop was at the very epicentre from the start. As Michael Denneny,* one of the first openly gay editors in American publishing, wrote in the *Harvard Gay and Lesbian Review* (1994):

> What was decisive was not the event itself, but how people responded, the immediate, spontaneous and utterly decentralized flurry of organizing, leafleting and pamphleteering that resulted ... it was this response, and perhaps above all the late Craig Rodwell's determination to commemorate the event the next June with the world's first Gay Pride March, that made Stonewall the shot heard round the gay world.

---

* Michael Denneny (1943–2023) was a pioneering book editor and the first openly gay editor at a major American publishing house. At St Martin's Press, he co-founded the Stonewall Inn Editions imprint, the first dedicated to gay and lesbian literature. His work gave voice to LGBTQ+ writers at a time when few mainstream outlets would, shaping queer literary and cultural visibility in the US.

Craig's tiny bookstore acted as a communication hub in the aftermath of the uprising. People made a beeline for Mercer Street, hungry for the latest news. Meanwhile, the NYPD carried on with its raids, most notoriously at the Snake Pit bar on 8 March 1970, when a frightened twenty-three-year-old Argentinian named Diego Viñales leapt from a second-floor window onto sharp railings. Fire crews had to cut through the iron spikes and rush both man and railings to St Vincent's Hospital where a vigil was kept, praying for his recovery. He did recover, but still the raids continued.

By this point, Craig sensed that momentum was seeping away and if they didn't do something significant, people would lose focus. As John Van Hoesen recounts, it was at Craig and Fred's apartment on nearby Bleecker Street where the notion of a protest march was dreamed up, along with fellow activists Ellen Broidy and her girlfriend, Linda Rhodes. It would be called the Christopher Street Liberation Day March.

Now was the moment to speak up in their own voices, or others would do it for them. Greater visibility was leading to an increase in homophobic attacks, physical and written, with *Time* magazine publishing a deplorable cover story asking whether homosexuals were 'sick', while segregating them into 'types' including 'the blatant homosexual', 'the desperate' and 'the bisexual'. All to be reviled.

Craig spearheaded preparations for what would effectively become the first Pride march by another name, with the Oscar Wilde acting as the central node for the various organising parties. It would coincide with another of Craig's ideas: a 'Gay Pride Week' including movie screenings, demonstrations and dances, run by the newly formed Gay Liberation Front, the Gay Activists Alliance and the Daughters of Bilitis. In fact, Craig had conceived of the idea months before the Stonewall uprising, following a disappointing fifth 'Annual Reminder' protest that summer. These 'reminders' were organised by the Eastern Regional Conference of Homophile Organizations and consisted of a peaceful picket at Philadelphia's Independence Hall, calling for equality under the law. Participants were expected to dress smartly, presenting strictly within their own gender boundaries and walk in single file with no same-sex handholding.

There were disagreements about the nature of Craig's proposed march; he opposed floats because they gave a chosen few a platform above others, creating the unwelcome perception of stars and their followers. 'On this day, let's just be a community', he said. 'Just a mass march. Just masses of all of us in all of our splendor and ugliness.'

The Christopher Street Liberation Day March went ahead under a clear blue sky at 2 p.m. on Sunday 28 June 1970, starting at Waverly Place leading up the west side of Sixth Avenue to Sheep Meadow three miles away. An estimated 5,000 people walked (and danced) the route chanting 'gay power' and 'out of the closets and into the streets'. It could not have been further from the staid and sombre marches organised by the Mattachines. Lesbian, bisexual, gay and trans marchers wore whatever they liked, some stripped to the waist, while couples held hands and kissed. It was the biggest queer demonstration in history, organised by the world's first proper lesbian and gay bookshop.

By the following year, an estimated 50,000 people came to march for their queer rights, the idea of an annual march taking hold. In Kay Tobin Lahusen's crackly recording, Rodwell gives a sense of his excitement but also his surprise: 'Every day I talk to people in the shop', he says, 'and literally everybody is coming and this year everybody knows about it because of last year.'

And so, the birthplace of all queer bookshops set the score: an LGBTQ+ bookstore must be visible to the outside world, and must offer a place where people can commune, learn and connect in safety. But there was a price to be paid.

By 1970, Craig was receiving death threats, the shop's location advertised publicly to enemies as well as friends. 'Windows have been smashed,' he wrote in *QQ Magazine* at the time, 'shelves torn down, books ripped and piled on the floor.' Once, a swastika was painted on the door, along with the slogan: 'Kill All Fags!' Staff were beset with at least ten threatening phone calls a week, along with 'a rash of hate letters' threatening to kill them and burn the shop down. Craig sent two of the letters to the FBI. Both were dismissed. Craig was certain their lack of interest was directly connected to the lenient sentences handed to murderers, who pleaded self-defence on the basis of 'indecent homosexual advances'. The local police offered little protection, at least not for free. Once, a beat cop came in looking for $5 a week protection money but Craig sent him packing. Ever stoic, he installed shatterproof glass and eventually hired a security guard, coaching the staff on how to protect themselves from assault. The important thing was to remain resolute and, above everything, stay open. Far from cowering in their shell, they should advertise and speak to the media. His integrity won him some notoriety in local newsrooms, one of which would approach the bookshop with a special and historically significant request.

In December 1970, twenty-year-old WBAI-FM radio producer and feminist Liza Cowan was preparing a report on the connection between gender and clothing. She had no previous experience with people who referred to themselves at the time as 'transvestites', 'transsexuals' or 'cross-dressers' and didn't know how to contact potential interviewees. She asked a colleague for some leads and he directed her to the Oscar Wilde Memorial Bookshop. The young journalist headed over to Mercer Street to ask this mysterious queer oracle for help. Trusting in her good intentions, Craig gave her an address on the Lower East Side. Up several flights of stairs she found Marsha P. Johnson, just twenty-five years old at the time, and Sylvia Rivera who was barely nineteen. The two friends had met when Marsha was seventeen and Sylvia eleven, forming an indefinable bond, somewhere between friendship and sisterhood.

The archive recording is a rare glimpse into the lives of trans women at the time, Sylvia and Marsha speaking freely about their difficulties, laughing and interrupting each other as they answer questions. Mostly, they talk about their discomfort around men and about male oppression and the choices they were making about their bodies. 'I have hormone treatments', says Marsha, 'and my bust is, uh, about a, a small ... It's a small bust, but it's a nice handful and they feel that nice handful and they automatically go into the illusion that I might be real.'

Her voice sounds a little slurred and faltering; she is unaware she will soon become one of the most prominent figures in queer history. Today, there are statues, plaques, books, articles and parks named after Marsha and Sylvia, but at the time of the WBAI-FM interview they existed in the wilderness, on the most marginalised outskirts of the margins. It is Sylvia who speaks most painfully through the buzz and fuzz of the cassette tape, going off on a tangent about how isolated she felt from the world of gay activism. She describes being misgendered by a member of the Gay Activists Alliance:

> I was there when GAA first started ... when it was four months old. I made a phone call from Jersey and said, 'Do you accept transvestites?' At that time, I was still using the word *drag queen*. I said, 'Do you accept drag queens?'
>
> 'Sure, come on down.'
>
> So we walked in, and like, um ... 'What's your name?' At the table, you had to write your name. I said, 'My name is Sylvia.'
>
> He says, 'What is your name?' I said, 'I'm Sylvia!' He says, 'Well, we can't accept that name.' So, I wrote down 'Sylvia

Lee Rivera,' but in parentheses I have the habit of putting 'Ray Rivera,' my real name.

Even butch-identified, even men, you know, homosexual males that are dealing with their sexism are always discriminating against transvestites because they just can't … We're threatening their masculinity. That's the way they feel.

There was no such discrimination at the Oscar Wilde Memorial Bookshop, at least from the owner and his staff. Rodwell established a broad queer church, where all members of the congregation could commune, protected from division, whether it came from the rest of society or within the queer community itself. He would never lose sight of his moral compass and was willing to offend fellow activists if need be. In 1978 he steadfastly refused to stock books by the aforementioned NAMBLA, leading to astonished paedophiles accusing him of bigotry. On a radio interview he spoke about the power imbalance between adults and children – something he understood from personal experience – and told the organisation's co-founder, David Thorstad, to 'Leave young boys alone.' Then in 1979 he objected to a tenth anniversary statue to the Stonewall uprising because it didn't include any people of colour. Equally, he pushed back against certain groups claiming glory from the riots. Speaking in 1986, with his usual disdain for revisionism, he said:

There were drag queens at the Stonewall riots, there were women, however the vast majority of people there were men. Nobody can deny that. My basic way of answering that question is simply to say that no one group or person was responsible for the Stonewall riots. It was an event that happened in history that came at a time when every component came together at a certain time. Almost a mystical experience or spiritual experience. No one group or person is responsible for it.

By 1973, the Oscar Wilde had moved to new premises on Christopher Street in the heart of the Village, just a couple of doors up from the Stonewall Inn. It was a larger space, and while he kept both shops open for a few months, he had to choose business over sentiment in the end and let the Mercer Street shop go. The shop was consistently in the red and there were a number of approaches from investors, but Craig wasn't interested. 'I didn't want to do that', he told Lahusen, 'because it would turn it into a commodity, but it's an extension of me, quite frankly it expresses my own personality about society, myself and others.'

A happy note. When his once hostile landlord heard that the original shop was closing, he said he'd gained respect for Craig and his customers and had learned to be more accepting. Perhaps that landlord's change of heart is as significant as Stonewall in its own small way. And maybe those shy customers who plucked up the courage to step inside the shop for the first time are as meaningful as the huge crowds marching for Pride.

Christopher Street would remain the Oscar Wilde's home for a further three decades, its contribution to queer culture undoubted, not least its impact on Craig's former boyfriend Harvey Milk. Harvey was radically influenced by the Oscar Wilde Memorial Bookshop, his Castro Camera store becoming a focal point for the growing LGBTQ+ community in San Francisco, before serving as his political campaign headquarters. The similarity to the Oscar Wilde was unmistakable and, though Craig and Harvey's relationship was brief, it was formative and in their exchange of ideas, they will stand, forever united.

On 27 November 1978, Craig heard the news that his former lover had been shot and killed along with Mayor George Moscone at San Francisco City Hall. In his short tenure, Harvey had, amongst other things, introduced a ban on discrimination against homosexuals.

Craig wrote: 'To be in love with Harvey Milk was an incredible experience because Harvey was a real man, a term often and usually misused in Gay male culture today. A real man to me is one who does not despise or fear the feminine aspect of his being.'

Craig Rodwell ran the Oscar Wilde in a state of unshakeable disarray until 1993 when, on Friday 18 June, he died of stomach cancer. As we'll see, his bookstore was never the same without him and amidst so many personal relationships – his mother, his partners, his friends and indeed his foes – there was no partnership so lasting as the world's first true bookseller and his invention: the queer bookshop.

When a nurse asked him at the end whether he had any unfinished business, he replied: 'No, I've accomplished my dream.'

Glad Day Bookshop
TORONTO
1970–still open

'*A naked man dancing in the spectral light of a rainbow.*'

JEARLD MOLDENHAUER

CANADA'S FIRST LESBIAN AND GAY BOOKSHOP BEGAN ITS own peculiar journey with a secretive boy in a thoroughly ordinary home in Niagara Falls. Jearld Moldenhauer stood out from the crowd. As he recounts on his eponymous website, he spent his days learning to bake, nurturing a vegetable garden, keeping caterpillars in his bedroom and sitting for hours pretending to conduct performances of Wagner and Strauss. He remembers being bullied and beaten by his older 'masculine' brother who, he says, felt shamed by his younger sibling's 'unmanly' character.

For a time, Jearld kept up a relationship with a girlfriend, more interested in her German heritage than anything else. 'I had been unconsciously brainwashed into believing that homosexuality was everything that could possibly be bad. At the time it was criminal, sinful, considered a psychological abnormality.'

Jearld first confronted his repressed feelings for other men at Cornell University where he studied biological sciences, coming out in 1965. A year later, three years before the Stonewall uprising, he began making trips down to Manhattan during school breaks. Then in 1967 he discovered Craig Rodwell's recently opened Oscar Wilde Memorial Bookshop. It was a momentous visit, planting the seeds of what was to become his own lifelong passion for bookselling.

In those days, the literary offerings were pretty slim and Jearld found only partial comfort in the few titles arranged on Craig Rodwell's shelves. Back at Cornell, his feelings amounted to 'psychological torture' and for a short time, he attended counselling at the university health clinic: 'I was assigned to a crusty old shrink, and I suppose if anything, my experience with him pushed me down the path of activism.'

In time, great writers, philosophers and scientific thinkers proved better counsel and Jearld set about finding scientific books on sexuality as well as novels with homosexual characters and themes. He took an interest in the Kinsey Reports, two scholarly books on human sexual behaviour: *Sexual Behaviour in the Human Male* (1948) and *Sexual Behaviour in the Human Female* (1953). The books were based on a pioneering study which asked around 5,000 young men and the same number of young women about their impulses and sexual history. By questioning his cohort, curious Dr Kinsey found that a surprising (at the time) thirty-seven per cent of males and thirteen per cent of females had had at least some overt homosexual experience to orgasm. His research begat the Kinsey Scale whereby researchers somewhat unscientifically assigned interviewees a numbered rating based on how gay they seemed.* For the first time, science had invented a graph to tell human beings what they already knew – and what society and the Church refused to acknowledge – that an awful lot of people are at least a little bit gay.

Other than Kinsey, however, Jearld describes the scientific books he found as 'consistently evil in intent'. All he could dig up was 'the same dreadful anti-gay psychiatric tracts that littered shelves in the Pre-Stonewall days'. The American psychoanalyst and proponent of gay conversion therapies, Irving Bieber, was being sold. So too Charles Socarides, who spent his career 'curing'

---

* 6 = Homosexual, 1–5 = bisexual, 0 = homosexually deficient.

his gay patients of their 'neurotic adaption' caused by overweening mothers and rejecting fathers.*

Jearld despised the 'English Canadian mentality' that kept gay books off the shelves, wondering whose fault it was – the publishers? The distributors? The booksellers? After a month or so of rumination, he decided to create his own book service to fill the void. Publishers at the time offered generous credit terms, with sixty to ninety days to sell books before paying the bills. He used his adolescent knowledge of gay history, culture and literature to buy in titles which informed his own coming out, furnishing his list with new books when he could afford them.

The name he chose, 'Glad Day', owes its heritage to a 1796 watercolour by British poet and painter William Blake. As Jearld explains: 'It depicts a naked man dancing in the spectral light of a rainbow, with the colours spread out behind him, almost as if the man himself were the prism through which light passed.' Allen Ginsberg had just given a week of free lectures at Jearld's university campus, citing Blake as his inspiration, and in 1970 Jearld embarked on a European odyssey, stopping for several weeks in London where he rented a bedsit. A coveted reading card gave him access to the Rare Book Room of the British Museum where he called up copy after copy of Blake's original books. He was struck by the writer's radical perceptions of religion and conformity. 'When it came time to choose a name for my knapsack full of books, *Glad Day* struck all the right notes for the greater task at hand.'

Jearld had a name, but no shop and in those early days he sold his books out of a knapsack which he carried from meeting to meeting. He managed to pull together a mimeographed catalogue which he advertised in the scandalous Toronto 'newspaper',

---

* Was Socarides a rejecting father? A question best answered by his eldest son, the philanthropist and Washington guru Richard Socarides, who is gay.

Tab. It was a rag for straight men filled with sleazy photographs of women, but Kinsey must have been onto something with that scale of his because Jearld's 'little ads' managed to find an audience.

Soon, his knapsack was struggling to keep up with demand and it was around this time that he moved to a house and arts centre in the Kensington Market neighbourhood. No. 4 Kensington Avenue had a shared unheated annex (basically a shed) in the backyard. It was here that a group of activists first met under the somewhat forced acronym: Gay Alliance Towards Equality (GATE). The group combined gay and feminist analysis of heterosexism and patriarchy with a Marxist analysis of capitalist society. It must have been quite a lively shed. In 1971, it also became home to the *Body Politic*, a magazine run by an informal collective associated with the underground publication *Guerilla* [*sic*], which had been seen as gay-friendly until the straight guys working there became threatened. When *Guerilla* [*sic*] editors altered Jearld's article about a Parliament Hill demonstration, he resolved to launch a gay-focused publication of his own, and so the *Body Politic* was born. They narrowly avoided cataclysm by deciding not to call it *Radical Pervert*.

The *Body Politic* hit the streets on 28 October 1971, sold by hawkers for a quarter an issue. The paper ran from the shed as a volatile collective, where articles were read aloud and given approval by a makeshift senate to save on photocopying costs, cranking out the text on an IBM Selectric typewriter. It included pages of political invective, setting out a manifesto demanding:

- Removal of the terms 'gross indecency' and 'indecent act' from the Criminal Code.
- A uniform age of consent for all sexual acts.
- Equal employment rights.
- Revisions to the Divorce Act regarding gay parents.

The publication quickly fell into disrepute when it caused understandable outrage by publishing a clumsy article (not by Jearld) about paedophilia, describing it as a sexually revolutionary activity. It was catastrophic and offered the mainstream media an opportunity to regurgitate the age-old accusation that gay people were a threat to children. It also gave Jearld's landlords – a gay couple named Amerigo Marras and Suber Donald Corley – good cause to evict their noisy tenants. Accounts differ, but this seems to have been in or around 1973.* Having jettisoned the *Body Politic*, Jearld re-potted Glad Day Bookshop in Cabbagetown, establishing a gay male commune close to Church and Wellesley Village,† Toronto's queer enclave. One member of the commune was a man named John Scythes who will return to this chronicle in approximately two decades.‡

Here, Canada's first manifest gay bookshop took recognisable form with its first 'Glad Day' shop sign swinging proudly on the porch of 139 Seaton Street. Jearld had hand-painted it himself. Still, it wasn't quite the open style of bookstore seen in New York. Instead of a shop window, the 'store' was hidden behind a locked residential door, customers having to ring the doorbell to

---

* Important honourable mention here. Librairie L'Androgyne opened the same year in Montreal, a pioneering gay, lesbian and feminist bookstore, founded by Will Aitken, Bruce Garside and John Southin. It closed 2002.

† In the 1800s, the land where the village now stands was owned by Alexander Wood, a merchant and magistrate. In 1810, Wood claimed to be examining a rape case in which a woman named 'Miss Bailey' had managed to scratch her assailant's penis. Wood enthusiastically launched an immediate and thorough investigation. Several young soldiers came under his suspicion and, to clear their names, they dropped their pants for the magistrate's close inspection. After a careful look, Wood found them innocent, but word of his unusual investigation spread. He was branded a molly (still a pejorative term in the 1800s) and was mocked as the 'Inspector-General of Private Accounts'. A subject of high ridicule, he bought fifty acres of Toronto land in 1827, which earned the nickname Molly Wood's Bush. Church Wellesley Village ought to be known as Mollywood.

‡ See Part Six: Pride Before a Fall, 'O Canada'.

gain access. Once admitted, they could peruse titles on cramped shelves in the ground floor hallway. It didn't seem much but, one day, Jearld's collection would grow into the Canadian Lesbian and Gay Archives.

After a couple of years, things had gone well enough for Jearld to finally emulate Craig Rodwell's shop, opening Glad Day Bookshop next to the Central Library on Toronto's Collier Street in 1976.

But by 1978, Jearld realised his business was being strangled by Canadian border controls and business costs. Books from the United States were already priced at the upper limit of the consumer's budget, especially for nice clothbound and hardcover editions. Add to that the weak Canadian dollar, and American books were just too expensive. Then there was the issue of imported titles being confiscated by Canadian Customs. Arbitrary censorship by the government would be a constant threat, with parcels being seized, incinerated or 'returned to sender'. There was an obvious solution to it all and Jearld made the decision to go on a trip across all forty-eight states of the US to scout for a possible new location for an American sister shop. Jearld had bigger ambitions than Craig Rodwell and this is the first recorded time a queer bookseller decided to build an empire, not to mention the only example of a queer bookseller expanding beyond his or her own national borders.

Jearld bought a cross-country Greyhound bus ticket and headed south. Hotels and motels were not an option for a young man scraping by, so he stayed with fellow activists or found shelter and security in gay saunas where he could lay his head. His journey of discovery took him to Seattle, Portland, San Francisco, Los Angeles, Denver, Houston, Chicago, New Orleans, Miami, Key West, Charleston, Baltimore, Philadelphia and Boston.

It was the last of these cities that won his heart. He returned to Toronto after two months on the road, certain that sports-crazy, racially divided and socially conservative Boston was ripe for a lesbian and gay bookshop. In spite of its challenges, Massachusetts had also become the first state in the US to elect an openly lesbian or gay state representative. Elaine Noble was elected in 1974 and sworn in on New Year's Day 1975.*

Jearld could sense the energy in Boston and resolved to open his second bookstore there. The city already boasted innumerable mainstream bookstores, several big publishing houses and some of the most renowned universities in North America. It had a vibrant gay scene too, packed with political activists, an active gay press, plus a 'very lively cruising scene, along with plenty of bars, clubs and saunas'. The feminist bookstore New Words had a focus on women's liberation more than homosexuality, but it did serve a nascent lesbian community across the Charles River. There had been an earlier attempt to open a lesbian and gay bookshop which had failed, but Jearld was undeterred. He opened Glad Day Boston in 1979, establishing twin lesbian and gay bookshops spanning two countries, stocking queer literature in Spanish,

---

* Noble described the campaign as 'very ugly'. She won with fifty-nine per cent of the vote despite a campaign of intimidation, including the destruction of her car, vandalism of her campaign headquarters and gunshots through her windows. The persecution didn't end there. Following her election, she faced terrible harassment in the House, with human faeces left in her desk and obscene profanities shouted at her by colleagues. At the height of the racial desegregation of public schools, she arranged for adults to ride on the school buses with black children, and she was the only white member of the Boston delegation to do so. Her support angered conservatives – no surprise there – but also many of her gay and lesbian constituents who felt she ought to focus solely on lesbian and gay issues. Her house was subsequently vandalised, and she was threatened with a gun.

Away from mainstream politics, she was told women couldn't vote on the board of the Homophile Union of Boston, so she went to work for the lesbian civil action group, the Daughters of Bilitis, instead. She also once had a relationship with Rita Mae Brown, author of the legendary lesbian novel *Rubyfruit Jungle*. Someone needs to write the screenplay.

French, German, Italian, Greek, Portuguese and Mandarin. The international focus of the two bookshops would have a formative effect on queer people from ethnic minorities, beginning with a young East Asian man named Siong-Huat Chua.

Known as S.H. to his friends, he visited the new Glad Day bookstore and found himself advising Jearld on Asian literature. He'd emigrated to Boston from Malacca, Malaysia, and founded Boston Asian Gay Men And Lesbians (BAGMAL), the first co-gender lesbian and gay Asian organisation in the United States. It was at Glad Day Boston that Chua formed the group, with two lesbian friends and another gay man. The organisation sought to offer a place where Asian gay men and lesbians could come together and learn to confront internalised gay shame, challenging the ingrained idea amongst the Asian community that being gay was a Western contagion. Chua's work helped his peers come out to family and friends and he wrote the definitive article on gay Asians in Routledge's *Encyclopedia of Homosexuality* (1990). It was a huge loss to the community when S.H. died of AIDS on 15 August 1994 at Beth Israel Hospital, Boston. He was just thirty-nine, but his work had already done a huge amount to change lives and free gay people from shame, and it was Jearld's bookstore that first facilitated his work within a hitherto hidden minority.

Meanwhile, back in Canada, the gay rights activist Alan Li would help Glad Day Toronto source Asian literature to connect with the city's own underground queer Asian community. Having struggled with his sexual identity in Hong Kong as a young teenager, Li moved to Winnipeg in the 1970s. It was in bookstores he came to understand his sexuality and discovered the notion of queer liberation, a concept he never imagined existed. He placed a mail order through Glad Day Bookshop before making a pilgrimage to Toronto to visit the shop in person, a trip that changed his life. Looking at the notices in the store, he saw an advertisement for a benefit run by a group called Gay Asians

Toronto. He attended and it was a revelation. He'd met gay men as a young person in Hong Kong, but this was the first time he'd met queer people finding love and confronting oppression as a group. Li would go on to carry out pioneering work with Gay Asians Toronto, changing queer lives and campaigning for AIDS awareness as a community organiser, activist and artist. His work would come to revolutionise the way the Asian community in North America perceived homosexuality.

In Alan Li and Siong-Huat Chua, we find two defining individual stories which reflect the impact a queer bookstore was having at a seminal moment in queer rights activism. From a few books in a knapsack, Jearld Moldenhauer had established a safe, open space where people of all identities and ethnicities could come together and change the world, free from judgement, racism and the particular prejudices of their own communities. Queer bookstores were not limited to white, Western, middle-class culture; they were proving just as valuable – whether deliberately or not – to all classes and ethnicities. The infusion of literature and the peaceful gathering together of disparate lives was creating a new hive of ideas.

Meanwhile, Jearld's queer bookstore had not gone unnoticed by the authorities and the young bookseller could never have known the trouble that lay ahead. But for now, in blissful ignorance, he could take pride in his considerable achievements and welcome a third bookselling pioneer, this time in Washington.

Lambda Rising

WASHINGTON AND BEYOND

1974–2010

'We refused to take that homophobic crap anymore.'

DEACON MACCUBBIN

DEACON MACCUBBIN WAS SITTING WITH HIS BEST FRIEND in his car in Norfolk, Virginia, the engine rumbling ominously as he tried to summon the courage to speak. The two attended the same church and were active members. They had been hanging out at the church's coffeehouse and, just recently, they'd started double-dating a couple of local girls, taking them to the cinema and going to the diner for milkshakes. But something had been eating away at Deacon. He was keeping a secret and he wasn't sure how his friend would respond. That night in the car, he took a deep breath and said: 'I have something to tell you.' Knowing he was about to risk losing a friend, he added: 'I feel like I've been lying to you. I don't want to do that anymore. I'm gay. I'm a homosexual.' His friend looked puzzled. 'Is that all that's been bothering you?' said the boy. 'Heck, I knew that all along, I don't give a fuck.'

And that's when Deacon knew he didn't care anymore that he was gay. If his straight friend, who meant more to him than anyone, could accept him for who he was, so should everybody else. He made a pact with himself in that moment: he would never hide again.

It wouldn't be an easy promise to keep. After being drafted into the US Army to fight in Vietnam, he burned his papers and refused to report. He was promptly arrested and placed in confinement at a special holding detachment at Fort Belvoir, Virginia. Many of Deacon's fellow inmates were opposed to the war in 'Nam, 'some probably gay, but we didn't talk about it'. After being in the lockup for about a month, Deacon decided to take a risk and make a bid for release, so he booked an appointment with the base psychiatrist and came out to him. Two decades before Bill Clinton's craven 'don't ask, don't tell' policy, Deacon had revealed his 'moral defect', but the psychiatrist had heard it all before and didn't believe a word. 'You're just saying that to get out of the Army', he told the young absconder, but it was no use. Deacon would never make a good soldier and he was released in December 1969 and booted out of the army with a general discharge under honourable conditions. He decided to stop in nearby Washington DC for a couple of weeks with a fellow soldier and the two spent most of it having sex and resting in bed.

Deacon's plan was to return to anti-war organising in Norfolk, Virginia, but, while the appeal of his GI lover waned, he was falling in love with DC. He called home and told his parents to sell his stuff, then moved into a room in a boarding house a block from Dupont Circle, a lively and growing queer neighbourhood just north of the White House. There was a bath down the hall and a tiny balcony that could, at best, hold one person. But it was only $15 a week and he knew he could panhandle enough to survive.

It was 1969, the same year as the Stonewall riots and, like New York and San Francisco, the Washington gay scene was coming to life. Washington at the time was in the throes of the so-called 'Lavender Scare' in which thousands of government employees were fired or forced to resign from the federal workforce for being gay.*

---

* Much can be said about the anti-gay witch hunt orchestrated by Senator Joseph McCarthy. Suffice it to say, he was apparently a frequent patron himself of the White Horse Inn gay bar in Milwaukee where it's said he had a taste for younger men. An FBI file also contains numerous accounts of his homosexual tendencies, including an army lieutenant who accused McCarthy of getting him drunk, taking him home and sodomising him.

By the dawn of the 1970s, Dupont Circle was crawling with gay men, powerful marijuana and talk of gay liberation, but gay literature was hard to find. Deacon went to a general bookstore one day and asked them where their gay books were but the man behind the counter wrinkled his nose. 'We don't carry *those* sorts of books', he said. Next, Deacon went to his local library and began searching through the card catalogue to see what they had. He found a lot of likely-looking books and went to find them, but there were only gaps on the shelves where they should have been. Returning to the counter, he asked the librarian whether they'd all been taken out. 'No,' she answered, 'we can't keep them on the shelves long enough, they're either stolen by embarrassed men, or torn up and thrown in the trash by religious sorts.'

At that moment, Deacon realised he'd uncovered an untapped market. People like him wanted to shop for lesbian and gay literature without shame. The idea had been percolating for a couple of years, ever since Deacon's trip to New York. By chance, he'd happened to stumble on the Oscar Wilde Memorial Bookshop and was struck by what he'd seen:

> Rodwell's was the first and, I think, the only non-porn gay bookstore when I stumbled upon it on Mercer Street. It wasn't a very impressive bookshop … it had a very small selection of books … but the *idea* of it is what struck me.

He was also intrigued by the political organising going on in NYC at that time. There was a palpable sense that change was coming, that the anti-war movement might spread into other movements for women and gay people too. 'Someday Washington should have a lesbian and gay store like this', he thought, without realising he would be the person to do it.

In 1970 and 1971, he was mostly unemployed, working odd jobs, making money on the side selling underground newspapers or comics on the streets in Georgetown, home of the hipsters and anti-war protestors. Deacon was sleeping with a young woman then. 'She knew I was gay, but we had a great relationship.' Irene was running her own small sewing shop called the Alternative, but she'd lost money on it two years running. One night when they were snuggling in bed, she announced she'd decided to close the store. Deacon was surprised. 'Well,' he responded, 'don't close it. Sell it.' She shook her head. 'I couldn't get $100 for it.'

'I'll give you a hundred', Deacon joked.

'Sold!'

So that was that.

'Heck', thought Deacon as he stood in the little shop, looking around at a bare, dingy space, 'I own a shop. Better figure out how to run one.'

There wasn't much in the store; the scanty merchandise was there on consignment and there wasn't any equipment, not even a cash register. Deacon noticed that the only popular items were the small hand-carved marijuana pipes, so he began building up his stock of those.

There was a lot of demand for the pipes and business was steady, with young people and Washington politicos alike enjoying a smoke. But Deacon hadn't forgotten about the gay bookshop idea and, in 1972, he cleared two shelves and lined up his own meagre selection of gay books with price tags, just to see how it went.

It went *very* well, and Deacon started ordering more stock.

His shop was called Earthworks then and it was located on the first floor of the Community Building, home to several leftist organisations. The DC Switchboard was there; so too the lesbian feminist monthly, *On Our Backs*. Another resident was a non-profit legal service called the Drug Offenders Rights Committee, along with the *Washington Blade* gay newspaper and – fighting for racial equality – the Black Panther Defense Committee. In all, the building made up nine rooms, a Rubik's Cube of radical organisations. Deacon became the manager of the building, joking with his fellow tenants that the only thing holding the building together were all the wiretaps the FBI had run through it.

Then, in 1974, he learned that the hippie leather shop occupying the other retail space on the first floor was moving. That's when he decided to give a bookshop a proper go. The space was only 300 square feet, but it had three large front windows facing the street. He borrowed $1,000 from a local gay activist and another $3,000 from Earthworks. It was just enough to give the walls a lick of paint, install some displays, buy a cash register and stock the store with about 200 titles. The shop was named Lambda Rising and made the following declaration on opening day:

> We are proud of the history of gay culture and of the struggle for political and social equality. We want the shop to be a showcase for the wide variety of happy, healthy gay lifestyles found among the quarter of a million gay men and women in the Washington metropolitan area.

It was a time of change. The previous year, the American Psychiatric Association had at last ceased classifying homosexuality as a mental illness, and Deacon realised his bookstore had the power to show the publishing world how much demand there was for queer literature. Sales wouldn't just put dollars in his till; they would support lesbian and gay authors *and* galvanise publishers to print and commission more. Who could say? Maybe then, some way down the line, mainstream bookstores would display lesbian and gay books on their shelves too.

Deacon's approach to curating his stock was very different from Craig Rodwell's. The Oscar Wilde Memorial Bookshop refused to sell anything remotely lascivious; even *The Advocate* magazine was banned because it included classified ads for sex workers. Lambda Rising was less strict, welcoming all kinds of magazines, including 'one-handers'* as long as they didn't show penetration. It was the same open approach with books. In fiction, he carried any title with a significant queer character in it. *Maurice* by E. M. Forster† was big in the 70s. So too James Baldwin's *Giovanni's Room*. *Rubyfruit Jungle* by Rita Mae Brown was popular with lesbian customers, the author living just down the road in Charlottesville.

The Lambda Rising corporate slogan was: 'The Bookstore that Celebrates the Gay Experience', later changing it to '… the Gay and *Lesbian* Experience'.

Deacon needed to earn $25 a day to keep the store open back then, and nobody expected him to accomplish much more. Earthworks was busy enough to subsidise the bookstore for a while and, if it didn't take off, nothing was lost. 'I just thought it was something that would be helpful to the community', Deacon recalls.

But it *did* take off, and it was the paraphernalia shop that ran into trouble. The laws changed on weed and Earthworks was an obvious target for the police, leaving him with the bookstore as his only source of income. Fortunately, Deacon had not lost his flair for marketing. He should do a TV advert!

It's been stated by various sources over the years that IKEA ran the first openly gay TV commercial in the United States. The Swedish chain's advert, aired in 1994, shows a gay couple finding prophetic symbolism in their dining table. Hopefully, they're still together hosting dinner parties of all sizes, but in fact, it was Deacon's advert that came first, way earlier in 1975. The low-budget, home-made commercial aired on the *Phil Donahue*

---

* Erotic magazines, cough.
† A tale of passion, bravery and defiance, *Maurice* was completed in 1914, but Forster kept it from publication throughout his life. It was at last published in 1971, a year after his death.

Show on the local NBC channel, WRC-TV. It was repeated a week later on a prime-time medical show on CBS affiliate, WUSA. It depicted gay men and lesbians wearing the lambda character (λ), explaining that it was an international symbol for gay liberation: 'And now there's a bookstore for gay men and lesbians, their families and friends: Lambda Rising, the bookstore that celebrates the gay experience.' Deacon also advertised in the *Washington Blade* as well as a couple of 'bar rags', and printed flyers. Saturdays were especially busy, while a gay bridge club, garden club and youth group made the shop their home.

In 1975, Craig Rodwell offered more inspiration. Deacon was talking to friends about going to a Pride celebration in New York. Somebody said, 'Why don't we do something in Washington?' Deacon thought it was a great idea and decided to make it happen. He went to work instantly, organising a Gay Pride block party right in front of Lambda Rising's shopfront at 1724 20th Street.

There was some opposition in the lead up. City officials made him check with his neighbours that they were okay with a Pride march on their doorstep. Deacon organised a petition to close off the block for the day and needed to get fifty-one per cent of the local residents and business owners to sign it. Had a gay bar tried to organise such a gathering, there would likely have been considerable opposition, with worries about street drinking, loud music, troublemakers and just a general seedy vibe, but even the most hostile members of the community struggled to object to an event run by a *bookshop*. Only a single person on the block refused to sign the petition and the Pride event went ahead. Another mini superpower of the queer bookshop was added to the growing list: the ability to appease, charm, or at least bamboozle, hidebound community leaders and bureaucrats. Meanwhile, Deacon got the word out by putting flyers in every gay bar in DC.

And so, at 1 p.m. on 22 June 1975, the DC Gay Pride Party was born... although, not quite. Nobody was there. With only a few minutes until the gathering was set to start, the street was almost deserted. Deacon's co-organiser was wringing his hands, nervously fretting that nobody would show up, but Deacon knew his customers' social habits as well as their taste in books. 'Don't worry,' he said, 'they'll be here. They're just on "gay time".'

Sure enough, a quarter of an hour later there were 2,000 people on the street, including politicians and, importantly for the bookshop, his neighbours, showing their support. The local TV news crew rolled up and Deacon made a deal with them: they could only film one side of the street. Anyone who didn't want to be on TV could stand on the opposite side. Amongst the thousands of attendees were people concerned about their colleagues or family members seeing them in that evening's bulletin. It was a Pride block party, but with a bookshop owner's sensitivity to people's safety.

By now, Deacon was able to take a small salary from the bookstore, never more than $35,000 a year, and there were frequently long stretches when his pay cheques sat in his desk drawer uncashed so he could make sure his staff got paid. And just as Craig Rodwell was finding in New York, being an openly lesbian and gay bookshop came with a price. There was constant harassment over the phone, the windows of his bookstore were broken and they received bomb threats. Undaunted, he and his staff would head to the bookstore day after day and kept going. They had to stand up and be counted: 'We weren't going anywhere; we refused to take that homophobic crap anymore.'

Over the next four decades, Deacon turned Lambda Rising into a successful chain of four stores stretching right across America. By the 90s, his Washington shop had moved to a much bigger 5,000-square-foot premises on Connecticut Avenue. There was also a second store in Baltimore, opened in 1984. His third store had opened in Rehoboth Beach in Delaware in 1991, while a fourth appeared in 1996 in Norfolk, Virginia, Deacon's hometown. 'That store touched my heart', says Deacon. 'Norfolk is a very conservative military town, home of the largest naval base in the world, and in the past, it wasn't a place people felt comfortable coming out in, so to be able to take my celebratory experience to my hometown did make me feel really proud.'

From that nervous teenager coming out to his friend, then the defiant soldier and the resourceful pipe shop owner to the inventive pioneer, Deacon would transform the queer bookstore from a personal project to a fully-fledged business empire with an annual turnover of $4 million. He was the first true business brain to step onto the field, but while his various stores would span the country, the next unlikely success story would build a revolutionary network that spanned the globe.

Giovanni's Room
PHILADELPHIA
1973–still open

'I often wonder what I'd do if there weren't any books in the world.'

JAMES BALDWIN

IN 1973, GAY ACTIVISTS TOM WILSON WEINBERG, BERN Boyle and Dan Sherbo decided to open a lesbian and gay bookstore. Unaware of the Adonis Bookstore in San Francisco, Glad Day Bookshop in Toronto or Lambda Rising in Washington, the three men were primarily inspired by the Oscar Wilde Memorial Bookshop in New York. It was closer to them geographically and philosophically. Like Craig Rodwell, they had all the qualifications they needed to be fearless young radicals: determination, political passion, hunger for change, no business plan, no money and no experience. Enthusiasm, pluck and optimism would have to do.

They joked about calling their store 'The Well of Loneliness', before deciding on something less bleak. Instead, they turned to James Baldwin and his 1956 groundbreaking novel, *Giovanni's Room*. They were ready to go.

Almost. Tom, Bern and Dan had a name, yes, but no actual shop, and the process of finding one would prove humiliating. 'For a while, we thought we'd just say we're opening a bookstore,' says Weinberg, 'but then we realised the landlord would know what we were doing the second we opened, and they'd be upset. So we were honest, and people thought it would be a porn store or something like that. They couldn't imagine a gay bookstore selling anything else.' Eventually, they found premises at 232 South Street, Philadelphia, opening their doors on 1 August 1973. The entire street was tabled for demolition if the state went ahead with construction of a new highway running from the Delaware River to the Schuylkill River. The area's uncertain future made rent cheap, creating a 'jumping' bohemian enclave in South Philly. A local chant at the time went: 'South Street, South Street, that's where all the hippies meet.' With a local movie theatre running midnight screenings of *Pink Flamingos* and *The Rocky Horror Picture Show*, it's where the gays met too. Rent was only $85 a month and, despite the landlord's hostility, neighbouring businesses welcomed the new bookshop with open arms, stopping by to wish them luck with their new venture.

'The gay community was mostly hidden in 1973 Philadelphia', says Tom. 'And "Gay" was the word used for what is now gay, lesbian, bisexual, transgender and the rest. I like "queer" better, but that's how it was then. There was a gay church, the Gay Activist Alliance, gay bars and bathhouses. We wanted to add a place that would be wide open for everyone to see it as they walked by.'

As with the Oscar Wilde Memorial Bookshop and Lambda Rising, they had a big plate-glass window allowing people to peer inside. And many did, though there wasn't much to look at in those early days. The trio needed help finding stock, so they reached out to Craig Rodwell at the Oscar Wilde Memorial Bookshop as well as the lesbian activist and editor of lesbian magazine *The Ladder*, Barbara Gittings. With book list in hand, the three men started making regular trips to New York, pushing shopping carts up and down the aisles of wholesale bookstores like Bookazine in the West Village. They paid in cash, then raced back to the store, leaving the big city for a less established lesbian and gay scene. There were days when they stared longingly at an undisturbed door. Some customers came in from day one and instantly fell in love with a new experience, but others hovered outside, then skittered away. As Tom recalls, one man circled the block repeatedly for weeks before finally plucking up the courage to dash in when nobody was looking:

> He bought a book though! He came back a few days later and became a regular customer and friend. Fifty years later, a few people still come up to me and say that Giovanni's Room was the first environment where they belonged and felt safe.

Tom, Bern and Dan ran the store for almost two years, hosting poetry readings and discussion groups, but it was hard going. They barely managed to fill the shelves with an inventory of fewer than 100 books, and in September 1974, they sold the business to their friend, Pat Hill, for $500.

An artist, activist and Quaker, Pat escaped her job in the civil service to be a bookseller, saying it was 'like running away with the circus'. At least, financially, it was a high-wire act. There was little money to be made, every cent being ploughed back into the shop. But as a lesbian with a determination to make a change, she wasn't in it for the money. She continued to host events, adding women-only evenings, welcoming live bands for parties and kicking off a series of gatherings for her female friends and customers called 'Wine, Women and Song'.

In the mid-70s, Pat was asked to appear on a gay-themed episode of the *Edie Huggins Show*, a daytime show on WCAU, bringing the gay, lesbian and feminist bookstore to a mainstream audience. It didn't lead to more customers though. Back then, a person could be spotted through the window of Giovanni's Room and get fired the next day.

Tommi Avicolli was one customer who didn't care so much if he was seen. He would go on to become a bookseller at another queer bookstore some 2,500 miles from Philadelphia but his journey there wouldn't start for another ten years. 'Seeing those books arranged on the shelves changed the way I saw myself and the way I saw bookstores', he says. 'I didn't know it at the time, but it was a moment that would affect the rest of my working life.' We'll return to Tommi in a decade or so but visits like his were helping to bring the previously rundown block of shops back to life. Philadelphia was also experiencing a 'restaurant renaissance' and on Valentine's Day 1975, the Knave of Hearts opened next door, attracting a new crowd to the area. Unfortunately for Pat, the restaurant was successful enough to persuade the landlord it should expand into the South Street premises, threatening to spell the end of Giovanni's Room a second time.

Pat celebrated her fortieth birthday in the store, throwing a champagne party which spilled out onto the street. Around this time, she was expressing her wish to sell Giovanni's Room to new owners so she could move on to something new. One of her guests was Arleen Olshan, who knew Pat from their days of community activism. In the summer of 1976, Arleen bought the business from Pat for $500, taking the shop on with her friend Ed Hermance, fellow volunteer and treasurer at the Gay Community Center of Philadelphia. Now Giovanni's Room would have a prudent moneyman at the helm, as well as two passionate advocates for the community. With a name, a short customer list and what amounted to an eviction order from the landlord, Arleen and Ed became the first female-male queer bookstore owners. First things first, they managed to find new premises at 1426 Spruce Street, much closer to Philly's business district, and set to work tearing out walls and building bookcases, helped by a gang of volunteers.

Arleen ran the shop full time while Ed kept his job at the University of Pennsylvania library, working during the day then going down to the store in the evenings. Twice, they made the now established trip to the Bookazine wholesaler in New York, paying cash before they realised there was no way they could drive all that way every time they wanted a book. Ed had once worked as manager of a natural food co-op where he got to know a young guy who happened to have opened a book wholesaler across the Ben Franklin Bridge in Camden, New Jersey. He gave the pair credit, meaning they could sell a book before they had to pay for it. After nine months of careful management, Ed was able to quit his job and join Arleen at Giovanni's Room full time.

One fall, Ed and Arleen were at the Gay Academic Union's national convention in New York City when they took a paltry few books to try and sell, thinking it would be a good chance to introduce themselves to the academic world. That same weekend *Gay American History* was released (by Jonathan Ned Katz, the young author we met in the early days of the Oscar Wilde Memorial Bookshop), but Ed and Arleen had no clue about it and certainly had no copies to sell. It was the only book people were interested in, and they were about to pack up and head home, feeling a little dejected, when up popped none other than Craig Rodwell carrying a healthy stack of copies. He dropped them on the Giovanni's Room table and told Ed and Arleen to sell them. 'Don't worry,' said Craig, 'pay for them later.'

Other people were less supportive. One day in 1979, Ed heard a voice coming from the hallway and realised there was a woman out there, calling through to him. After some confusion it became clear she was trying to deliver an important message without having to step inside the shop. Ed and Arleen were being evicted. Turns out their landlord hated the idea of a queer bookstore in their building, so they'd sold it to a suburban family who owned parking lots around the city and wanted office space nearby. They only had a three-month notice period and finding the right location proved difficult. For four to six weeks they scavenged about for new premises without any luck; one realtor telling Arleen that her business would attract too many homosexuals to the apartment building. Nobody seemed willing to rent them a storefront, at least not in the downtown district of Philadelphia.

Ed and Arleen had no money to buy their own place, but they were forced to consider the impossible and explore buildings in the very heart of the city. One day, they came upon a cheery-looking corner building in red brick dating back to 1820. The property at 345 South 12th St was going for $50,000, a considerable but not insurmountable price tag for a business premises in a prime location. Ed and Arleen raised the down payment of $12,000, with Ed's mother lending them another $3,000 while a further $1,000 was borrowed from nine loyal customers, each of whom would be paid back on time with interest. Over 100 volunteers helped them renovate the building, painting walls, fixing floors, installing shelves and putting in a skylight. No other queer bookstore would rely so heavily on volunteers in the decades to come, offering hundreds of helpers the chance to bring the store to life and leave their fingerprints on a small but significant patch of queer history.

Home at last, Giovanni's Room grew in popularity. In the late 1970s and early 80s, it would become an internationally significant phenomenon, its stock ballooning from hundreds of books to tens of thousands.

Around that time, the American publishing industry's first openly gay editors like Michael Denneny began to push for more work by LGBT authors and for reprints of discontinued titles, such as those by James Baldwin and Christopher Isherwood. Ed and Arleen did exactly the same, harassing publishing companies to bring older titles back into print. At the American Book Association's annual conference, they'd hand publishers a list of out-of-print books they wanted to sell. Those publishers listened, realising they could make money from the gay and lesbian community and, thanks in no small part to Giovanni's Room, once-mothballed queer titles came back to life.

Soon, Giovanni's Room was being visited by every leading light in queer fiction, from Alan Hollinghurst and Alison Bechdel to

Audre Lorde and Jeanette Winterson, though its most significant visitor was probably its briefest. James Baldwin visited Giovanni's Room (named after his own novel) in 1987, but it was an awkward encounter. He was in town to see rehearsals of his play, *The Amen Corner*, at the Zellerbach Theater, and it seems he'd been cajoled into visiting by his PA. Perhaps cautious of seeming grand, he popped in for a few minutes, completely unannounced. He climbed to the second floor, greeted Ed and offered to sign some books. Having finished with the stock available (Ed would have ordered more if he'd known in advance), he attempted to light a cigarette only to be told the building was non-smoking. So he left, no fanfare. In truth, Baldwin's low-key visit left a positive impression, better than if he'd expected adulation; his humility complemented a store where everyone was treated the same, even if their most celebrated book was painted above the door.

By the 1980s, Giovanni's Room had become a lifeline for a breathtaking network of queer booksellers around the world. Their wholesale business had begun as an effort to offer their customers books published abroad, trading with Gay's the Word, Prinz Eisenherz and Les Mots à la Bouche, but soon it was clear that foreign demand for American books outstripped American demand for British and European titles. To get prices down, Ed set up wholesale accounts with the big LGBT publishers in the US and Giovanni's Room soon became the world's leading distributor of feminist and queer literature, the established wholesalers missing a trick. 'We were satisfied with a low profit margin,' says Ed, 'because it was so much fun establishing contact with booksellers in Europe and the rest of the world.' Ed's often clandestine shipments of American titles supplied clients the world over, including – believe it or not – the Vatican. 'We were the international distributor for Naiad Press, by far the largest publisher of lesbian books', explains Ed, 'and this one letter arrived, and the return address was in Latin from a religious library in the

Vatican. I told them they had to pay in advance, so they ended up sending a cheque.' The order was for *Lesbian Nuns*.

A full client list from the mid-80s, the zenith of Ed's distribution empire, offers a fascinating insight, never published before. Not all of the stores are queer, but they were all stocking queer books:

Athenaeum, Amsterdam
Biff's, Richmond (Virginia)
The Bookshop, Sydney
Broadsheet, Auckland
A Brother's Touch, Minneapolis
Bruno Gmuender, Berlin
Category Six, Denver
Christopher's Kind, Atlanta
A Different Light, Los Angeles
A Different Light, New York
Dulle Griet, Louvain
Erlkoenig, Stuttgart
Exclusive, Cape Town
Exclusive, Johannesburg
Exclusive, Westdene
Feminist, Lilyfield (Sydney)
Frauenbuchladen, Nuremberg
Frauenzimmer, Vienna
Friends Bookstore, Des Moines (Iowa)
Gaia, Leiden
Gay Christian Movement, London
Gay's the Word, London
Glad Day, Boston
Glad Day, Toronto
Gleebooks, Glebe (New South Wales)
Grass Roots, Manchester

Homologie, Amsterdam
In Other Words, Plymouth
Intermale, Amsterdam
Intervention, Sydney
Kate Sheppard, Christchurch
Kvinnobokhandeln, Stockholm
Lambda Passages, Miami
Lambda Rising, Washington
Lammas, Washington
Lavendelschwert, Cologne
Lavender Menace, Edinburgh
Lilith, Berlin
Lillemor's, Munich
Lioness Books, Sacramento
Little Professor, Champaign (Illinois)
Little Sister's, Vancouver
Lumen Books, London
Maennerschwarm, Hamburg
Juul Moeller, Oslo
Les Mots à la Bouche, Paris
Murphy Sisters, Norwood (South Australia)
John Neal, Greensboro (North Carolina)
News from Nowhere, Liverpool
Old Wives' Tales, San Francisco
Oscar Wilde, New York
Oslo Bokkafe, Oslo
Outrage! (magazine), Australia
Papers and Books, Auckland
Paths Untrodden, New York
Raymond Port, London
Prinz Eisenherz, Berlin
Purple Print, Napier
Revolt, Hamburg

Rosa Rummet, Stockholm
Savannah Bay, Utrecht
Scharf, Bielefeld
Shrew Women's, Fitzroy (Melbourne)
Siegessaeule, Berlin
Silver Moon, London
Sisterwrite, London
Snapdragon, Auckland
Sodom, Munich
Tempo Ritrovato, Rome
Unabridged Books, Chicago
University Bookshop, Auckland
Volume One, Boise (Idaho)
Von Heute an, Hamburg
Vrouwen … De Feeks, Groningen
Walt Whitman, San Francisco
A Woman's Place, Oakland
A Woman's Place, Portland
Womanzone, Edinburgh
Women's Book, Gift …, Brisbane

A daunting list, and we'll visit those we can. Starting with one queer bookstore that would one day become the biggest LGBTQ+ chain in America. Its origin story takes us back to Jearld Moldenhauer and the heady days following the commune's eviction from the shed.

A Different Light
LOS ANGELES
1979–2011

WE RETURN TO TORONTO IN AROUND 1973, DURING THE heady days of Jearld Moldenhauer's Cabbagetown commune. A young, handsome man named Norman Laurila had just arrived, suddenly feeling a very long way from his hometown of Nipigon, Ontario. Just like most of his new comrades, he was carrying emotional baggage in his backpack as well as underwear.

Norman's mom Bernice was a softly spoken teacher, endlessly kind to the schoolchildren she taught, no less so to her only son, whom she'd raised alone since his twelfth birthday. Norman had sat on her lap every day when he was in kindergarten while Bernice read him classic children's stories. *Pinocchio* was a particular favourite; about a boy trying to hide his differences and become 'real'. Bernice shared her passion for writing, buying Norman lots of books for Christmases and birthdays.

But, while Norman's mother was nurturing, 1950s Canadian society was somewhat stifling. At five, Norman remembers the other boys refusing to play with him because he was 'different'. His community prized old-world masculinity over freedom of expression, demanding Canadian boys speak and walk like 'real men'. He was hassled in class for growing his hair long and dressing in 'fancy' clothes, not to mention committing the age-old gay crime of 'sucking' at sports and excelling in his studies, expressing himself by playing violin and piano, and – most egregiously of all – wearing shorts in the summer. Norman remembers the rules vividly. 'Back then you had to wear black, you had to dress conservatively in pants. I wasn't butch or athletic or what you were supposed to be as a man.'

His awakening as a high school student came thanks to a countercultural newspaper out of Vancouver called – with intentional irony – the *Georgia Straight*. He was flicking through it when he saw an ad for a booklet. It was titled *A Guide to the Naïve Homosexual*, by Roddy Green. At seventeen, Norman from Nipigon was 100 per cent the target market, and he ordered it straight away. It arrived soon after, and teenage Norman tore it open. It offered various tips and tricks of questionable wisdom, most of which are lost to memory, but Norman can still recall one piece of advice: a pinch of peanut butter could serve as anal lubricant. The article failed to stipulate crunchy or smooth but no matter, it seemed like wisdom from a far-off land, so Norman hid the booklet under his mattress, excited, confused and wondering if there was any peanut butter in the house.

He quickly worked out that he needed to find some sensible gay literature, but he had no way of accessing it. There certainly wasn't that sort of book in the school or local library – there would have been outrage – and of course nothing even approaching a lesbian and gay bookshop. So, when he moved to Toronto for university in 1975, he was completely starved of information.

That's when he discovered a magazine called the *Body Politic* which was being printed from a Cabbagetown gay commune by a mysterious Wizard of Oz-like figure called Jearld Moldenhauer. Young Norman decided to pay a visit and next thing he knew he was being admitted through the front door of a suburban house into a long hallway, lined with shelves of books. Within days, Norman was working as Glad Day's volunteer bookkeeper… and dating Jearld.

Norman is polite about his relationship, describing his ex as 'very intense and highly opinionated'. They dated for about a month. 'He was very smart, well read and radical. I learned a lot from him. Not an easy man, but a very fine bookseller.'

The next year, Norman helped Jearld move his stock into the shop's first proper retail space next to the big central library in the heart of town. He devoured every lesbian and gay book he could get his hands on, and was particularly impressed with Andrew Hodge and David Hutter's searing treatise, *With Downcast Gays*,* cementing his politics as a gay activist.

It was around this time that Norman decided to drop out of school, where he was studying landscape architecture, to become Glad Day's first full-time manager. Glad Day had secured its first senior staff member, but as much as the new recruit enjoyed his job, he wouldn't stay for long. It was all the fault of George Leigh.

George Leigh, a forty-something Toronto corporate attorney for an oil giant and Glad Day regular, met Norman while browsing for books. The two dated briefly but though the romance didn't last, their shared passion for books set them on an adventure that would endure, establishing LGBTQ+ bookselling as a serious force in the North American publishing industry.

While George had never involved himself much with the gay community, he saw something in Norman that inspired him, and he was impressed with Glad Day as a concept. With a sharp eye for business, he envisaged something on a grander scale that would take queer bookstores nationwide. Between them, George and Norman agreed to open a flagship bookstore, far from Toronto, where they could establish a truly radical retailer.

---

* Hodge and Hutter rail against the politics of shame, urging gay people not to accept straight ideas of good and bad. They describe gay children as growing up in a way that's unnatural to them, like cuckoos in the nest, and shake their heads at heterosexual women for laughing at jokes about fey men who are, they contend, laughing at queers for being feminine and for lacking power and are, therefore, laughing at themselves. Hodge was also a serious mathematician and author of the definitive 1983 biography of Alan Turing.

Several cities were considered. Chicago was too cold, Atlanta too humid, New York too big and already claimed by the Oscar Wilde Memorial Bookshop. So, they took a gamble and chose Los Angeles. The LA gay and lesbian community was vibrant and relatively wealthy, and the businessman and bookseller reckoned there was enough of a lesbian and gay population to support a bookstore.

George provided seventy-five per cent of the startup costs while Norman – then only twenty-four – provided the rest of the cash plus his expertise, contacts and elbow grease.

In September 1979, Norman and his then partner Richard Labonté – one day to be a significant bookseller in his own right – moved to Los Angeles to set up the store. It was Richard who came up with the name A Different Light, taking it from the title of a science-fiction novel from the previous year. The author, Elizabeth Lynn, was one of the first writers to introduce lesbian and gay characters into science fiction.

Los Angeles at the end of the 1970s was already a city rich with queer heritage. The Merced Theatre between Chinatown and Little Tokyo had been famous for holding masked balls in the 1920s offering a chance for people to cross-dress, overdress and undress, forming the precursor to drag balls of the 1930s, 40s and 50s. By the 1970s, the Merced was a lodging house offering a refuge to broke gay men who were flocking to the city from far and wide.

To the north, Griffith Park spread out beneath the famous Hollywood sign in a green blanket of chaparral and toyon which prickled the bare legs and bottoms of gay cruisers after dark. It gained a little respectability in 1968 as the site of a mass 'Gay-In' organised by the Gay Liberation Front; a kind of proto-Pride, starting with a primer on police harassment, ending with an all-night bar crawl.

Then there was Redz Bar, originally Redheads, an *ensalada* of class, gender, race and sexuality which opened in the 1950s in

Boyle Heights, east of downtown LA. It was still going strong when Norman and Richard arrived, though it catered predominantly to a Mexican lesbian clientele.

One of the first black discos in the US, Jewel's Catch One, was opened in 1973 by a singularly impressive woman named Jewel Thais-Williams. It served queer people of colour when racist nightclubs hassled black patrons and turned them away. Thais-Williams, a black lesbian, received threats from authorities when she purchased what was then the Diana Club in a white neighbourhood, but quickly found success, later attracting 80s megastars Whitney Houston, Janet Jackson and Madonna.

And then there was a gritty 'roadhouse' named Barney's Beanery in West Hollywood, infamous for a sign over the bar – first mounted in the 1940s – which read, 'Fagots* stay out'. The sign would stay up until 1984 when the city introduced by-laws forcing its removal.

A Different Light opened in 1979 at 4014 Santa Monica Boulevard. In the last days of the 70s, the Silver Lake neighbourhood was expected to become LA's answer to San Francisco's Castro district. Their rented building was a lofty 600-square-foot structure designed to house and repair electric trams for the Pacific Electric Railway Company. With a façade slanting onto Sunset Boulevard, mock-Tudor detailing and double-height ceilings, it was predestined for its bookstore glow up. There were a couple of businesses sharing the site already: a florist and a motorcycle repair shop. Neither seemed too concerned about their unusual new neighbour.

Norman decided from the start to make the interior just as innovative. While Glad Day, Giovanni's Room and the Oscar Wilde Memorial Bookshop had taken a more traditional approach

---

* If you hate something, you really ought to be able to spell it. Then again, if people insist on basing their entire moral code on an ancient and poorly translated book, it probably helps to be illiterate.

to their aesthetic, Gordon had the ingenious idea of putting the freestanding shelving on wheels so they could be rolled to the back of the polished concrete floor, creating a large open space for live events. They added basic lighting, some carpet and a splash of paint and in no time at all, the space was ready to be filled with books. Here, too, they took an eclectic approach, as Norman explains:

> With my radical gay politics and George [the money man] being a libertarian, neither of us was interested in practicing any form of overt censorship, but we carried very few homophobic titles. It was all meant to be uplifting or educational.

The fact they carried *any* homophobic titles reflects just how little censorship they wanted to impose on their selection. If it was a book about homosexuality – positive or negative – or written *by* a homosexual, it was a valid title for consideration. Far from trigger warnings and boycotts, it was about considering all sides of an issue to confront oppression. Their approach also meant they were early adopters of literature for trans people and books that centred the queer black community, who struggled to find representation beyond the doors of Jewel's Catch One. Norman explains: 'If we thought we had the customers for a particular book no matter the slant, we'd carry it.'

In queer publishing at the time, Avon Books were the largest distributors of lesbian and gay material in the United States and Norman packed the shelves with their books, including Patricia Nell Warren's bestselling novel, *The Front Runner* (1974), about a gay track coach campaigning to get an openly gay runner onto the Olympic track and field team while falling in love with his young protégé. Hardly a famous book today, but it sold an extraordinary ten million copies and was the first work of contemporary gay fiction to make the *New York Times* bestseller list.

Thanks to George, Norman stood out from the crowd of early lesbian and gay booksellers, paying himself a tidy $750 a month from the start, the store opening with a comfortable $15,000 of investment to back it up.

The Canadian invasion continued when Norman's close friend Gordon Montador took a year off work as an editor – his parents funding his sabbatical – and flew in from Toronto aiming to write *the* great Canadian gay novel. It wasn't great though, as it turned out, perhaps because he was distracted by his passion for the new bookshop. He was already a prominent gay activist, having hosted *Gay News and Views* on cable television in 1977 ... which actually ... yes, it's worth a moment's attention.

The show was produced by the same bull-in-a-china-shop activists behind the *Body Politic* magazine of Jearld Moldenhauer's shed. The first episode aired at 6 p.m. and was promptly axed by Rogers Cable due to an apparently overwhelming number of complaints. Under pressure from gay rights activists, the show was reinstated three weeks later, revealing that there'd been fewer than twenty objections. The storm continued to rattle the teacup, however. The show was filmed at the Maclean-Hunter studios where executives tried to impose a special code of conduct whereby – amongst various ill-conceived directives – producers had to include a straight person in every episode by way of 'balance' and all episodes would be watched by heterosexual in-house censors before being broadcast. Naturally, there was no directive instructing straight programmes to include homosexuals in every episode or pass a homosexual jury. Their dreadful haircuts proved as much. Maclean-Hunter executives were also worried about the 'gays' using their television facilities to 'recruit' unsuspecting heterosexuals to their evil ways. Unsurprisingly, things didn't work out and Maclean-Hunter cancelled the show in 1978, issuing a statement describing the programme as, amongst other crimes, 'disrespectful to the establishment heterosexual community'.

Toronto's loss, A Different Light's gain, as Norman recalls. 'Gordon was a brilliant ideas man, and I was very good at making ideas gel into reality. He was a lot of the creative driving force behind the fledgling A Different Light. (I was the workhorse!)'

Gordon* certainly left his mark and by the end of its first year, A Different Light was so successful, Norman and Richard expanded into the lot next door by opening up a wall, more than doubling the floor space. With ample room above the shelves, the bookstore welcomed local artists and photographers to showcase their work, making the bookstore a destination for art and literature lovers alike.

But it was always a bookstore first and foremost, welcoming any author coming to town for readings and signings. Gordon was close friends with the author, poet and activist Paul Monette as well as Christopher Isherwood, who in typical flirtatious form referred to Gordon as a Greek god. The artist David Hockney paid a visit too, and took part in an event, further establishing the new store as a serious destination for queer creatives.

One of the biggest early events was with English raconteur and flamboyant icon Quentin Crisp† in 1979, the same day as

---

* Gordon Montador left Los Angeles after a couple of years to become organiser of Gay Days, one of the precursors to Pride Toronto. While changing the world with his talent and tireless enthusiasm, he became gravely ill with AIDS and died on 27 May 1991.

† Hardly necessary to footnote such an idolised figure as Quentin Crisp – the self-titled 'great stately homo of England' – but worth noting that his visit came only four years after the 1975 television drama *The Naked Civil Servant*, based on his autobiography of the same name. Broadcast in the UK on ITV and the US on WOR, it caused outrage with American conservatives, though the *Los Angeles Free Press* praised the dignity at the core of John Hurt's characterisation, which they thought turned every negative situation towards the positive. The author of this very book had the honour of scripting and directing Hurt in a Second World War documentary for BBC Radio in 2011. When asked to name his most important role from a long and illustrious career, Hurt threw a patterned scarf over his shoulder and uttered in that unmistakable rumble: 'Crisp, I expect. Not *fucking Alien*.'

his seventy-first birthday. Norman and the gang rented a Russian cellar bar and threw a drinks party for him. The elderly raconteur proved as mercurial as he was fascinating. 'He was such an unusual character,' says Norman, 'because there was an element of homophobia built into his personality. A sort of performance that went with the drama. Crisp was very formal and while people adored him, it was a slightly odd encounter. He was just who he was, I suppose, without any sexual politics – while the audience wanted him to make being gay political.'

Soon, A Different Light was importing books as well as celebrity speakers from all over the world: Japan, the UK and Europe, and when Norman travelled abroad, he'd be on the lookout for new titles to add to his stock. British versions of American titles were a particular hit, their curious covers differing considerably from the American designs. While other early lesbian and gay bookshops prided themselves on their worthy ideals, Norman's store was about revolution with a high gloss. And that revolution was picking up speed, though women were being left behind.

While the revolution had begun with Sylvia and Adrienne in wartime Paris, the warriors of the twentieth century were overwhelmingly male. There was Pat and her successor Arleen at Giovanni's Room, yes, but our shops have been predominantly owned and run by men.

Things were about to change.

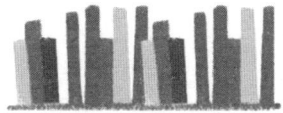

Part Four

A BOOKSHELF OF ONE'S OWN

Amazon Bookstore Cooperative
MINNEAPOLIS
1970–2012

> *'A lesbian is the rage of all women condensed to the point of explosion.'*
>
> THE LAVENDER MENACE RADICALS

IN THE FLUORESCENT-LIT ROOMS OF EARLY FEMINIST meetings during the 1950s and 60s, a quiet tension simmered beneath the shared goals of equal pay, reproductive rights, and liberation from domestic life. For the lesbian women present – often sitting silently, gauging how much of themselves to reveal – the movement for women's liberation could feel as alienating as the patriarchy it sought to overthrow.

From the very start of second-wave feminism, lesbian activists were central to its momentum. They marched, organised, wrote and agitated, but they also fought a battle within the movement itself: a battle to be seen not as a liability, but as visionaries, the purest form of feminism, untainted by sexual desire for the oppressors. While feminists publicly debated 'respectability', lesbians were dismissed as distractions at best and, at worst, saboteurs of feminism's credibility.

The Daughters of Bilitis (DOB)* was founded in 1955 in San

---

* The Daughters of Bilitis (DOB) was the first major lesbian civil and political rights organisation in the United States. It started as a social club in San Francisco, founded by Del Martin and Phyllis Lyon, providing a safe space for lesbians to connect and socialise, amidst the anti-homosexual climate of the McCarthy era. DOB evolved into a national organisation with chapters across the country, advocating for lesbian rights and identity through education, publications and activism.

Francisco and though it was initially focused on assimilation and safety within a hostile society, it provided one of the first spaces for lesbians to meet, publish (through *The Ladder* magazine) and begin articulating a collective identity.

Perhaps no individual encapsulates the internal conflict of the feminist movement more sharply than the founding member of the National Organization for Women (NOW) Betty Friedan* who, in 1969, warned that the high-profile presence of lesbians in positions of power could cost feminism mainstream support, calling it a 'lavender menace'. 'The women's movement is not about sex but about equal opportunity', she said. 'The lesbian issue is a red herring that will divert attention from the real issues we're trying to fight for.' This public stance alienated many lesbians and spurred a radical response.

The following year on 1 May 1970, at the Second Congress to Unite Women in New York City, upcoming authors Karla Jay, Rita Mae Brown and ten other lesbian activists donned lavender T-shirts and set their sights on sabotage. They switched the lights off as the first speaker approached the stage, then jumped up when the lights returned and declared, 'We are the Lavender Menace and we are not going away!' They seized the stage and distributed their manifesto, *The Woman-Identified Woman* (1970), which cut through the silence with a radical battle cry: 'What is a lesbian? A lesbian is the rage of all women condensed to the point of explosion.'

---

* The famed author of *The Feminine Mystique* (1963), Friedan sold a million copies of her book in its first edition, puncturing the veneer of 'respectable' 1950s misogyny. Nevertheless, while a leading light in the women's movement, her notion of equality stretched only so far as her own identity and she has been criticised for excluding any woman who was not white, heterosexual and middle class. She described homosexuality as a 'murky smog' spreading across America and in her righteous campaign to free oppressed women by demonising gay women, she also found time to rail against what she called 'bearded undisciplined beatnickery', while blaming 'feminine' men for a 'deterioration of the human character'. Feminists against femininity… go figure.

The document reframed lesbianism not merely as a sexual identity, but as a direct rejection of patriarchal structures and heterosexual norms. They weren't asking for inclusion. They were demanding transformation. Adrienne Rich's essay 'Compulsory Heterosexuality and Lesbian Existence' was published in 1980, but its intellectual roots were planted in the contested soil of the early 70s. Lesbian thinkers insisted that feminism without queer voices was incomplete, dishonest and complicit in its own form of erasure. As doors were slammed shut, lesbian feminists took their sledgehammers to the wall, conjuring their own bookstores into being. They would be built in the image of the lesbian feminist movement itself, rooted in empowerment and a deep understanding of women's needs. Makeshift sanctuaries that carried books no one else would stock, that played records no one else would play, sold art nobody else would exhibit, breathed words nobody else would say.

But which was the first? Exact dates seem a little foggy, but while Oakland's A Woman's Place is usually thought to be the first bricks-and-mortar lesbian-led bookstore in the United States – opening its doors in 1970 – another less-developed shop in Minneapolis might, effectively, have predated it by a matter of weeks. There was no shop window or, for that matter, four walls, nor any shelves to speak of, nor a proper till, but as we shall see, it *was* a shop of sorts, selling printed books that touched meaningfully on homosexuality. So it stands.

In the fall of 1970, feminists Rosina Richter and Julie Morse carried several boxes of books to an anti-war commune called the 'Brown House' in Minneapolis's Seward neighbourhood. They placed them on the porch and duly named the boxes and their contents the 'Amazon Feminist Bookstore', thus founding the first independent feminist bookstore in the United States. It was open every afternoon from 3 to 6 p.m., or by appointment. Whether bleached by sunlight or dampened by rain, their books were the voices of women ignored by dominant publishing houses: titles by Audre Lorde, Judy Grahn, Monique Wittig and others who dared to write what mainstream feminism was afraid to vocalise.

In 1972, following a couple of years of sporadic sales, Rosina Richter and Julie Morse* stepped away to found a women-only karate school. They sold their inventory to Cindy Hanson and Karen Browne for $400, at which point the 'store' was moved to the new owners' home on Cedar Avenue South, complete with a painted sign which declared: 'Amazon Bookstore: Feminist Literature'. Their stock included everything from feminist poetry to self-defence manuals.

Six months later, the Amazon Bookstore moved again, this time to the basement of the Minneapolis Lesbian Resource Center, a somewhat gloomy and cloistered women's collective just opened in the Wedge District next to Hum's Liquor on 22nd Street. The books were still being sold out of boxes then and customers had to descend down a dark stairwell and brave cobwebs and worse before they were able to rummage through the jumbled stock. In spite of this, Hanson and Browne somehow managed to scrape enough money together for their first proper storefront.

The Amazon Bookstore opened in September 1973 at 808 West Lake Street. An advert in the local lesbian magazine *Gold Flower* announced they would be open six days a week and called for new volunteers with the intention of establishing a cooperative. It wasn't a very safe neighbourhood, mind you – 'shady' by all accounts – and working conditions were dreadful, with

---

* Morse's politics eventually shifted rightward, as described by author and journalist June Thomas in her 2025 book, *A Place of Our Own*: 'In 1987, she married Allen Quist, a Republican state representative who was a passionate opponent of abortion and gay rights. She later worked for Rep. Michele Bachmann and became an ardent supporter of President Donald Trump.' Asked for a quote by the Minnesota Women's Press on the bookstore's twenty-fifth anniversary, she is reported to have replied: 'I don't think it's a tremendous accomplishment.'

no heating and frozen pipes. Members of the cooperative had to wear gloves, shivering as they stocked the shelves. They quickly relocated a fourth time to a storefront next to the corner of 25th Street and Hennepin Avenue in the more salubrious Uptown area. The heating was still shonky, and the pipes were leaky just like before, but the location was a step up and there was space for a lending library with comfortable seating, allowing a new flock of women's studies students to mingle with activists and community feminists in a welcoming and – crucially – *safe* space.

From 1975 to 1985, the store's exterior featured a large handpainted sign that included the labrys, a double-headed axe symbolising the ancient origins of women's strength. This sign, along with the large window and central location, attracted new customers as well as the attention of the FBI. Tasked with infiltrating and disrupting supposed threats to national security, suited agents identified the shop as a hive of dangerous lesbian feminist liberationists, but in spite of their questions the investigators achieved little.

The bookstore became a lifeline, especially for lesbians who lived far from coastal cities or outside of activist circles. The Amazon Bookstore Cooperative – as it was now titled – was how young lesbians discovered they weren't alone – that there was an entire world of literature, politics and art which affirmed their lives. It was a hub for music labels like Olivia Records,* as well as feminist newspapers, poetry readings and community organising.

---

* Founded in 1973 by a group of lesbian feminists, Olivia Records was a radical feminist music label. In 1977 the radical feminist scholar Janice Raymond published a book titled *The Transsexual Empire: The Making of the She-Male*, in which she likened male-to-female gender reassignment to rape and publicly criticised the label's trans sound engineer, Sandy Stone. Olivia Records stood by Sandy but she ultimately decided to step away. The experience inspired her pioneering essay, *The 'Empire' Strikes Back: A Posttranssexual Manifesto* (1987), which became a foundational text in gender studies.

Over the years they built a strong connection with the women's studies centre at the University of Minnesota, while bookseller Mev Miller ran her own campaign to improve women's literacy. An estimated forty to fifty per cent of women in the city had less than a fifth-grade reading level (kids around ten or eleven years old) and they were missing out on books and articles about women's health, domestic violence, housing, workers' rights and all sorts of important lesbian and feminist issues. Effectively, the women being shut out of the movement were those who needed it *most*.*
'Those voices weren't necessarily in the conversation', says Mev. 'It really started to grate on me, so ... we kept a bookshelf with lower literacy level reading materials. I don't know that any of them sold that much, but I just felt good that we had that shelf.' Lesbian publisher Seal Press was printing books for women with a lower reading ability. One, written in large, clear print, was on battery and domestic abuse, another discussed sexual violence, a third was about women's health.

As well as books, they sold pottery, jewellery, cards, bumper stickers, candles and – following fiery debate – sex toys. Mev was against it. 'They [dildos] were phallic, and I was a lesbian ... Who knows, maybe I was a prude. It was a whole conversation around lesbian sexual practices and whether or not ... the toys represented maybe, maybe not, some kind of coercion.'

The debate around explicit material was based on much more than basic prudishness. It went right to the heart of the women's rights movement which railed against the objectification of women's bodies and endemic sexual violence. One young bookseller with 'fire in her belly' was so angry about some of the magazines they were carrying, she threw red paint over them during a Gay

---

* Mev, along with other members of the Cooperative, discussed her time at Amazon in an interview for the Minnesota Lesbian Community Organizing Oral History Project in June 2021, with project founder Lisa Vecoli.

Pride event. Throwing paint was a relatively tame protest for the time, as one particular incident proved.

It was just an ordinary day when the phone rang. A man from Hennepin County Coroners was calling to gather information about the body of a woman in their morgue. He wanted to know if the booksellers knew anything about her. Turns out they did. She'd been a slightly eccentric regular. They gave what information they could, then asked how she'd died.

Ruth Christenson was an anti-pornography and women's rights campaigner who'd testified earlier that year in favour of an anti-pornography ordinance at Minneapolis City Council. A vote was being held that week and it was facing strong opposition, having been vetoed by the mayor the first time round.

On 10 July 1984, Ruth headed to Shinder's Bookstore, downtown, which was selling explicit magazines. She was carrying 'Stop Pornography Now' leaflets. She paused near the door, poured gasoline over her head and set herself on fire.

A store clerk named Tom Dolan watched in horror as her crop of curly blonde hair went up in flames. 'There was a *whoosh* sound', he told reporters at the scene. 'I turned around and saw a girl ... on fire.' Another witness reported, 'It was really strange – no screaming or anything.' The young woman stood there engulfed in flames for as long as a minute before shop staff and customers wrapped her in floor mats and bundled her to the ground. She was rushed to hospital, but it was too late. Only one thing was found on the young woman's body to help identify her. An Amazon Bookstore Cooperative loyalty card.

The Amazon Bookstore Cooperative was a nexus for the anger women were expressing at the time, as well as the empowerment, though it struggled to attract lesbian women of colour; something the bookwomen acknowledge in hindsight. Things blew up at one point when they welcomed a white author for a reading of her book about Native American healing. 'That garnered a lot of protests and opened my eyes', chief music buyer Lori Schroeder remembers. Protestors showed up at the reading and confronted the author. 'I think that was my first exposure to the concept of cultural appropriation', says Lori. 'It was like "oh my gosh. Yeah, absolutely right. Thank you for that."'

By 1985, Amazon had outgrown its Hennepin location. It moved to a bigger premises facing Loring Park on Harmon Place, the store's most iconic address, warm and comforting with an event space, wide-open windows and a reading loft, that became famous as 'Madwimmin Books' in the make-believe world of *Dykes to Watch Out For*, a landmark comic strip created by era-defining lesbian cartoonist Alison Bechdel.

At the dawn of the 1990s, Ruby's Café moved into the lot next door, attracting a huge new crowd of lesbians, particularly on Sundays when couples would head there for hash browns after hooking up the night before. A doorway was cut into the wall between the two, a match made in heaven. The new premises and new neighbour led to a big rise in takings, but then another new arrival turned out to be the bookstore's worst nightmare…

A new-fangled invention called a 'personal computer' allowed the Cooperative to digitise their index cards, putting their entire inventory at their fingertips. Imagine. A bookshop called 'Amazon' on a computer. What could possibly go wrong?

We shall return.

A Woman's Place
OAKLAND
1970–1989

'Mainly we look at things through a feminist anarchist, lesbian, paranoid schizophrenic, dope fiend perspective, whatever that means.'

A WOMAN'S PLACE NEWSLETTER, 1970

THE WORLD'S *second* FEMINIST-LESBIAN BOOKSTORE, BY a matter of weeks or short months, challenged white supremacy as well as the patriarchy while slapping its manifesto up front for all to see. A Woman's Place opened on 5251 Broadway in Oakland, California, its full name written on a circular sign forming the top part of a painted women's symbol: the Information Centre Incorporate: A Woman's Place. The seriousness of the name was quite deliberate; conceived by 'dykes with a vision' to claim the space as a resource centre, not just a place to buy books. It was a locus for women to congregate safely and exchange information and ideas. Sometimes telephone numbers. Leaflets were printed to explain:

> This bookstore is different from other bookstores. It has tables and chairs to sit and relax at, and coffee and tea and nibbles. There are bulletin boards that women can use to get in touch with other women. And of course, a bookstore run by feminists is different from a bookstore with a feminist section in it. The store is a pretty good size, so we can have rap groups, poetry readings, movies, etc.

HOW QUEER BOOKSHOPS CHANGED THE WORLD

How many lives have been saved and enriched by those bookstore noticeboards? Impossible to say, but without a meeting to decide on the matter, all queer bookstores – gay or lesbian – seemed to know instinctively that they had to be a signposting service as well as a literary destination. Inside A Woman's Place, those early customers found a resource centre with shelves of theory, history books, novels and activist pamphlets written by women for women, while the bulletin board was quickly plastered with flyers announcing community events, clubs, meetings, women-only residencies, performances and signings. There was information on everything from coming out to divorce, curated by knowledgeable bookwomen who guided visitors to pamphlets on abortion, single motherhood, care for lesbians with cancer and how to get published.

But this unprecedented space didn't simply host feminist and lesbian thinking, it helped *create* lesbian and feminist thinking, with women meeting amongst the shelves in a way they never had before, discussing the books they'd read while sharing their own experiences.

The very fabric of the shop was designed specifically with women customers in mind. Traditionally, independent bookstores of the 1960s and 70s were somewhat dark and musty with jumbled books stuffed into narrow aisles, the classification system impenetrable. Meanwhile, the new wave of 1960s shopping mall bookstores like B. Dalton and Waldenbooks took on a sleeker style with an emphasis on self-service, modern materials, bold signage and iridescent lighting, wide aisles and low shelves. A Woman's Place took the middle ground, matching polish and natural lighting with cosy furnishings and a personal touch. The feminist-lesbian collective understood that a bit of jumble could be comforting and while books had to be categorised to help customers find what they were searching for, the most important category was the shop itself. It was an oasis in a man's world. Spaces were created away from the windows so women couldn't be spied upon by jealous husbands or suspicious male family members.

The store's defiant name and open storefront meant the staff regularly had to scrub misogynistic graffiti from the steps and replace broken windows.

And when it came to choosing which books to stock, the collective worried less about what would sell and more about curating a selection of feminist and lesbian literature to inspire, inform and comfort. A Woman's Place set it out clearly in an early newsletter:

> We are acquiring books, magazines, and newspapers in a discriminating manner, and plan to have a book list available, with our thumbnail description of each book. It will indicate what we think of a book, why we feel it is important. If we like a book for certain reasons, but dislike it for others, we'll indicate that. Mainly we look at things through a feminist anarchist, lesbian, paranoid schizophrenic, dope fiend perspective, whatever that means.

There was a specific request for people to bring professional journals to the store since, to quote, 'the average person (us) never gets to see stuff like that, and it's very informative, especially if stoned.'

They were distancing themselves deliberately from strict academia – a stance future stores would shuck – but their emphasis was on the average American woman who simply didn't have access to academic texts, didn't feel equal to them and knew that most of the essays published about her life and her body were authored by men. A Woman's Place gave women permission for the first time in the history of bookstores to read about themselves on their own terms, in their own time, to explore life-affirming ideas without judgement.

They needed more books and, thanks to the first ever all-women's press, they were doing something about it. It was born a few years earlier, thanks to a cat and a coma.

In 1965, twenty-five-year-old Judy Grahn was scratched by a cat. The wound was small, but the area grew inflamed and she developed a fever and a headache. Unbeknownst to her, she'd been infected by the bacterium *Bartonella henselae*, leading to so-called 'cat scratch fever', which can lead to swollen glands and, if untreated, death. Judy was rushed to hospital and put into a coma. When she came around, cured of her cat fever by antibiotics, she had one of those 'back-from-the-dead' epiphanies. 'I decided I would not do anything I didn't want to do that would keep me from my art.' So, four years later, Judy joined forces with her partner, an artist named Wendy Cadden, and founded the first lesbian-led press focusing on lesbian writers in the United States, indeed the world: the Women's Press Collective.

The Women's Press Collective started life in Grahn and Cadden's living room with a mimeograph* and the most basic rudiments of the printing process. With barely a clue how to print books and no one there to teach them, they took the machinery apart by hand, figured out how it all worked and then reassembled it.†

Based in Oakland, the WPC stood at the vanguard of a hitherto underground movement of lesbian insurgent women poets, reflecting their place as gender outlaws in a world where the bourgeoisie, the straight publishing industry, the gay publishing industry and the heterosexual feminist collective treated them as delinquents. The WPC published some twenty-four books between 1969 and 1977, from poetry and memoir, to novels, essays and non-fiction, even a manual on gun ownership for women.

---

* A mechanical duplicating machine with an inked barrel and tray, a bit like a pre-digital photocopier.
† Metaphor klaxon.

The press was set up as a direct act of defiance following the refusal of the publishing industry to print Grahn's own first work, *The Psychoanalysis of Edward the Dyke*, in which the medical profession attempts to 'cure' a lesbian of her 'disease' and 'depravity' with a hare-brained and cruel dismissal of her lesbian identity. Grahn was unfortunately used to such indignities. As a younger woman, she had admitted to being a lesbian in the US Air Force and was immediately thrown out with a dishonourable discharge. Her rage comes through loud and clear in her poetry:

> I am the dyke in the matter, the other
> I am the wall with the womanly swagger
> I am the dragon, the dangerous dagger
> I am the bulldyke, the bulldagger
>
> Excerpt from the *She Who* poetry collection

With the opening of the Woman's Place bookstore, the Women's Press Collective found the ideal home and customers in the bookshop could hear the typing and whirring of machines right next door as they browsed for books, picking up pamphlets still warm from the press. The women running it would work overnight, churning out their pages on a weighty Gestetner roller press,* handing their materials to the booksellers in the shop the next morning, freshly 'baked'. It was a highly effective collaboration, with the writers and printers on one side of the door in real-time dialogue with the women booksellers on the other, all inspired by the diversity of their growing community.

---

* A more advanced duplicating machine than a mimeograph. Pages are typed onto a wax sheet to create a stencil which is wrapped around a revolving drum, while a second drum is coated with ink. A single full rotation of the drum handle creates one printed page, so laborious work.

By 1974, the shop boasted a racially diverse membership, including supporters from Jewish, Filipina, African American and Korean backgrounds. Amongst many titles, they published Willyce Kim's poetry compendium *Eating Artichokes* (1972) and Pat Parker's *Child of Myself* (1972). While in other parts of the country the term 'racially diverse' meant black women and white women or Latina women and white women, A Woman's Place boasted a rich diaspora.

The trailblazing black lesbian activist Pat Norman* became part of the collective in the early days, having created the Lesbian Mothers Union in 1971. So too Pat Parker, who had a close creative relationship with Judy Grahn and was an activist with the Black Women's Revolutionary Council.

The symbiosis between feminist-lesbian bookstores and the Black Power movement was solidified – according to Judy Grahn in her memoir, *A Simple Revolution* (2012) – by the shared experience of being outsiders from poor and immigrant communities, because 'we ourselves, as Lesbians and as single women, were defined and treated as marginal, displaced and oppressed.'

A Woman's Place had established something radical and empowering, pushing lesbian bookselling *and* publishing to the foreground of the feminist bookstore movement. It was only

---

* Patricia Elise Norman was born on 21 October 1939. Her mother was a community activist and civil rights leader in the 1940s. She was a longtime leader in the fight for lesbian and gay rights, and in 1971 she co-founded the Lesbian Mothers Union to address and defend child custody issues. Lesbian mothers in the US were having their children taken from them, with courts frequently citing concerns about the potential impact of a lesbian parent on a child's development and sexual orientation. In 1972, Norman became the first openly gay person hired by the San Francisco Department of Health and she was the second black lesbian to serve on the San Francisco Police Commission. She was the first openly homosexual employee at the San Francisco Department of Public Health, where she co-ordinated the response to the HIV/AIDS epidemic in San Francisco. She died on 4 August 2022.

a matter of time before other cities got in on the game. The Toronto Women's Bookstore opened in 1973 and New Words opened in Cambridge, Massachusetts the next year. New York's first feminist-lesbian bookstore opened relatively early in 1972. We can go to Labyris, but they might not let us in.

Womanbooks
NEW YORK
1975–1987

*'We are the custodians of the world's best kept
secret: merely the private lives of ½ of humanity.'*

CAROLYN KIZER,
WOMANBOOKS FLYER, 1975

THE LABYRIS LESBIAN BOOKSTORE IN NEW YORK WAS WELL intentioned and pioneering but a tad inhospitable. It was already closing down by 1976, four years after it was opened by three women who liked to vet customers by requiring them to ring a doorbell and undergo an inspection before they were admitted. A defensive measure, for sure, and radical bookstores *did* encounter vandalism, threats and perverts, but still, it wasn't quite the open spirit of A Woman's Place or the nearby Oscar Wilde Memorial Bookshop. So it's perhaps unsurprising that this quirky addition to our history managed to bunker itself into oblivion. Still, not before three customers decided to open a feminist-lesbian bookstore of their own.

Socialist, feminist lesbian Karyn London and lesbian linguistics scholar Eleanor Olds Batchelder met at a feminist group one night in New York and became lovers. Joining forces with their straight friend and fellow activist Fabi Romero, they decided to establish a bookstore that was tailored specifically to the needs of women New Yorkers. They came from very different political origins. Eleanor and Karyn were queer, while Fabi was married to a man. Fabi was Latina, a radical feminist and a heterosexual mother; while Karyn saw herself as a socialist lesbian feminist. Eleanor, who was a lesbian mum, was most interested in building a profitable business. All three had discovered the feminist bookstore movement in the pages of *The New Woman's Survival Catalog*, which was available by mail order from its publisher: the Women's Press Collective in Oakland. The mail-order catalogue carried pictures of A Woman's Place's cosy reading nooks complete with coffee mugs, couches and chairs. The Lesbian Herstory Archive in New York holds the package of material collected by the three women, revealing how one lesbian bookshop, in this case A Woman's Place, influenced those that followed. The trio collected mail-order lists, newsletters and letters from Oakland, learning from their mother-shop how to strategise for success.

Womanbooks opened its doors in 1975, squashed into the leaky storefront of a rundown hotel on 255 West 92nd Street on the Upper West Side of Manhattan. A flyer announcing their opening concluded with a quote from poet Carolyn Kizer: 'We are the custodians of the world's best kept secret: merely the private lives of ½ of humanity.'

It was an instant success. In the very first week, word had spread all the way to Australia with a female customer flying over to buy hundreds of dollars of books before taking them home.

Womanbooks became an influential space in the academic world, hosting young scholars who were researching papers on the nascent field of women's and gender studies. Worth drawing a line under this: a network of customers at a tiny, somewhat damp bookstore on New York's Upper West Side were inventing the field of women's studies and gender studies in America.

Of course, the store served everyday women too, those simply searching for books about romance (lesbian and otherwise) but the shop also stocked books on sensitive topics including rape and abortion. In so doing, Womanbooks helped a hidden cohort of women make sense of their trauma and substantiate their experiences, drawing them out of the shadows. Such things have mostly gone unrecorded (less so now, thanks to the field of women's studies and gender studies) and the bookstore's impact on countless lives cannot be underestimated. If a single book empowered just one woman, then perhaps it chastened an abuser or defied an employer or challenged politicians, or indirectly inspired the reader's children. One way or another, that single book will have fed the future of women's lib.

The boundless energy within the cramped walls at 255 West 92nd Street was quickly too much for the space. By 1976, Womanbooks moved up 92nd Street to no. 201. It was nicely situated just a few doors down from the Lesbian Herstory Archives and the two institutions helped to create a never-before-seen centre for lesbian identity in the heart of Manhattan.

The new store consisted of a single 1,000-square-foot rectangular room. There was the 'Poetry Corner', the 'Children's Books' area and the 'General Reading' area. And now, as a divergence from A Woman's Place in Oakland, the entire shop was clearly visible from the street. It was a statement the three owners were determined to make, declaring in their first newsletter from the new address:

> The large expansive corner windows flood the store with sunlight and make us more visible within the community. Women living nearby are passing on their way to work and school, who would not have sought out a women's bookstore, lured inside out of curiosity, they are surprised to find out how comfortable they feel being in a woman-defined space.

A woman-defined space and, crucially for this history of queer bookstores, a *lesbian*-led space, which in 1978 welcomed a far-flung visitor with a funny accent and an air of determination. She wandered around the expansive floor with a notepad and Biro, turning in circles to see so many titles in the same place.

Lynn Alderson was fresh from London and on a mission.

Sisterwrite

LONDON

1979–1993

'We had something called the "head fuck" where you spent the night just bloody talking and we would fall in love with each other without anything sexual.'

LYNN ALDERSON

BY THE 1970S, LESBIAN FEMINIST LYNN ALDERSON WAS throwing herself body and soul into London's Women's Liberation Movement. 'It was a whole new way of *being*. For those of us raised in the 1950s and 60s, to be suddenly let loose on an ocean of ideas was exciting.'

Lynn looks back on that time as a moment that challenged almost every aspect of their lives as women and all assumptions about sexuality. Deeply passionate bonds arising from new relationships between women led to a whole new conversation about what it actually *meant* to be attracted to other women. 'Even if you'd never seen yourself as a lesbian', explains Lynn, 'you could find yourself admiring female warriors and falling in love with them. You were turned on in a way you'd *never* been with men.'

While the British feminist movement was united in its battle against male dominance, it was also split between radical feminist lesbians and *socialist* feminist lesbians. One group called Lesbian Left liked to joke: 'you can sleep with a radical feminist but for God's sake, don't *talk* to her!' Nonetheless, the various tribal divisions were an intrinsic source of energy, driving the feminist movement along.

The ground was fertile for Britain's first women's bookshop and in 1978, Lynn Alderson travelled to New York on a mission to meet publishers and set up an American bank account. Sisterwrite defined itself as a feminist cooperative and although lesbians were involved in setting it up, and as staff and customers, and lesbian literature was always an important part of the stock, it wasn't a lesbian bookshop. Lynn's trip offered an exciting, formative few days. She went to the feminist bookshop Womanbooks and asked if she could go through their stock. She'd been running the women's and lesbian section at the radical Compendium Bookshop in Camden, but there were many more books to be found, published in the US and not yet distributed abroad. The staff in Womanbooks generously agreed, perhaps expecting their British customer to be gone after a couple of hours, but Lynn was there for *four days*, digging through their shelves from top to bottom for titles that would add to Sisterwrite's collection.

> I was standing on stools, going around their shelves through every single one of their books, writing title, author and distributor on a big stack of index cards. I was a bit surprised that the shop gave me as much access as they did.

While at the shop, Lynn met the renowned lesbian poet Marilyn Hacker,* who allowed the young visitor to crash in her flat. At night, Lynn went out to explore the lesbian clubs – a much more sophisticated concept than at home, where lesbian Londoners tended to drink pints together in unglamorous rooms above

---

* A native of New York City, Hacker attended New York University in the early 1960s, and married the gay science-fiction writer Samuel R. Delany in 1961. After thirteen years of marriage and the birth of her daughter, she spent much of the early 70s living in London, working as a book dealer. She returned to the US in 1976 and came out as lesbian soon after.

pubs like the Crown and Woolpack in Islington.* 'How can I describe the New York scene? They seemed very sophisticated to me, drinking cocktails in cocktail bars and looking very glamorous, whereas in London we went to the pub and had half a lager.'

She ordered boxes and boxes of books that weren't available in Britain, including a few, such as *The Joy of Lesbian Sex*, which would later fall foul of Customs and Excise censorship. Already, a gulf was opening up between the sort of books you could buy in the States compared to Europe.

Since Samuel Roth's many obscenity trials and tribulations in the 1950s, Uncle Sam's once rigid stance had continued to soften. In 1964, in the *Jacobellis v. Ohio* case,† the Supreme Court held that a work could only be obscene if it were 'utterly without redeeming social importance'. Justice Potter Stewart famously stated that obscenity is 'constitutionally limited to hard core pornography', adding in a possibly unwitting fit of personal transparency, 'I shall not today attempt further to define the kinds of material I understand to be embraced within that shorthand description ... But I know it when I see it'. Quite how often he saw it, and in what circumstances, was left to everyone's imagination.

Come 1966, and the *Memoirs v. Massachusetts* case, which dealt with the banning of the eighteenth-century book, *Fanny Hill*.‡

---

* The Crown and Woolpack pub was built on St John's Street in 1851 and was used for meetings in the early 1910s by exiled Russian revolutionary Vladimir Lenin, who was not a lesbian. But by the 1970s, it hosted a wildly popular lesbian disco night, reputed to be the first 'real' gay women's pub disco in the UK.
† Over the screening of the erotic French arthouse film, *The Lovers* (none of whom are queer, so of no interest to us).
‡ You may recall we briefly touched on *Fanny* during our visit to the Highlander & Dove in the mid-1700s. She took a tumble after catching a pair of mollies playing hide the weasel. Extraordinary, really, that she was still being censored more than two centuries later. If she hadn't been banned so regularly, she probably would have been forgotten. There really is no better mode of promotion than censorship.

The court could now apply the 'Roth-Jacobellis test' to determine that *Fanny Hill* had redeeming social value after all, and was therefore protected under the Constitution.

That opened things up for the *Miller v. California* case* in 1973, which established the three-pronged 'Miller test', designed to delineate whether books and films were merely erotic – and thus protected by the First Amendment – or obscene. The test asks:

a) whether 'the average person, applying contemporary community standards' would find that the work, taken as a whole, appeals to the prurient interest;
b) whether the work depicts or describes, in a patently offensive way, sexual conduct specifically defined by the applicable state law; and
c) whether the work, taken as a whole, lacks serious literary, artistic, political, or scientific value.

More than enough loopholes for gay fiction to slip through, unlike the United Kingdom, which remained comparatively stringent. America generally took the view that material should be published under the protection of the First Amendment and challenged *after* the fact if legitimate legal objections were raised, whereas the British Parliament (under the monarch of the day) answers to no such constitution – there isn't one – granting politicians of the day free rein to ban things *before* publication, rather than in retrospect. That made publishers considerably

---

* In 1971, Marvin Miller, owner of a Californian mail-order business specialising in porn, mass-mailed a brochure stuffed with books and films depicting straight sex. Five of the brochures landed on the doormat of a restaurant in Newport Beach, California. The owner and his mother opened the envelope and nearly choked on their bread rolls, then called the police. So began another court case.

more risk-averse – why spend money on a product that might be banned before anyone has a chance to buy it?*

So Lynn's jaunt to Womanbooks was like stepping into a treasure trove. Buzzing with enthusiasm, she flew back to London and the three collective members and many helpers got the shop ready for business. Feminist bookselling in the UK was different, however, homogeneous with the 'alternative society' of the 1970s: 'We had something they didn't: an existing and long-standing socialist underground, which meant there was a pre-existing understanding amongst young, particularly educated young people of social activism at a political level.'

They also had Onlywomen Press, the first fully kitted out lesbian printer and publisher in the world. It was set up in 1974 thanks in particular to two Jewish American radical lesbians who studied print production at Camberwell College, Lilian Mohin and Sheila Shulman. The lesbian collective who ran Onlywomen realised early on that women couldn't claim the freedom to publish lesbian books unless they put themselves in charge of the entire process from commissioning and editing to the actual physical printing of books. Book-printing was not a woman-friendly industry in the 1970s. Printers were nearly all cigarette-puffing

---

* Unlike the US, England also had the law of blasphemous libel (repealed in 2008), making it a crime to insult, offend or vilify Christ or the Christian religion. In 1979, *Gay News* magazine was found guilty of blasphemous libel for publishing a poem portraying Christ as gay (empathetic to women, keen on dinner parties, likes to put on a show, great hair …). Prosecuting Counsel John Smyth told the court: 'it may be said that this is a love poem – it is not, it is a poem about buggery.'

One woman was not amused. The case was brought against the magazine's editor Denis Lemon in a private prosecution by the grand high witch of the National Viewers' and Listeners' Association, Mary Whitehouse. 'I'm rejoicing', she trilled outside the Old Bailey following the guilty verdict, 'because I saw the possibility of Our Lord being vilified. Now it's been shown that it won't be.' Denis Lemon was given a nine-month suspended jail sentence and a £500 fine, while *Gay News* was fined £1,000 plus £9,000 costs. Denis Lemon died of an AIDS-related illness in 1994.

blokes, employed by cigar-puffing blokes, so there'd been little to no hope of getting lesbian books into the world. Those men would have laughed at the women's collective simply for trying, while none of the publishing houses were interested at the time in radical feminist titles. So, the collective bought their own presses, learned the craft and taught themselves how to build, fix and use print presses without the need for men.

The machines were outdated goliaths of lacquered metal with tubes, wires and cartridges of ink sticking out all over. More than that, they were expensive. Not to be beaten, Lilian remortgaged her flat to set up the printing house in Clerkenwell, creating a completely autonomous literary powerhouse, from author to publisher, printer to bookshelves. Now British lesbian books could be published and distributed with pure, unadulterated, female expertise.*

Lilian was, by all accounts, a fierce bookseller as well as publisher and printer, who managed against the odds to get Onlywomen titles into a considerable number of mainstream bookshops. And she had a strong range of titles to sell. Lesbians were writing prolifically by the mid-70s. There was a burst of British poetry and pamphlets, romances and coming-out stories which readers devoured. Booklets like *Love Your Enemy*, *Women and Honour* and Adrienne Rich's *Compulsory Heterosexuality and Lesbian Existence*. They created discussion and led to a sense of shared experience, energising and informing the second-wave feminist movement.

But there wasn't a single women's space in Britain to *buy* any of these books. That's where Sisterwrite came along, building bridges not only with American feminists but also, when the shop became well known, offering an essential port of call for lesbians and feminists around the world.

---

* There was only one concession to male involvement: they had to use the Publications Distribution Co-op which had some male employees, but there were lesbians too, so Lilian and her comrades made peace with their compromise.

There was a measure of hostility to London's first feminist bookshop when it opened in 1979. Local youths sometimes ran by shouting insults, a few customers didn't like the emphasis on books by women and the lock was glued at one point. A year or so later when they'd opened the Sisterbite Café upstairs, a wine bar a couple of doors down reported them to the council for not having the correct licence and it had to close. But other alternative bookstores in London were facing worse.

On 15 March 1973, Unity Bookshop – a black bookshop in Brixton – was firebombed, endangering staff as well as the lives of those living above. On 10 August 1977, a separate bookshop going by the same name was firebombed and destroyed. There was a string of systematic racist attacks against black bookshops. Bogle-L'Ouverture in West Ealing had been attacked earlier that spring with Ku Klux Klan slogans smeared across the shopfront, while others had bricks thrown through their windows, obscene fascist telephone calls, locks gummed up, shelves and books destroyed and warning calls threatening the owners with arson and bombing.

Attacks didn't stop at black-owned businesses themselves. Those *supporting* the black community were targeted too, but Sisterwrite was uncowed. It went from strength to strength as it grew and became a home for lesbian women of all backgrounds seeking literature and refuge from very real dangers in the outside world. Being homosexual wasn't illegal in the way it was for men, but gay women faced the very real threat of violence at home and on the streets. It was common for men to invade lesbian gatherings above pubs and threaten women for not having sex with them. The word 'dyke' was being reclaimed by lesbians, but it was still a swear word in the mouths of bigots. Women who came out risked ruining their lives and losing their children in homophobic custody cases.

'The usual rule of "children go to the mum" didn't work if you were gay', remembers Alison Hennegan, a gay rights campaigner who was literary editor of *Gay News* at the time. 'When you're looking for your identity – maybe in secret – and being a lesbian feels unsayable, you've got to find safety somewhere, the security of being part of something, and that place is often best found in fiction and poetry.'

Lynn Alderson remembers: 'I would see women who'd been at lesbian clubs over the weekend, but we'd ignore each other at work because we wanted to keep our jobs. There was a real fear of blackmail.' The bookshop became an important space for lesbians to just meet friends and relax as themselves.

There had been an earlier struggle to get the rights of lesbians into the 'Seven Demands' of the Women's Liberation Movement. And, as part of the politicisation of sexuality, arguments rolled on to the opening of Sisterwrite and beyond. One of the best-remembered pamphlets of that time was titled *Love Your Enemy*, which – to paraphrase – asked straight women: 'why are you remaining heterosexual when you could be a lesbian? You have a choice.' It wasn't satire; it reflected the questioning of how sexuality was constructed and the social structuring of 'compulsory heterosexuality'. Still, it caused some bad feeling amongst heterosexual women in particular who felt challenged. The notion that 'every woman can be a lesbian' was popular at the time and equally controversial.

Lesbian feminists won their fight and sexuality was included in the Seven Demands:

1. Equal pay.
2. Equal education and job opportunities.
3. Free contraception and abortion on demand.
4. Free 24-hour nurseries.
5. Legal and financial independence for women.
6. An end to discrimination against lesbians, and women's right to define their own sexuality.

7. Freedom from intimidation by the threat or use of violence or sexual coercion.

Within its first year of opening, Sisterwrite was a nexus for lesbian life in London, offering information on the latest political news, notices for feminist meetings and activism as well as a broad range of books celebrating gay and straight womanhood. Women would come from all over the world and make a beeline to Sisterwrite before going anywhere else, treating it like a lesbian tourist information centre. The shop was effectively a key to a hidden network, a women's community which was blossoming everywhere, from culture and the arts to politics. These were the days when a full-blown gender revolution was being discussed, as part of a wider societal revolution, complete with an envisioned collapse of modern society whose time had passed.

At one early radical feminist meeting, a group of activists discussed how to communicate after the revolution. There was no internet of course, but there were 'telephone trees' with one person spreading the word to a list of comrades, and them doing the same, but that could be tapped by 'Big Brother'. Carrier pigeons were a serious suggestion. Everything was very serious. Radical feminists were exploring the idea of a woman-centred world, some even abandoning their sons as well as their husbands in a bid for freer lives of their own.

In fact, it has been claimed in various articles that Sisterwrite maintained its own form of strict gender segregation, with a complete ban on any males entering the premises, including boys older than five. This isn't true. Men *were* admitted, but most of them kept their distance by choice. Were a man to enter, he may have found the atmosphere a little chilly, and if he'd lingered next to the lesbian bookshelves, he'd have received a questioning glare from a bookseller. But no man ban.

The overtly political atmosphere made some young lesbian visitors feel awkward. Today, Sarah Waters OBE is a writer of international renown, but when she visited Sisterwrite as a recent graduate from university, she found it a little daunting. 'I thought they would greet me with open arms', she says, 'but they were quite political and much older than me. It was *serious* feminism, you know, which at that stage I found a bit intimidating.' Still, Sarah took a fancy to an array of badges for sale. One of them read: *LESBIAN AND GAY PRIDE*, while the other had the single word *PRIDE* above the pride triangle. 'I asked the woman whether I could have the triangle one, and I'll never forget her saying: "Oh … you're not *that* proud then?"'

Back in the late 60s and early 70s, Lynn Alderson remembers the pre-feminist lesbian scene was often focused on sexual practices and roles with more rigid 'butch and femme' stereotypes. 'One half with manicured nails, a suntan and a bikini, and the other wearing suits, working in a garage, binding their breasts and fighting like blokes when they got drunk.' Many of the new wave of younger lesbian women, feminists in particular, jettisoned those roles, refusing to adhere to the identities they felt were oppressive and reductive.

Books reflecting changing lesbian life were still few and far between. One of the biggest-selling authors in those first years before the dawn of the 80s was Mary Daly, the radical American lesbian feminist and philosopher. Hundreds of copies of her 'lesbian orientated' book *Gyn/Ecology* went through the till, helping it reach a wide audience of lesbian women across the UK. Many more copies were sold via the Sisterwrite mail-order service which had been developed to make sure that as many women as possible could get their hands on feminist books. The shop delivered abroad too, posting books to women in countries where being a feminist or lesbian could put a woman in real danger.

Sisterwrite was fast becoming a bellwether for publishers judging which books to bring over from the States. Effectively, London's first feminist-lesbian bookshop was influencing the very future of women's literature by allowing women themselves – and lesbians particularly – to express what they wanted to read and talk about. Marge Piercy's fantasy, *Woman on the Edge of Time*, sold a huge number through Sisterwrite, giving the Women's Press* the confidence they needed to buy the rights and publish it in the UK.

It's a little acknowledged fact that gay women brought queer bookselling to the UK before gay men. Yet still, there was no substantive and exclusively lesbian and gay bookshop in Britain. That was about to change. A new decade was dawning and Oscar Wilde, Lambda Rising, A Different Light, Glad Day and Giovanni's Room were about to welcome the first British lesbian and gay bookshop to the party. Oh and naturally, like any self-respecting gay party, there would be *drama!*

---

* Onlywomen Press, the lesbian printers and publishers in Oakland, first used the name Women's Press in the UK in the early 1970s, but this refers to the Women's Press founded in London in 1977, apparently unaware they were treading on toes. Onlywomen then decided to change their name, allowing Women's Press to continue until it went out of business in the 1990s.

Part Five

ROUGH TRADE

Gay's the Word

LONDON

1979–still open

*'I'm not quite sure what they expected to
find in a lesbian's cat litter in Kilburn.'*

AMANDA RUSSELL

WHEN A GROUP OF LONDON ACTIVISTS DECIDED TO SET up the UK's first lesbian and gay bookshop, they had no idea their business would one day be saved from destruction by a tireless team of campaigners, press support and 432 rubber sex dolls.

Gay's the Word bookshop was first conceived a decade before it opened when a young Englishman named Ernest Hole visited New York. It was 1968 and he was exploring Greenwich Village when he met Craig Rodwell and visited the Oscar Wilde Memorial Bookshop. He was instantly taken by the store and its owner, and became involved with the Gay Lib movement. In 1969, he joined the New York contingent of that year's 'Annual Reminder' march in Philadelphia, catching a chartered bus from the Mercer Street shop with fellow protestors Craig Rodwell and Kay Tobin Lahusen.* The Stonewall riots blew up not long after that, and Ernest was inspired by the Oscar Wilde Memorial Bookshop's formative role in the aftermath of the uprising. Here he is, some fifty years later, writing in *Polari Magazine*:

---

* The same march that insisted on a dress code and zero homosexual handholding, inspiring Craig Rodwell to invent Gay Pride following the Stonewall riots.

> In the early 60s, Craig [Rodwell] had an affair with Harvey Milk, the first openly gay politician elected to public office in California. Craig is credited with radically influencing Milk's politics, and he certainly influenced mine. His example inspired me to try and create a similar bookshop in London.

Ernest Hole returned to England determined to set up his own lesbian and gay bookshop. Tricky thing though; he didn't have any money. Or books. Ernest shared his vision with fellow members of the Gay Icebreakers telephone helpline, including Peter Dorey, a softly spoken BBC sound technician, who agreed to put up a small amount of money. Like those early feminist and gay bookshops in America which sprouted out of knapsacks and boxes, so Ernest's venture started life as a portable pop-up, visiting gay venues and conferences. The shop was successful and by the late 70s, the dream of a bricks-and-mortar bookshop was within reach. Surprisingly enough, their first hurdle was Ernest's surname.

> We were looking for somewhere central but cheap and I found out that Camden Council had some empty shops in Marchmont Street due to the cancellation of the second phase of the Brunswick Centre. I applied for the lease of one with no response. I discovered, through a gay friend who worked for the council, that the officers were not taking it seriously – my surname, Hole, being the reason for that. I was advised to get in touch with one Ken Livingstone, not famous at that time, who was a councillor there. A word from him and they hurriedly changed their tune and offered me No. 66.

So Mr Hole got his shop, and Gay's the Word opened its doors at 66 Marchmont Street in January 1979. It was a bleak midwinter, the same year Margaret Thatcher brought her radical government to power. Police were raiding gay clubs and saunas, indiscriminately harassing men for half-baked transgressions. The aforementioned Adelaide bookshop at no. 14 Cecil Court was subjected to repeated and co-ordinated raids, even targeting the owner's home. He was sent to jail and ordered to pay fines and costs totalling £11,500.90. So ended Adelaide Books on Cecil Court and the clandestine owner was never seen again. It sent a shockwave through gay booksellers in the area, with David Leonard and John O'Brien at Dance Books deciding they'd gotten away with their racy stock for long enough and they 'pulled the plug'.

Young thugs joined in with their own attacks, lurking outside pubs, bars and cruising spots hunting gay men. Journalist Graham McKerrow, who had just co-founded the newspaper *Capital Gay*, recalls:

> I got queer-bashed twice. Young men, teenagers, early twenties mostly and they would go and bash some queers for fun. They'd go to Clapham Common or Hampstead Heath or some gay bar, you know, and could be fantastically brutal, fantastically horrific. They were knocking people down and using our heads as a football, kicking and kicking and kicking to do maximum damage, they were jumping up and down on men's faces. If people survived – and not all survived, lots were killed – they were left with massive injuries.

One night, Graham was out cruising when he was very badly attacked. A man knocked him to the ground and was kicking him. He knew he had to get up.

> There's the instinct to go into a ball but you have to stand up if you want to live, otherwise they won't stop. I was able to run away covered in blood and take sanctuary with a kindly shopkeeper nearby. I got a fractured nose, fractured ribs and

a broken arm. For a long time, I was too frightened to step outside my front door.

Thugs were emboldened by a British justice system that empowered homophobia. Anyone who killed a gay man could get a lighter sentence or escape prison altogether by using the 'homosexual panic' defence, reminiscent of Lucien Carr and his escape from a murder charge in 1940s New York. Attackers could explain to sympathetic juries that their exit had been blocked and they'd committed murder in a fit of heterosexual terror. Men were arrested for kissing in public while handsome young police officers in London and Manchester dressed up in leather jackets and torn denim to entrap homosexuals. Known as the 'pretty police', they'd charge men with 'importuning for an immoral purpose', sometimes forgetting to make an arrest until they'd been thoroughly purposed. The same year Gay's the Word opened its doors, a handyman at a Scottish school camp named John Saunders was sacked for being gay. In 1981, the Court of Session ruled that it was reasonable to assume that homosexuals were automatically a risk to children.

It was amidst this madness and intimidation that Ernest opened his bookshop. He named it after a play by Ivor Novello,* the renowned gay dramatist and composer and one-time lover of Siegfried Sassoon.

With help from volunteers, Hole and his friends stripped the small unit back to its previously condemned walls, furnishing it with tables and chairs, adding a small makeshift café at the

---

* Like many creatives before me, I find myself delighted to accommodate Sir Ian McKellen. In his documentary *McKellen: Playing the Part*, the venerated thespian recounts an experience, aged nine, when watching Novello on stage, in which he experienced his first tumescence, marking a significant moment of self-discovery and a feeling of being 'other'. For the uninitiated, Ivor Novello was openly gay, very dashing and presented with many such standing ovations.

back and, last but not least, a thin smattering of lesbian and gay books. On the day of opening, Ernest stood back on the street and looked up at the sign. Suddenly, the word 'GAY' seemed starker than he'd expected: 'No one had ever opened a place so up-front gay on the street before', Ernest would later recall. 'The name alone was enough – and we were worried about vandalism, if not direct attack. The shop windows had no protection, and so I decided to sleep in the shop the opening night.'

As it turned out, Ernest and his friends got a good night's sleep, undisturbed by peaceful Bloomsbury. The windows were still boarded up every night however, the glass protected with heavy wooden shutters; a stoic routine that would remain until the mid-90s.

Ernest's friend and future co-director Charles Brown treasures the moment he saw the shop's collection of queer books on display for the first time.

> Actually seeing those books on a bookshelf was – I can't express this enough – *explosive*. To read a book written by someone gay that didn't have a sad ending was revolutionary. Yes, these new books were often poor quality, but they filled people with confidence, that's why so many lesbian and gay people came to the shop in the early days.

Working behind the till, Charles would see people lurking outside the window, working up the courage to come in. One of them was Jim MacSweeney.

Jim would one day become the world's longest-serving bookseller in a queer bookshop (still counting) and his own journey began with a visit to Gay's the Word in 1983. He was twenty-three years old and hadn't been out of the closet for long. He'd grown up in Cork, a small city on the River Lee tucked into the south coast of Ireland. He'd grown up helping his parents run a venerable bookshop by

St Patrick's Bridge, selling everything from second-hand Agatha Christie paperbacks to treasured tomes from the nineteenth century. Isolated from anything approaching gay culture, he'd assumed he was the only boy in the world who liked other boys. 'I remember vividly the horror, thinking: "what the hell is going on with me?" I had no idea there was a whole world out there.'

The reassuringly dusty and familiar bookshop of home seemed rather a long way away from London and as Jim hopped from the Tube and made his way to Bloomsbury, he grew nervous. He'd already plucked up the courage to buy *Gay News* in WHSmith, blushing bright pink as he approached the counter; and now he was going to step inside an actual lesbian and gay bookshop. As he walked through Bloomsbury, his heart was beating fast, certain everyone knew where he was going. 'I was excited but frightened too. Going to a bookshop with the word "Gay" above the door meant you were effectively naming yourself.' Jim remembers the big open window in broad daylight, the boldness of the sign on a busy street. Like so many before him, he walked past the shop the first time, then around the block before resolving to go inside. He got as far as the front section then dashed out again, but the die was cast. Jim returned soon after and started attending groups where men spoke confidently about their sexuality, owning who they were. 'It was a revelation', says Jim, 'it changed my life.'

The supply of lesbian and gay books was still gathering momentum at that time, but that wasn't the only reason the shelves were a tad bare on opening day: the shop was determined to adhere to a strict policy on the books it stocked. Gay's the Word wanted to distinguish itself from other purveyors of gay material like Modern Books, Man-to-Man and other magazine-heavy shops.

In fact, it's worth taking a pause here to explain that while Gay's the Word was absolutely Britain's first lesbian and gay bookshop in any substantive sense, it was not the UK's first shop selling gay books to a gay clientele. By the definition of gay bookshops laid out at the beginning of our chronicle, we are duty bound and rather excited to qualify.

During research for this chronicle a pamphlet was discovered which gives a surprising and illuminating glimpse into queer bookselling prior to Gay's the Word. The *Gay–Z** is a long-forgotten guidebook, published by an erotic bookshop, listing the best spots for gay men to visit in London.† It's not completely clear when precisely it was published but it would be astonishing if any were produced before the 1967 Sexual Offences Act. The second half of the 1970s seems about right, based on evidence from the map itself.‡

---

* A pun on A–Z maps, those paper things people used to use before GPS. Legend has it, they were single-handedly created in 1935 by pioneer map-maker Phyllis Pearsall who worked alone, spending eighteen hours a day walking a total of 3,000 miles charting 23,000 streets from scratch. She was turned away, so the story goes, by Hatchards before making her first delivery to WHSmith using a wheelbarrow. However, her brother Alexander Gross takes us down an interesting track. He was evidently so outraged by the mythology surrounding his sister that he set up a website to debunk it, stating: 'Phyllis absolutely did not publish the A–Z Atlas on her own. It was largely our father's work, based on one he had published years earlier'. Turns out their father was one of the world's foremost cartographers. Gross's last word on his sister: 'Phyllis could be – and a bit too often in fact actually became – a pathological liar.'

† It wasn't a new idea. In 1937 a book titled *For Your Convenience* was published as a very thinly veiled cottaging guide to London, with a map of public toilets with their own distinctive reputations eulogised. It was widely understood: if you wanted to make a bargain with a bit of trade you'd head for the cottages in Covent Garden. For 'theatrical trade', pop round the back of Jermyn Street. For a better class of trade, visit the cottage at Waterloo Station.

‡ The inimitable antiquarian bookseller who rediscovered the *Gay–Z*, Tim Bryars (of Cecil Court, *naturally*), carried out his own detective work. The Man-to-Man Bookshop opened in Notting Hill in May 1974. And there's no mention of Gay's the Word which would surely have been included, meaning the book *had* to have been published prior to 1979. There's also an advert announcing over 1,000 performances of *The Rocky Horror Picture Show* at the King's Road Theatre, which provides the best clue. Allowing for matinées and working on the assumption that the advert would be updated every couple of hundred performances or so, a date in 1976 or 1977 seems most likely.

The *Gay–Z* offers a smorgasbord of gay destinations including restaurants and hotels, saunas and clubs, complete with a stark warning in English, German and French:

> British Law permits homosexual activity IN PRIVATE, between two consenting adults of 21 and over. But any sexual contact in public is forbidden!

But here's the surprise: when each category is placed in descending order, the second most popular attraction is… gay bookshops.

> Bars and clubs x 10
> Booksellers x 6
> Restaurants x 5
> Masseurs x 3
> Hotels x 3
> Enigmatic unknowns x 3
> Theatrical show – Rocky Horror x 1

The term 'bookshop' might be a polite term for porn mags in some cases, but we shouldn't be too hasty to discount them all. More detail is offered inside the listing.

> Man-n-Mates, Berwick Street W1: MAGS / FILMS / BOOKS: *Film Shows 7 days a week*
> Man-to-Man, Pembridge Road W11 [the publishers of the map]: *magazines, books and films, everything from toys to text*
> Pages of Fun, Victoria: *Your gay bookshop*
> Don Busby, Railton Road, SE24: *We've stacked it right up solid with magazines, books and leather things*
> Tunnels of Love, Wardour Street and Berwick Street [which may or may not have been a bookshop in the loosest of terms]: *'The largest selection of gay material in Soho'*

> Modern Books on Monmouth Street WC1 [this appears to be a typo, as revealed by the owner's son – below – who corrects that the shop was on 283 Camden High Street]

The last on the list, Modern Books, boasted: '*the best gay books, 200 titles from 20 countries*'. Much more than a mere magazine shop then.

Turns out, it was opened around 1971 by Philip (Pip) Hindle-Briscall, an Edwardian-born married man who came to bookselling and fatherhood in his fifties. His son Adrian remembers his dad's literary tastes well: 'My father was always interested in porn. He was a friend of Harrison Marks, the most famous name in UK straight porn in the 1950s and 60s.' Pip opened the bricks-and-mortar bookshop on 283 Camden High Street (not Monmouth Street, as stated in the *Gay–Z*), just up from Compendium Books, a famous radical bookshop. At the beginning, Modern Books sold a mix of gay and straight stock but by the mid-70s, it was selling exclusively gay romance and erotic novels as well as magazines, many of them imported from the United States. Sadly, it wasn't to last, and Pip's son Adrian remembers the end of the shop with a mix of pride and sadness. 'The shop had done very well at times,' he says, 'though my father never seemed to make much money. It was doing very badly at the end due to competition and legal restrictions on what could be sold. Then dad got lung cancer and the business worries didn't help, and he died in April '78.'

To seal his place in the annals of gay bookselling history, Pip also ran his own publishing company called Millivres and was behind some of the most popular and influential gay magazines of the day, including *The Drag Queens: Secrets of the Female Mimics*, diarising drag culture of the 1970s. This is from the social diary of the legendary drag queen of her day, Jean Fredericks.

I have just been contacted by a 24-year-old engineer – would I do a theatrical makeup and dress up to see how authentic he looks? Apparently at college they had a cod beauty contest and although he would love to have entered did not as it was in public and the other students might tease him. We'll do our best!

Another article describes the booming popularity of drag balls at the time, stating confidently: 'fancy dress balls have been popular in all parts of the western world since pre-history and still attract a lot of people, even in these sophisticated times.'

Jean Fredericks was busy organising three or four balls a year at Porchester Hall at the top end of Queensway in Paddington, attracting more than 1,000 people, many wearing 'the apparel of the opposite sex'. Some guests intended to show off their elaborate and often beautiful costumes while others were in a comedy get-up. 'But', cautions the article, 'these events are not just a get together of the amateur drag Queens or to use the correct term transvestites; there is always a big crowd of normally dressed people who enjoy the fun.' The author of the article proudly states that the balls had been featured in *The Sunday Times* colour supplement.

It might be tempting to overlook booksellers like Pip on our journey, but his shop and publishing business – selling gay novels and magazines and employing gay staff – is a timely reminder that the queer bookseller has taken many forms over the years while serving the needs of a broad and kaleidoscopic community. All of them paved the way.

Anyway, we might need a *Gay–Z* map after this excursion, but let us find our way back to Gay's the Word, no less respectful of its pioneering credentials but better informed about its heritage.

Ernest Hole's vision was for a bookshop that rejected the erotica-focused model of Modern Books and its ilk. Even volumes on therapy weren't allowed, nor any on religion, and titles about gay icons like Judy Garland? Over the rainbow perhaps, but certainly not in Gay's the Word. Meanwhile anyone searching for a biography of Maria Callas would be singing up the wrong tree: there were no books on opera, none on high art, none on ballet, unless they were written by queer people about queer people for queer people.

Some gay visitors in those early days found the approach a touch self-defeating and po-faced, scented with a faint perfume of inverted snobbery and sexual shame, but that would have been to misunderstand Ernest Hole's intentions. More akin to the Oscar Wilde Memorial Bookshop or A Woman's Place than, say, Lambda Rising or A Different Light, the shop was determined to edit stock and cut out inappropriate titles. Nor would it please the bourgeoisie or excite the horny. Ernest and the directors who took over from him a year or so after opening wanted the shop to take itself seriously, allowing thoughtful customers to access books that nourished their desire for empowerment and revolution. Not that books couldn't be light-hearted. Queer activist Leslie Jones was dating one of the shop's staff, Amanda Russell (more on Amanda to come) in the early 80s. She chuckles, thinking back to the pulp fiction that lesbian customers were loving back then.

> Women were lapping it up, if I can put it that way? Lesbian pulp fiction, we'd never had those books before. We had *The Well of Loneliness* where somebody has to die or get married to a man. In the 1960s you had lesbian fiction but there had to be death or going straight in the end because that was the only way they could get published. Then in the 80s there were romantic stories, and they were loved not because they were well written, but we could identify with them, even though the characters had their own swimming pools and drank cocktails by the beach. A world away from London.

Mainstream booksellers would have blushed at those brightly illustrated covers of young, naked bodies, their titillating titles causing half-moon spectacles to steam up and Y-fronts to twist. Even volumes that had been doing the rounds for a decade or more were eschewed by the mainstream but given a home in Gay's the Word. Monique Wittig's *The Lesbian Body* (translated into English, 1975) was prominently featured, as was Donn Teal's *The Gay Militants* (1971) and suggestive novels by generally respected authors, like L. P. Hartley's *The Harness Room* (1971).*

The 1980s were a breakthrough moment for a chosen few highbrow queer writers, however. Larry Kramer's novel *Faggots*, Edmund White's *Nocturnes for the King of Naples*, Jeanette Winterson's *Oranges Are Not the Only Fruit* and Andrew Holleran's *Dancer from the Dance* were all published by commercial or 'trade' publishers to critical and financial success. They were widely reviewed and available in bookstores, including those that usually wouldn't touch lesbian and gay titles. However, one of these authors didn't break the mould so much as glue a gay Caucasian penis to it, proving that gay books could be a success for big publishers so long as they adhered to a white, cosmopolitan sensibility. They tended to concern the lives of doomed white middle-class queens living in gay enclaves, spending their afternoons at the gym before heading out to bath houses or dance bars, surviving with trust funds or the kindness of benefactors to enjoy a bacchanalian life of sex, drugs and dancing. Sounds awful. Even in the era of Day-Glo tracksuits and yuppies, many queer books were reminiscent of the literary world of F. Scott Fitzgerald and Ernest Hemingway.

---

* Wherein a retired and frankly naive army colonel commissions the services of a handsome ex-guardsman to toughen up his seventeen-year-old son. The boys get on fabulously and by all accounts the young man *does* harden.

This is not to snark. The upswell of gay writing was almost double the output of the 1950s. In Gay's the Word, lesbian and gay readers had found their home. 'The bookshop rapidly became what I had always wanted it to be', Ernest explained.

> A meeting place as well as an information point for lesbians and gay men, tempted by the ever-increasing stock, good coffee and home-made cake. I remember Andrew Hodges taking breaks from writing his marvellous biography of Alan Turing. And runaway teenagers seeking refuge. The director of the new discotheque, Heaven, seeking advice. Friendships and relationships were formed; heated discussions took place.

As well as a new influx of books, there was a ready supply of political pamphlets from the Gay Liberation Front and a host of gay journals. One of them, published by Pomegranate Press, suffers from the astonishing 1970s obsession with the colour brown, emblazoned in a Hanna-Barbera font: *With Downcast Gays*: *Aspects of Homosexual Self-Oppression*. Inside, the reader is greeted with a waft of damp paper and a searing treatise against internalised homophobia:

> We have been taught to hate ourselves – and how thoroughly we have learned the lesson ... We seldom recognise the queer-basher's fist in the liberal's guiding hand. 'How can you be sure that you are homosexual?' asks the psychiatrist. Whenever does he ask heterosexuals the converse question?

Demand for these pamphlets and the thin selection of 'serious' books being distributed in the UK far outstripped supply and Gay's the Word soon realised they would have to order books from the United States. A quid pro quo deal was set up with Ed and

Arleen at Giovanni's Room in Philadelphia, who agreed to supply boxes of American books in exchange for hard-to-get European stock. By this point, the Philly booksellers were already supplying around eighty bookshops with queer titles, from Australia to South Africa, Germany to the Netherlands.

All was going well, but Her Majesty's Customs and Excise were circling. Remember those rubber sex dolls mentioned at the beginning of this chapter? As court records show:

> On the 7th and 11th of October 1982 Conegate Ltd. sought to import into the United Kingdom through Heathrow Airport a number of articles which were described on the air waybills and the invoices as 'window display models'. The company has contended that, because of their realistic physical features, they were sold for use as models for the display of ladies' dresses and underwear.

Unfortunately for Conegate – which ran a number of sex shops around the UK – the consignment of inflatable life-sized dolls from West Germany were obviously not mannequins. Not only were they described as 'Love Love Dolls', 'Miss World Specials' and 'Rubber Ladies', they were also travelling with a crate of what was described as 'Sexy Vacuum Flasks' (as opposed to the unsexy variety). The Customs authorities duly seized the articles as being indecent or obscene under Section 42 of the Customs Consolidation Act 1876.

What does any of this have to do with Gay's the Word? We'll find out very soon.

By the summer of 1980, Ernest had left Gay's the Word, realising with good cheer that he was a brilliant gay activist but a hopeless bookseller. John Duncan replaced him as manager, supported by a number of investors. The stock had swollen to around 500 titles, thanks to Ed Hermance in Philadelphia, who turned out to be a cunning operator when it came to evading international Customs authorities.

'We tricked 'em!' grins Ed, looking back on his career as the world's foremost bookselling swashbuckler. 'We addressed deliveries to Archbishop Runcie to fool Customs. I think that helped get a lot of stock through.'

It's true. Buried in the Gay's the Word archive, papers show deliveries being made from Philadelphia to director John Duncan's house, specifically stipulating: 'Gay's the Word should not be put on the parcels.'

By January 1981, Ed's most popular dispatch to Gay's the Word, *The Joy of Gay Sex* by Edmund White and Charles Silverstein, was struggling to get through Customs, no matter what he put on the delivery. The Gay's the Word archives hold a letter from Ed expressing his anxiety: 'I have been a little nervous about the recent shipments of *Joy of Gay Sex* because of the recent burning of same by British Customs.'

In February 1981, ten more copies were seized. In March, *A Lover's Cock* was duly blocked. Twenty more copies of a book titled *Chicken* were also intercepted at the border. It was not a cookery book. The seizures extended to gay women's titles too, including *A Woman's Touch* and *What Lesbians Do*, both seized that same August.

At one point, the police tried to have Gay's the Word reclassified as a sex shop. They failed. On and on it went, with ever more seizures of *The Joy of Gay Sex* along with *Below the Belt & Other Stories* and *Roman Conquests* (*not* a history book). Towards the end of 1983, directors were noticing more seizures and longer delays with stock; then in 1984 Ed received a call from London he won't forget. Gay's the Word had been raided by Customs and $10,000 worth of stock had been seized. Ed was shocked. 'I remember thinking, wow, England's as crazy as we are.'

It turns out Gay's the Word had been subject to long-term surveillance and at 9.20 a.m. on Tuesday 10 April 1984, Customs and Excise launched Operation Tiger. Two officers walked through the nearby Brunswick Centre, arriving at the flat of one of the shop's directors, Glen McKee. Glen woke to the sound of fists thumping on his door and was forced to admit the officers who effectively trapped him in his own home for six hours while they searched the property. 'They went through everything,' he said, 'every piece of paper, my videos, minutes of board meetings. And they wouldn't let me talk to anyone.'

At around 1 p.m. that afternoon, officers stormed Gay's the Word itself, ordering the bookseller and assistant manager Paud Hegarty to eject his customers so they could rummage through every single book in stock. An agent suitably named Dave Odd seemed to be in charge, while the listing of books was supervised by a balding man with unkempt sideburns, dirty trainers and a hideously patterned shirt.

Graham McKerrow tells the story of the raids in his article for the book *Queer Between The Covers* (2021). His newspaper *Capital Gay* took photographs as the officers rummaged through the shelves:

> They were just ordinary people, one woman and three men, very straight, in naff straight clothes. It was bizarre in its drabness; there was nothing official about it. They were bemused because they didn't deal with words in books, they dealt with magazines filled with pictures they could just look at and decide were dirty, but here they had to sit down and actually *read*.

They left three hours later with no fewer than eight hundred volumes, bundling them into a beige Vauxhall to be taken for closer inspection. Till rolls, invoices, address books and various documents were placed into a polythene bag and stuffed into the footwell. It was absurd, but genuinely frightening, as Graham explains:

> Alarmingly they also took the list of names and addresses of everyone on the mail order service. Only a couple of years earlier the police had been methodically going through the gay community in Huddersfield on what was called a 'fishing trip': searching men's homes, taking their address books then visiting everyone mentioned as an act of intimidation. They weren't only harassing people, they were outing people at work and at home. So the fact they were taking this list of names and addresses was very alarming.

To add insanity to harassment, Customs and Excise officers were actually asking Gay's the Word staff which books they should seize, calling HQ in a state of confusion. As they would come to admit in court, they were given no guidance on obscenity and they received no clear instructions on precisely what to take back to base.

Operation Tiger agents raided the home of director Jonathan Cutbill later that day, with officers overheard complaining to superiors: 'we're meant to be looking for pornography, but he's got about 10,000 books here!' Jonathan was a book collector. Bookshop manager Amanda Russell was also raided, spending most of that afternoon being grilled at Customs and Excise headquarters in nearby Woburn Place. 'They interrogated me for hours', she says in an interview with her lifelong friend Janet Jones in 2018.*

---

* Amanda Russell died in 2023, rendering her short interview an invaluable historical record. Along with her former lover and ex-Gay's the Word volunteer Lesley Jones (no relation to Janet), she established the Gay's the Word Lesbian Discussion Group which still meets in the shop on Wednesday evenings, by far the oldest such group anywhere in the world.

When I finally got back to my flat, they had a writ from the Queen, signed by Queen Elizabeth II herself, allowing them to search wherever they wanted without a warrant. They even took the cat litter, but didn't find anything. I'm not quite sure what they expected to find in a lesbian's cat litter in Kilburn. They found our letters to Ed from Giovanni's Room though, talking about a "safe house" and evading Customs, which is what did for us really.

Officers also seized Amanda's VHS tapes of *Dallas*, *Coronation Street* and *Crufts*, adding them to a mountain of seized titles by Tennessee Williams, Oscar Wilde and Jean-Paul Sartre. Hundreds of titles were seized, about a third of the shop's stock, from Charles Hirsch's ambiguously authored *Teleny* to the laconically titled *Cum*. It was a potential death blow after a flood at the start of the month which had already caused serious damage. Furthermore, about £11,000 worth of stock at wholesale prices had been seized on its way to the shop.

There is a farcical aspect to the raids, but the shock and pain of those present can be felt in paperwork prepared for the subsequent court case. The now-faded documents are stored in ripped plastic wallets in a filing cabinet in the basement below Gay's the Word's creaking floorboards. There, the blue painted brickwork once rattled to the sound of typing and ringing phones. One document reads:

> Over the first five years, Gay's The Word has come to occupy a central role in the lesbian and gay community. It has informed, entertained, and provided a meeting place for new – and as yet insecure – groups. It has encouraged new authors, provided the setting for some of the key debates in the lesbian and gay community. Gay's The Word is the largest book shop of its kind in the country and has a worldwide reputation.

The existence and success of Gay's The Word is one of the gay community's most cherished achievements. The effects of the raids are devastating.

As Gay's the Word director Jonathan Cutbill said at the time: 'Can we afford not to fight?' In June 1984, the mail-order service Essentially Gay announced it was closing after £1,600 worth of books was seized. The owner Terry Sanderson said he couldn't afford to go to court and he didn't believe he'd get a fair trial anyway. The Gay's the Word directors understood that this was a battle for more than the future of one business; either they made a stand, or queer businesses across the UK would be forced to shut down. Directors shelved plans to move into larger premises and focused on their fight for survival. A 'Defend Gay's the Word' fighting fund had raised £500 within the first week, and on 27 April, more than a hundred people demonstrated outside Customs HQ in Woburn Place.

In August 1984, copies of the French newspaper *Gai Pied* were seized on their way to Gay's the Word and in September, £250 worth of books and magazines were seized on their way to Lavender Menace bookshop in Edinburgh. In October the same year, another 132 titles were detained on their way to Gay's the Word, amounting to 2,265 items. In November 1984, fifteen copies of *The Joy of Gay Sex* were seized on their way to the Gay Christian Movement. Reverend Richard Kirker told a Defend Gay's the Word meeting that Customs had quietly offered not to prosecute him if he gave evidence against the bookshop. He refused to bow to blackmail.

Either Gay's the Word stood its ground in court, or the seizures would escalate. Campaigners made it clear: 'We have decided to go ahead with this as a political principle even though it is going to be quite serious for the shop financially.' As it transpired, events overtook them and on Wednesday 21 November

1984, assistant manager Paud Hegarty and the eight directors were charged with conspiracy to import indecent and obscene material.*

This was shaping up to be a major trial at the Old Bailey and publishers stepped in to help Gay's the Word target an estimated battle fund of £30,000. Penguin Books gave £500, as did Gollancz, while Chatto & Windus gave £200.† With a growing campaign and media coverage, the goal was reached and surpassed.

In June 1985, the committal hearing was heard, the defence extracting extraordinary details from witnesses for the prosecution. It emerged that Operation Tiger had been planned at quite a low level, and many of the surveyors who issued seizure notices were young men aged around twenty who'd left school at sixteen. These were the arbiters of British literary morality, deciding whether poems by Verlaine were 'indecent'. As was patently obvious during the raids, officers had been given no training or guidance on what 'obscenity' actually meant. Graham McKerrow's newspaper *Capital Gay* had already published a leaked set of secret guidelines sent to those young surveyors, section 1(2)b stating that offensive material included:

> Books and magazines. Sexual activities, including variations e.g. masturbation, lesbianism, homosexuality…

---

* The term 'directors' should not mislead the reader. They were unpaid volunteers who offered guidance and worked in the shop on Sundays on a rota basis. Some had painted the walls and built the bookshelves that remain in the hallowed shop to this day.

† *The Guardian* newspaper compared the case to the 1960 obscenity trial against Penguin Books over their publication of *Lady Chatterley's Lover*. In that instance, after three hours of deliberation, the jury returned a unanimous verdict of not guilty.

On 20 August 1985, the defendants were committed for trial at the Old Bailey, the magistrate Mr C. J. Bourke's sinister Note of Committal ringing in their ears:

> A committed homosexual may consider that detailed accounts of homosexual behaviour in such a way as to arouse homosexual feeling was [sic] proper. He would dispute the classification as indecent or obscene and challenge their description as such. That is not the point. The question is not what *he* thought, but what others, not of his prediliction [sic] would think.

The trial was set for October 1986. In January of that year, Graham McKerrow left *Capital Gay* to become a joint co-ordinator of the defence campaign, alongside David Northmore from the National Council for Civil Liberties. Together, they whipped up an international storm of protests, fundraisers and media interviews. A BBC documentary was being prepared and a London theatre director was busily writing *Operation Tiger – The Musical!*, scheduled to premiere at the Piccadilly Theatre just before the beginning of the trial.

It was all horribly embarrassing for the government, the once silent press taking an increasing interest in Operation Tiger which might as well have been renamed Bull in a Bookshop. The authorities desperately needed to make it all go away, which ultimately brings us back to those West German sex dolls.

The sex shop owners, Conegate, did not take kindly to the seizure of their 432 rubber ladies, let alone those sexy vacuum flasks, so they took the UK government to the European Union in Luxembourg arguing that Customs had broken the European Economic Community's rules on the free movement of goods. The EU agreed:

> A Member State may not rely on grounds of public morality within the meaning of Article 36 of the EEC Treaty in order to prohibit the importation of certain goods on the ground that they are indecent or obscene when its legislation contains no prohibition on the manufacture and marketing of the same goods on its territory.

Translation: if it's okay to manufacture something in Britain, you cannot then ban the same thing from being imported. The type of books coming in from America, and indeed some of the very same titles, were already being sold and produced in Britain, so how could Customs justify seizing them? If they were obscene, they would have to be banned outright, for everybody, in *all* shops and for *all* publishers. This was impossible.

On 27 June, after two years and two months of immense emotional strain but the most incredible show of force by the defence campaign, HM Customs and Excise dropped all charges against the nine defendants. Most of the seized books were returned, apart from the very naughtiest ones which went straight back to Ed in Philadelphia. The right loyal Reverend Richard Kirker from the Gay Christian Movement was allowed to pick up his fifteen copies of *The Joy of Gay Sex* from Woburn Place.

Gay's the Word bookshop led the Gay Pride parade in London that summer, waving and cheering from an open-top bus, swagged in rainbow flags and declarations of victory. Victory isn't quite right though, is it? Not after such rank injustice, so much fear and cost, not when people across the country were continuing to face a government ruled by the 'Iron Lady' and a will that seemed – for many of the downtrodden – pathologically homophobic. But queer people were not the only ones facing potential destruction and, even amidst its own war with Customs, Gay's the Word found time to stand up for some unlikely allies.

* * *

At the same time as the raids, another community far from London was under the cosh of the Thatcher government, and it was this sense of shared persecution that led to probably the most unexpected alliance in queer history.

The bitter dispute between Thatcher and the National Union of Mineworkers raged from 1984 to 1985, with mining communities across Britain torn to pieces by the closure of pits. Thirty years later, the Stephen Beresford movie *Pride* would tell the story of gay people and mining families overcoming considerable cultural differences to stand together. Gay's the Word appears in the film, with collections for Lesbians and Gays Support the Miners (LGSM) regularly held on its doorstep.

Ray Aller and Reggie Blennerhassett were two of the activists shaking their buckets, even in heavy rain and snow. 'It's impossible to imagine LGSM without Gay's the Word,' says Reggie. 'I guess we would have found somewhere else to collect money, but I don't know where, and it wouldn't have been the same.' Further collections were held outside supermarkets, but these locations could be dangerous. 'Gay men were too frightened of being attacked,' says Ray, 'but the lesbians were a lot braver. I remember someone collecting in Camden outside a general store, but they were arrested and cautioned by the police.'

Gay's the Word's assistant manager Paud Hegarty kept the young activists watered with regular cups of tea and when things became too much, they were allowed to retreat inside to the warmth and book-cloistered safety of the café. While most passers-by were supportive, others shouted homophobic slurs and spat on the campaigners; not just the usual boneheads, but businessmen and elderly women too, calling them 'disgusting perverts' as they bustled past with their briefcases and shopping.

Their busiest day at Gay's the Word was Saturdays, regularly collecting £50 by closing (a sizeable sum for the time) along with donations of food.

Early LGSM meetings were held on Sundays at 6 p.m. inside the shop and it was there, in November 1984, that Dai Donovan from the Neath, Swansea and Dulais Valleys Miners' Support Group met the LGSM campaigners for the first time. 'It was an incredible evening,' says Reggie, 'because people were very anxious about whether they would accept the money.' The miners hadn't been sure, at first, what to do about this group of 'poofs and dykes' reaching out from London, but Dai arrived, friendly and chilled, joining them for drinks at The Bell pub where he was presented with a cheque for £700. It was a lifeline for struggling families hundreds of miles away.

Young activist Colin Clews was also a member of LGSM. 'The Gay's the Word directors and managers were facing prison for conspiracy to import indecent materials at the time', he says. 'The entire bookshop [staff] was under threat of being sent to jail for decades and still, they supported us without fear.'

The police would occasionally come along and threaten to arrest Colin and his fellow activists. 'Imagine it,' says Colin, 'one lot of gays helping another lot of gays helping a vilified group [the miners] who would normally have been dead against us. It was a bizarre pantomime. We'd say "okay we'll stop now and go into the shop" and as soon as they went, we would be straight out again until the next coppers came along. For most people, the shop was there for books, but to us it was our hiding place and sanctuary from the law.'

* * *

The shop's notoriety in the public imagination was galvanised by the protests and moreover by the Customs raids. With support from MPs, barristers and journalists, the bookshop was quickly gaining respect from the liberal elite, though support from the gay community was far from universal.

Even amongst celebrated writers, there was a degree of sniffing and tutting about the shop from the beginning. In an article for *Christopher Street* magazine (the largest gay magazine in the United States in the 80s), writer Robert K. Martin describes a trip to London with dinner at a friend's flat. While bemoaning Margaret Thatcher's newly formed government, he suggests he might visit London's famous gay bookshop. His fellow dinner guest, who turns out to be the dashingly turtle-necked Greek poet Nikos Stangos, wastes no time serving up some classic European cynicism. A heated discussion ensues. Nikos can see no need for such a thing as a gay bookshop; England has always been liberated and gay bookshops are creating a 'ghetto mentality'. Martin argues that gay bookshops serve the needs of those already *in* a ghetto, alleviating their isolation rather than exacerbating it.

> I remind him that WHSmith, England's mass-market bookseller with branches in virtually every train station in this land of trains, refuses to stock gay books or periodicals if they are aware that they are gay. But Nikos will have none of it. Literature is literature, he retorts; there is no such thing as *gay* literature.

Nikos goes on, possibly ruining pudding, arguing that Americans are the enemy of culture, 'exporting a political strategy that can have no relevance to enlightened societies like England'.

This may surprise the modern reader: the idea that centring gay books can be perceived as a form of unwelcome provocation, but many writers at the time yearned not for queer status but mainstream approval. Indeed, in research for this book, a small number of venerable literary figures responded with triumphant hostility, echoing the view that 'there is no such thing as *queer* books or *queer* bookshops or *queer* authors or *queer* booksellers, only books and people'. This chronicle might suggest otherwise. Returning to Jim MacSweeney, who was manager of Gay's the Word from the late 80s until 2025. Sipping a glass of wine in a Kennington pub, he remembers people talking about the subject of ghettoisation at the time.

> The notion of having a gay section in a bookshop was inconceivable back then – even in the gay community – what was *gay* fiction? Just because an author's gay, should they be segregated? Perhaps the chilly reception Gay's the Word received from some in the community reflected the pain people suffered, being banished from their own families and communities and never quite shedding that longing to return 'home'.

The notion of a gay bookshop seemed to embrace otherness, when it was precisely that sense of being an outsider that caused so many people distress. Jim blinks, frowning at a passing traffic warden beyond the pub window.

> The thing about that is … it's fine until your identity is denied you, or you feel you have to monitor your behaviour because of the possibility of threat. But in a gay space you can cast that off. That's why gay bookshops are important as gay spaces. That's why it isn't about ghettoisation, at least not for people who need it.

Robert K. Martin did visit Gay's the Word, regardless of his friend's disapproval. He arrived to find a shop in the midst of a discussion about a baffling new illness. For a couple of years, staff at the bookshop had been noticing an increase in the number of men contracting hepatitis. It was the first tremor in a fast-approaching global disaster.

AIDS and the Queer Bookstore: Refuge and Resource
1981–present day

*'I finally thought to myself, bitch,
do something yourself.'*

ELIZABETH TAYLOR

ON 5 JUNE 1981, THE US CENTERS FOR DISEASE CONTROL published an article in their Morbidity and Mortality Weekly Report titled 'Pneumocystis Pneumonia – Los Angeles'. The article described cases of a rare lung infection, *Pneumocystis carinii* pneumonia (PCP), in five young, previously healthy gay men in Los Angeles. All the men had other unusual infections, indicating that their immune systems were not working. That summer, an unnamed thirty-five-year-old gay man exhibiting symptoms of severe immunodeficiency became the first known person with AIDS to be admitted to the Clinical Center at the National Institute of Health (NIH) in Maryland. He was never discharged and died on 28 October.

It wasn't until November the following year that the World Health Organization held its first meeting to assess the global AIDS epidemic and began international surveillance. At last, in spring 1984, the US Department of Health identified the cause of AIDS as a retrovirus they initially labelled HTLV-III. This, then, was HIV.

Around the world, hospitals and governments struggled to reconcile their alarm with their prejudice and though lesbian and gay bookstores never imagined they would come to bear such an incredible responsibility, it would often fall to them to offer terrified men comfort and information. In America, the federal, state and municipal governments were terrified of saying anything about AIDS for fear of 'promoting homosexuality'; thus, many sexual health clinics were directed not to offer information or support to the gay male community, even when they were begging for help.

In Philadelphia, Giovanni's Room was simultaneously selling books and offering a lifeline to customers. Looking back on a painful time, Ed Hermance clears his throat, shaking his head. 'Just a couple blocks from the store was a municipal health clinic', he says. 'Any rate, they were forbidden to tell their customers about AIDS – they couldn't tell people anything about it! Nurses would walk to our bookstore and take brochures to give to their patients. That information was produced by lesbians and gay men for themselves.'

If it weren't for lesbian and gay bookstores, countless gay men would have been left without any meaningful support or information. 'They were often in a stupefied state of shock,' says Ed, 'having been given a death sentence.'

Men would walk to the counter, pale-faced and shaking, asking Ed and his staff what they were going to do with the remaining time they had left. In tears, they'd ask how they were going to tell their families that they were gay; that they were ill with this disease; that they were dying. 'We had window seats on the first and second floors,' says Ed, 'and we'd guide people to them so they could sit in the light for a minute and just breathe. They were panicking of course, and so frightened.'

Soon enough, regular customers and beloved staff at Giovanni's Room started to disappear.

Joseph Fairchild Beam was born in Philadelphia in 1954. The son of a security guard and a teacher, he organised for the Black Student Union at Franklin College before joining Giovanni's

Room as a bookseller. While working in the bookstore, he wrote for various publications, including *Blackheart*, *Changing Men* and *Gay Community News*.

A young man of extraordinary drive and talent, he travelled the United States, compiling *In the Life*, a groundbreaking anthology of black gay lives. It was the first chronicle of its kind anywhere in the world. In the introduction he writes:

> There are many reasons for Black gay invisibility. Hard words come to mind: power, racism, conspiracy, oppression, and privilege – each deserving of a full-fledged discussion in gay history books yet unwritten.

He journeyed all over the US, building his anthology from scratch, visiting people at work and in their own homes, sometimes writing men's words for them if they were illiterate.

> We have been ministers, hairdressers, entertainers, salesclerks, civil rights activists, teachers, playwrights, trash collectors, dancers, government officials, choirmasters, and dishwashers. You name it; we've done it – most often with scant recognition. We have mediated family disputes, cared for and reared our siblings, and housed our sick. We have performed many and varied important roles within our community.

He spent every spare minute in Giovanni's Room, compiling his various testimonies, giving to the world stories that would never otherwise have been told, and when the book was published by Alyson Publications in 1986, he took a year off, promoting his seminal work on a countrywide tour. He returned on the brink of international fame, but he was poor, tired and struggling to cope with some devastating news. He asked Ed for his old job back. 'I told him we couldn't do it', says Ed with a pause. 'We'd have been forced to fire somebody to make room. I didn't realise he had AIDS until he was dead.'

Joseph Beam told no one he was sick. Ed shakes his head. 'To watch somebody with that disease was an excruciating experience, losing weight till they were just skin and bones. The fear and the shame were horrible.'

Ed heard the news that Christmas. Joe had taken his own life.

Beam's family church refused to have anything to do with his funeral, so his friends including Ed found another church in west Philadelphia willing to hold a service. A congregation of three hundred people, including black gay friends from all over the country, paid their respects.

Joseph Beam – activist, author, pioneer, queer bookseller (30 December 1954–27 December 1988) – is a bright star amongst so many lost heroes. There is no way to account for the phantom novels, poems and essays lost to HIV and the subsequent response of a society that didn't want to understand, or just didn't care.

Far from Philadelphia, a lesbian and gay bookstore in Hamburg named Buchladen Männerschwarm was facing its own wave of grief. By the mid-80s, it was a haven for HIV+ men. Joachim Bartholomae was a young bookseller at the time, barely six months into his new job, but he remembers the demand for books on the virus, sparse though they were.

> At a gala, gay men passed me by, all kinds: the neurotics, the tough leather guys, old, educated people and young cuties. Some came quickly, took a book and put their money on the table, others lingered. We had to put the change out on the table because they didn't want to touch our hands. After all, we were professional gays and guaranteed to be infected. I can see the image in front of me: this flood of all different people, and I, a young thing, sat there and just kept thinking: 'this is my family. We belong together'. It sounds cheesy, but this

deep feeling has given me the strength for decades to keep my passion [for bookselling] alive despite all the difficulties.

Men would enquire sheepishly about books on AIDS, followed by a torrent of questions, seeking information they were frightened to ask for anywhere else. Men would buy an innocent postcard so they could hide the real reason they'd gone into a gay bookstore. Joachim and his fellow booksellers became experts on the virus, long before health workers gained the same level of awareness.

In the UK, National Health Service nurses also found themselves unable to give their patients the advice and support they needed, and with a dose of sickening irony, some started ordering *The Joy of Gay Sex* from America to help train their staff, right when Customs were seizing the very same book from lesbian and gay bookshops. Journalist Graham McKerrow's hands shake as he thinks about it. 'I really don't know what word to use', he says with undimmed incredulity. 'Just the idea that they could do that to us. Even now I'm shocked that Customs did that. It seems to me of all the awful things they did, that's probably the worst; to take away books people needed so very desperately to stay alive.'

Graham's newspaper, *Capital Gay*, is credited in the *Oxford English Dictionary* as the first publication anywhere in the world to use the term 'HIV'.

At the time, black gay men in London realised they needed to establish their own groups, coping with the stigma around AIDS *as well as* racist discrimination. Lifetime activist and community leader Marc Thompson found himself at the heart of black gay activism, his philosophy nourished by the books he was reading and buying at Gay's the Word. 'Actually, my earliest memory of getting a gay book', he remembers, 'was at WHSmith in Lewisham in 1983. It was James Baldwin's *Giovanni's Room*. I knew I wasn't the only gay boy at the time, but I definitely thought I was the only *black* gay boy.' The book was a disappointment, because it wasn't about black gay men, but it did give him a window into a different world. Aged sixteen he started going to gay pubs and picked up copies of Graham McKerrow's *Capital Gay*, which carried a review of *In the Life* by Joseph Beam. It was Marc's 'Damascus moment'. A limited consignment of the book had been sent to Gay's the Word, so Marc hot-footed it to Marchmont Street and by the next day he was holding a precious copy in his hands. It was expensive but worth it.

By 1986 Marc was seventeen and the HTLV-III test (later, the HIV test) had just become available. He took the test in November and it came back positive. 'I'd only had two partners, so HIV wasn't really a part of my world so when the result came back, I was totally devastated. It was like everything crashed down on me and the first few days and weeks were really dark and lonely.'

In distress, Marc went to Gay's the Word.

> Buying books on HIV at Gay's the Word was really important to me as a gay man. I could get information on my condition as a positive man in a safe space. I could find stories about other gay men who had HIV or who'd lost lovers, so it wasn't always about race, there's other parts of my identity which places like Gay's the Word filled.

The Gay Man's Guide to Safer Sex VHS tape (1990) was being sold at Gay's the Word at the time, reassuring men that the virus couldn't be spread through 'piss, shit or tears', nor through 'spanking, wanking, beating, or bondage'. In one section of the video, it shows slides of contemporary newspaper headlines:

'Judge Raps Revolting Acts by Perverts'
'AIDS House Sealed Up by Council'
'Outlaw All Gays'
'Castration Cures AIDS'

'MENACE: He Carries Killer Virus but Works with Sick Kids'

For Marc Thompson, the video carried an important message, but it also reflected its own form of prejudice. He'd set up the HIV prevention and support charity Big Up, as a direct response to the group Gay Men Fighting AIDS which was allegedly failing to include black gay men. It was a general problem.

> The video didn't have a single black person in there. It wasn't intentional racism, but the message was: this is what 'gay' looks like. I think white activists felt like they were in this crisis, and they didn't have time to be thinking about race, but actually that meant they were leaving people behind.

The sentiment wasn't lost on the lesbian feminists working at Sisterwrite, who set up a buddy system, supporting infected men of all ethnicities by helping them get the support they needed, standing up for them, going to hospital appointments with them and – in too many cases – holding their hands at the end when their families didn't show up. 'There was so much love and kindness shown by lesbian women to gay men', says Lynn Alderson. 'They needed our solidarity and friendship at such a horrific time.'

Emboldened by networks of queer bookshops around the world, publishers printed the latest essays and health titles, as well as poetry and novels on the subject of HIV. In 1988, the gay publishing mogul Sasha Alyson – who'd published Joseph Beam – drew up plans for a radical project titled *You Can Do Something About AIDS*, with multiple publishers co-operating to produce a 126-page book distributed for free through lesbian and gay bookstores. Writers and publishing figures contributed articles, while Elizabeth Taylor, who took a stand in Hollywood to advance gay rights, wrote the book's introduction. An outspoken activist for AIDS awareness, she later said: 'I was made so aware of the silence, this huge, loud silence regarding AIDS. How no one wanted to talk about it, no one wanted to become involved. Certainly no one wanted to give money or support. And it so angered me that I finally thought to myself, "bitch, do something yourself."'

Every single copy of the first edition was snapped up in just ten days, and the book was printed in multiple editions, finally reaching no fewer than 1.5 million copies worldwide. As a result, Sasha Alyson received the first Lambda Literary Award – set up by Deacon Maccubbin at Lambda Rising in Washington – for Publisher's Service.

Back in the UK, Gay Men's Press published *AIDS: Your Questions Answered* (1984) by Richard Fisher, a defining book released at a time when it was still disputed whether AIDS was caused by a virus or a combination of factors. Fisher's book was up to the minute, stating unequivocally that AIDS definitively *was* caused by a virus, explaining how men could protect themselves. 'At least I hope we saved lives with that book', says Gay Men's Press co-founder David Fernbach with characteristic modesty. 'I'm sure we must have; it sold pretty well.'

Just like Giovanni's Room and Gay's the Word, The Bookshop Darlinghurst in Sydney would prove a lifesaver when men started dying of the disease. Books weren't being published on HIV in Australia, so readers were forced to wait for foreign titles to arrive. Owners Les McDonald and Wayne Harrison had to fly to mainland Europe, Britain or ideally the US to find books. By 1986, they'd opened a second store: The Bookshop Newtown, and both outlets lost many friends during that time.

Colin Clews was an early customer at the Newtown store. We last met him standing outside Gay's the Word in London, protesting with Lesbians and Gays Support the Miners. A new arrival to Sydney, he was working in Australia's largest AIDS unit. It was his job to support men who'd just been diagnosed with HIV.

In that clinic we often saw people who'd just been given their AIDS diagnosis. The doctor would tell them the bad news and hand them over to me. These young men in a blubbering mess, weeping: 'Fuck I'm going to die!' Back then we had no treatments at all, apart from specific medicines for things like pneumonia. It was like, 'Alright, you've got AIDS and we've no idea what the fuck is going to happen to you.' I felt like I was doing my duty for my community and yes it was difficult. I was trying my best to be brave.

Overwhelmed, Colin went to The Bookshop Newtown, searching for information from newspapers and magazines from around the world. There was the *Body Politic* magazine from Canada, *Christopher Street* magazine from New York and *The Advocate* from Washington. 'That bookshop was like a lighthouse giving people an idea of what to do,' says Colin, 'where to go, how to navigate this maze of people and how to access the right advice.'

The AIDS pandemic would rage for many years to come, reanimating society's worst prejudices *just* when the mainstream was beginning to be more accepting. Lesbian and gay bookshops were helping to unite the queer community, but one bookshop was facing a greater barrier than most: a reinforced concrete wall 155 kilometres long.

Prinz Eisenherz

BERLIN

1978–still open

> *'People were literally fainting on the floor when the Berlin Wall came down.'*
>
> PIET VAN DER WAAL

BY THE LATE 1970S, QUEER PEOPLE IN BOTH EAST AND West Germany were building their community, but they did so carrying the weight of a horrifying past.

The Weimar Republic of the 1920s had created one of the most progressive and vibrant queer cultures in the world. Berlin was alive with drag balls, same-sex cabarets and a blossoming queer press. But that brief period of openness was violently destroyed by the Nazis in 1933 when homosexuals, alongside Jews, were subjected to some of the worst cruelties of the regime. In 1935, Hitler tightened a pre-existing law known as Paragraph 175, effectively creating Germany's answer to Britain's Labouchère Amendment, criminalising not just sex acts but any perceived homosexual behaviour between men. Between 5,000 and 15,000 queer people were deported to concentration camps, forced to wear the pink triangle and often singled out for especially brutal treatment, including forced castration, medical experiments and executions. Very few survived.

Lesbian women were classified as 'asocials' or 'degenerates' and subjected to surveillance, imprisonment or institutionalisation if they refused to conform to the Nazi ideal of womanhood.

Paragraph 183 of the German Criminal Code prohibited 'sexual self-determination' and public exhibitionism. Many transgender individuals were deported to concentration camps, where they faced brutal treatment including dystopian medical experiments.

The end of the war did not spell freedom for those interred in concentration camps. Many queer survivors were reimprisoned by their supposed liberators, their cries for mercy either ignored or dismissed.*

Paradoxically, East Germany took a more liberal approach to the law. At the close of the 1960s, the secular GDR government reformed its criminal code, removing Nazi-era provisions and setting a uniform age of consent for homosexual and heterosexual acts. Yet still, queer life remained strictly controlled. Homosexuality was portrayed as a symptom of Western decadence and public expressions of queer identity were suppressed. There were no openly gay venues and activism was nearly impossible. What little community did exist often found shelter in the Protestant Church, which offered one of the only protected spaces for dissident thought. Still, that isn't to say there were no gay parties in East Berlin before the Wall came down. While clubs in the West were expensive and loud with techno music and flashy strobe lights, their equivalents in the East were more akin to underground social clubs in rented sports halls. No Western music but still some sweat and romance to go with the rum and Club Cola.

By the late 1970s, queer Germans in West Berlin were beginning to reclaim their history, and the Prinz Eisenherz bookstore was founded on Berlin's Bülowstraße in the freezing November of 1978.

---

* It wasn't until 1969 that West Germany began to roll back Paragraph 175, and only in 1994 was the law fully repealed. By then, tens of thousands of lives had been damaged by state prosecution. Former convictions were not officially annulled until 2002. Compensation would not come until 2017, when most of the violated men were dead. Paragraph 183 remains, but has been amended significantly, now pertaining to indecent exposure.

Activists Peter Hedenström, Lothar Lang, Michael Keim and Christian von Maltzahn were involved in radical gay left-wing student activism. Peter Hedenström remembers the time fondly. 'By the time of the 80s in West Berlin there was a very large gay and lesbian subculture. It was very friendly, not very dangerous, more vibrant. Above all, there were still lesbian bars, not like today.'

West Berlin already boasted two feminist bookstores and several radical booksellers but there were very few queer books in German to stock. Hedenström and his friends planned to bring queer literature to the forefront, not only for the community but for the public at large. They envisioned a shop that went well beyond bookselling, offering readings, exhibitions, community meetings and discussion groups.

The bookshop's regal name was chosen at the very last minute, the day before the business was ratified with local government. The four men convened in a pub to hash out some ideas. They considered 'Magnus Hirschfeld Buchhandlung', in honour of the famous exiled sexologist. They also thought of 'Klaus Mann bookstore' in memory of the German author known for his novel that exposed the evils of the Nazi regime. Resonant, but not particularly optimistic. Eventually, their brainstorming and beer led them to the name Prinz Eisenherz, alluding to Prince Valiant from the British Arthurian legend of Camelot. Depicted in a 1930s comic strip, rumours persisted that the fictional character was gay: he was a muscular and often bare-chested knight from Norway who fought for King Arthur and made friends with Sir Gawain and Sir Tristram. There's no immediate evidence the knights had a tug on Excalibur or rocked the Round Table but the founders liked the idea of answering the phone with a royal flourish, so the name stuck.

Unfortunately, opening in the middle of a snowy Berlin winter was exacerbated by a damp retail unit that lacked adequate heating, so the shop moved west to leafy Savignyplatz in

Charlottenburg which was packed with a multitude of bookstores at the time.

Their stock was growing, with many books ordered from abroad. American books and newspapers were ordered from Ed Hermance at Giovanni's Room. It was on a trip to Philadelphia that Peter first heard about HIV. 'From the beginning we took this very seriously', Peter says, 'and had all the important information and newspapers delivered from the States.' The Berlin gay magazine *Siegessäule* (meaning 'Victory Column', named after Berlin's famous gay landmark and meeting place) did a special issue on the AIDS pandemic, and customers rushed to buy it, frightened and hungry for information. Prinz Eisenherz staff co-founded the German support service AIDS Help. They would lose many customers, too many to count. A bookseller died from the virus, while a second was saved when new medication arrived just in time. Peter and his staff got used to attending funerals and made full use of the large shop windows, displaying books about sexual safety and how to cope with the syndrome.

In 1988, Prinz Eisenherz needed to expand from three staff to five, so it took on Piet van der Waal. His bookstore, Vrolijk in Amsterdam, had been supplying Prinz Eisenherz, so he was instantly at home. He'd only been in his job a few months when, in November 1989, the city experienced a cultural shock.

'People were literally fainting on the floor when the Berlin Wall came down', remembers Piet. 'They were overwhelmed to see a shop filled with gay books and magazines. It was a dream for them. They had heard rumours of a gay bookstore that looked right onto the street with open windows, but didn't believe it.'

These gay men from the East were filled with joy, laughing with delight, and in tears. But they left in shame because they were unable to afford anything to carry back across the rubble of the demolished Wall. The physical divide was gone, but it was still entrenched in the reality of people's day-to-day lives. 'In the early days men from the East would arrive at the store with no money', says Piet, 'because we had the Deutsche Mark and they only had East German money which was worth nothing, so they were looking at the books and magazines but couldn't buy them which was very emotional.'

Prinz Eisenherz asked the local community to hand in used books to sell for 20 or 50 cents and the staff put up two or three bookcases of good books which customers from the East could afford. The shop was now an established gathering place for a gay population at last free from persecution, no longer split by war, united for the first time since those long-distant days of the 1920s. Of all the bookstores featured in this chronicle, Prinz Eisenherz stands as the most visceral embodiment of the unextinguishable power of queer existence, even when it has been driven far underground by the weight of fascist bigotry.

In fact, Piet's bookshop in Holland – the first of its kind – is a fine example of a queer bookshop operating beneath the very feet of the mainstream. Let's pay a visit to Amsterdam.

Vrolijk

AMSTERDAM
1983–2017

'It was the first time we said: "we are open, this is who we are."'

PIET VAN DER WAAL

IN THE MIDDLE OF AMSTERDAM'S SPIDERWEB OF CANALS stands Spui Square, a collection of teetering seventeenth-century buildings in multicoloured brick, arranged like cakes around a cobblestone piazza. Here we discover the heart of Amsterdam's literary district where, next to the legendary Athenaeum Bookstore, we find a gloomy doorway leading down a narrow staircase. This is Vrolijk.

The subterranean shop had a bare concrete floor and low ceiling, forcing taller customers to crouch to avoid bumping their heads on the old wooden beams. The shop started life as a mere stockroom for Piet van der Waal's mail-order business but, when the Post Office went on strike, he invited customers to pick up their orders in person, for the first time revealing his address. That was 1983, and in April 1984, the Vrolijk Bookstore plucked up the courage to step into the sun with a sign at the top of the staircase reading: 'Bookshop Vrolijk Gay and Lesbian Bookstore'.

Vrolijk is Dutch for 'happy' or, similar to the English double meaning, 'gay'.

'It was the first time we said: "we are open, this is who we are,"' remembers Piet. 'It felt very good but also a risk.' Vrolijk was right next door to the exit for Madame Tussauds, which gave some unwelcome footfall. 'The English were pretty awful, trying to push into the store shouting "you are gay!", and drunk students at night were bad news too, peeing against the door, it was quite awful.'

Piet was effectively trapped in the basement with only one exit. 'I was robbed once at knifepoint, by a group of young men from Holland, and I gave up all my money in fear of being stabbed. It was very unpleasant.'

Piet had good reason to be alert. Another bookstore owner[*] had been attacked in Germany when a stranger pulled out a knife and slashed him across the stomach. The attacker ran off, followed by the victim, who was covered in his own blood, before collapsing to the ground. He was rushed to hospital and put into an induced coma. As doctors fought to save his life, staff from other gay bookstores across Europe stepped in to save his business.

Thus, while previous lesbian and gay bookstores had taken on their first staff to meet demand, Piet's first employee was hired, at least partly, for security. Bookseller Eric, a young gay man in his late twenties, joined the shop in around 1985. In spite of sporadic attacks, they never once thought about taking their shop sign down, partly because the other businesses on the square stepped in to keep them safe.

An orange light was fitted at the top of the staircase which Piet and Eric could flash on and off if they were under threat. There were many cafés dotted around the square and the second the mayday button was pushed, a waiter would respond to the signal, running in to help. Multiple attacks and attempted robberies were thwarted thanks to this valiant squad of rapid-response waiters.

---

[*] A request was made to speak to the owner, but no response was received. The name of the shop and the individual concerned are redacted here out of respect for their privacy.

By the mid-80s, Vrolijk was a beloved destination on the Dutch gay scene and customers were soon cramming the basement. There was no window down in the cellar, which appealed to those who preferred to visit unseen. In that sense, it was the absolute opposite of the other shops which defined themselves by having a large streetside window. As far as the stock went, however, Piet followed much the same sensibility as his fellow pioneers.

'We didn't want to be a sex shop', he says. 'There were enough of those in Amsterdam already, so we only put serious magazines outside.'

The bookstore's notoriety continued to spread and soon, Piet and his assistant Eric were extending their hours, rushing to the shop every day with bundles of stock in their arms, freshly collected from the Post Office. They desperately needed more helpers. That's when Vrolijk took on its first woman bookseller, a twenty-five-year-old self-described butch lesbian called Anneke.

At that time, there was still a split between gay women's and gay men's bookstores in Holland, so this was the first time in Dutch history that lesbian and gay books were set side by side. It was an important move for Piet, who'd always envisioned a mixed bookstore, championing gender equality on his shelves. It wasn't that way for other businesses nearby. A second gay bookstore named Intermale had opened hot on Vrolijk's heels in 1984. It was close to Spui Square, so it would have made sense to join forces rather than compete, but the new boys on the block were only interested in catering for men and early talks fell through. Intermale also wanted to expand into sex aids (who doesn't?) and erotic magazines. 'We were more serious,' Piet says, 'specialising in literary, scientific, and political books.' And thanks to new arrival Anneke with her considerable connections in the lesbian scene, a growing number of women started frequenting the store.

The shop had grown from one makeshift set of shelves to fifteen bookcases, stuffed floor-to-ceiling with titles from around the world. Here, buried deep beneath historic Spui Square, there blossomed a queer nexus, a space – by now a relatively *safe* space – for people to purchase and request lesbian and gay literature, advancing rights in just as meaningful a way as the university courses, activist groups, magazines and marches of the time. Piet remembers the store's popularity with a mixed sense of pride and exhaustion. 'Saturday evenings were packed with so many people it became a crush and yes there were some people stealing books because it was so squashed nobody could see.'

By 1988, Holland's first gay bookstore owner was growing a little tired, the thrill of revolution having given way to the drudgery of admin, covering overtime, agreeing leave, bookkeeping and stocktaking. That's when he decided to move to Berlin and join his friends at Prinz Eisenherz.

Let's travel now to a rural town in Scotland, where the idea of lesbian and gay rights would be considered more than a little exotic.

Lavender Menace and West & Wilde

EDINBURGH

1982–still open as archive

*'It was the first time I realised two
women could be together.'*

AN EARLY CUSTOMER
AT LAVENDER MENACE

NEWS ABOUT THE LESBIAN AND GAY UPRISING OF THE early 1970s hadn't yet reached Sigrid Nilsen's small town in rural Scotland. 'I knew one other lesbian among my classmates', she says, looking back. 'We had to pretend we were just friends.' In the days before the internet, she was isolated, searching for books about 'funny' women and 'Friends of Dorothy', always hopeful, always ready to be disappointed. She haunted the local bookshop and bought a copy of Ann Bannon's pulp romance, *Odd Girl Out*. It was something at least, but she had better luck in the sleazy newsagents nearby. It was all depressingly parochial and young Sigrid felt it was time for an adventure.

In 1979, she found herself standing in a bookshop in Edinburgh with a rucksack slung over her shoulder. She was enjoying her journey around Scotland, discovering new ways of seeing the world, new ways of seeing *herself*.

She cast her eyes around the shelves, maybe looking for something to read, just happy to be dry and warm. Her eye was caught by a stack of books which stretched all the way from the floor to the ceiling. It was a new bestseller in hardback, glossy in black, with red and white lettering: *Portrait of a Marriage*, the biography of author and garden designer Vita Sackville-West. Sigrid looked up at the great stack of books and thought: 'Now, what is this about?' She bought the book, fell in love with Vita and sensed her future was in bookselling. If only there were a bookshop selling lesbian and gay literature…

Bob Orr had set up the Open Gaze bookstall three years earlier in 1976, having grown frustrated with the lack of gay books available in mainstream bookshops. His literary awakening was *No End to the Way*, by Neville Jackson, a novel with a relatively uplifting climax. He'd had to buy it in a bus station because mainstream bookshops wouldn't touch popular gay novels. He saw an opportunity. By selling queer books, it could be argued that Bob was the first openly gay bookseller in the whole of the UK; he was most certainly a pioneer in Scotland. In those very early days, Open Gaze was part of the Scottish Homosexual Rights Group's Gay Information Centre, based on Broughton Street. A collective of bookselling volunteers took shape and one of them was Sigrid Nilsen.

Soon, the bookstall was thriving, but as demand grew, they had to make a tricky decision about the types of books they wanted to sell. Bob didn't want to stick to just literary books, but as he became more adventurous, the conservative members of the SHRG grew uneasy, and in December 1979 there was a bit of a stand-off. Bob and his fellow volunteers were accused of selling blasphemous greetings cards, and consequently, the collective gave up their membership and formed Lavender Books.

Untethered from the SHRG, the travelling bookshop evolved into a roaming co-operative, selling lesbian and gay books and paraphernalia at conferences and marches right across the UK. Between 1980 and 1981 they became a familiar sight for British lesbian and gay activists, supported in the background by Edinburgh's radical bookshop, First of May, and then by their new friends at Gay's the Word.

Inspired by their success and realising they could give Edinburgh what Ernest Hole and his fellow booksellers had given London, Sigrid and Bob decided it was their destiny to open a bricks-and-mortar bookshop. Not everyone supported the plan, however, and they were left to pursue the venture alone. They set up their business in partnership and raised funds through a new bookstall. Edinburgh had its first proper gay disco venue by then, 'Fire Island' on Princes Street,* which gave Bob and Sigrid space for a pop-up table of books. They also got an overdraft for their account with the Co-operative Bank and enthusiastic members of the queer community made donations towards set-up costs.

The name Lavender Menace was a neat satirical nod to the phrase coined in the 1960s by the aforementioned Betty Friedan, the homophobic feminist campaigner. They had lots of volunteers helping to kit it out, with new shelving and as much stock as they could afford. It was a basement space down a steep and treacherous staircase, but no ankles were broken and their dream was realised in August 1982, opening their doors just in time for the Edinburgh Pride March. The sign above the door declared: 'Edinburgh's Lesbian and Gay Community Bookshop', and there was a sincere emphasis on 'community'. '*Safe space* wasn't a phrase when we opened the bookshop', remembers Sigrid, 'but that's essentially what we were doing. People would come in and say "this is such a gay space!" Once, a man put his head through the door very timidly and said, in surprise, "Oh… it's nice."'

The arrival of Edinburgh's first lesbian and gay bookshop didn't seem to cause much more than a ripple in the local community. 'Most people in the neighbourhood seemed happy to ignore it', says Sigrid, 'unless they were lesbian or gay of course, or if they just liked books.'

---

* Funnily enough, the venue is now a Waterstones bookshop.

There was a little scepticism in the early days, however, including one supporter who wondered aloud: 'Are there enough books?' That customer was unwittingly voicing the refrain of early visitors to virtually every newborn queer bookstore from Toronto to Hamburg. They needn't have worried. Stock grew as publishers took courage, and so did the bookshop's reputation, with author signings and readings, discussions and book launches. Sigrid and Bob made sure women were at the heart of the bookshop, never a second thought as they so often were in the activist scene of the time. 'From the beginning, we made it clear that Lavender Menace wasn't just a name', Sigrid writes in the foreword to the 2017 play *Love Song to Lavender Menace*. 'It was important to be visibly *there* for women.' They took advice from the London feminist bookshop Sisterwrite, and for a while, the shop was women-only on Sundays. She also set up a women's mail-order catalogue, the Lavender Lesbian List, and in 1983, the shop sponsored the Edinburgh Feminist Writers' Conference. Writers Jeanette Winterson, Suniti Namjoshi, Anne Fine, Sarah Schulman and many others gave readings, along with gay male writers including Edmund White, Armistead Maupin, David Leavitt and Randy Shilts.

There were arguments about what books to stock, debates between Bob and Sigrid, colleagues, customers and random members of the public, who liked to pop their head through the door and comment on the books in the window. Once, a group of lesbian feminists disapproved of some of Lavender Menace's books and staged a boycott, with one woman announcing she'd stolen a book and burned it.

Meanwhile, a general mail-order service was set up, allowing lesbian and gay customers living in the remotest parts of Scotland to order books discreetly. In no time, they connected with Ed Hermance at Giovanni's Room, along with a few other international shops, so they could import the latest titles from abroad. Which led to some trouble.

Just like Gay's the Word, those imports caught the ever-searching eye of HM Customs. Many titles were seized at the border for being 'pornographic', including classic gay authors such as Jean Genet. 'The Gay's the Word raid was a problem for us too', Sigrid says. 'Boxes of our imported books were being seized all the time. A few were returned damaged, but most just disappeared.' To get around the raids, they ordered stock using the names Jane Pirie and Marianne Woods – the two Edinburgh teachers who went to court in 1811 after they were accused of being lovers – but that didn't work for long. Down in London, Gay's the Word had a third of its stock seized and there was no way Lavender Menace could have survived in those circumstances, so they hid their imported overstock in another room. When the day came, they were ready, perhaps even over-prepared.

The police had received a complaint about a magazine they were selling. Officers turned up and started rifling through the magazines, searching for the offending item. They scoured the shelves and cupboards and the backroom stock until they found it, the title lost to memory. And then they left. 'I was stunned', says Sigrid. 'A friend of Bob's was with me in the shop at the time and he said, "Well, they certainly tidied up after themselves, didn't they? I'll have to get them over to my house to do some cleaning." The other person in the shop and I started laughing with relief.'

A few weeks later, the magazine was returned along with a box of books, covered in cigarette ash, chocolate and coffee stains. Clearly someone had satisfied their curiosity with a thorough read. Sigrid and Bob weren't charged.

Trouble occasionally arrived at the door in other guises. 'We had a few incidents of harassment at Lavender Menace', says Sigrid. 'A school pupil once threw a book across the shop, and, to our astonishment, he was brought in by his teacher and told to apologise. Then there was a local fundamentalist preacher who stood next to the political pamphlets and sang hymns, but he was happy to move on when asked.'

In 1987, Lavender Menace changed its name to West & Wilde and moved to new premises on Dundas Street, then owned by Bob Orr and Raymond Rose. West & Wilde would continue to trade for another decade, welcoming writers from all over the lesbian and gay publishing world, including Karla Jay, one of the original New York Lavender Menaces.

The new premises were on the ground floor this time, and were firebombed twice. Thankfully, the bombs didn't properly ignite and nobody was harmed, at least not physically. Still, the attacks were far outweighed by the love people had for their bookshop. Sigrid looks back with pride on the difference they made.

> Many people have told me how a book encountered in the shop gave them a different view of life. One customer told me she met her life partner in the shop. She was a teenager when we opened and she bought *Patience and Sarah*, by Isabel Miller. It had a huge impact on her. She said: 'It was the first time I realised two women could be together.'

A sense of female empowerment shared by customers in our next bookshop. Let's join them.

Silver Moon

LONDON

1984–2001

*'We would prefer male customers not
to browse in the lesbian section.'*

CUSTOMER NOTICE, SILVER MOON

JANE CHOLMELEY WAS BORN IN 1948, THE DAUGHTER of a country parson who – though a doting father to his two daughters – craved a son to continue the family name. The Cholmeleys had first landed in England as part of the Norman Conquest of 1066, and, despite flourishing for nine centuries, they were at risk of dying out. Jane may not have satisfied in the agnatic sense, but she'd inherited more than her share of Cholmeley pluck.

After a year's scholarship at Randolph–Macon College in Virginia, she returned to England and managed to get a job in publishing as a secretary – more or less the only role available for a university educated woman at the time. After cutting her teeth at Yale University Press, she moved to children's publisher Macdonald Educational and there she discovered both feminism and her first love. Sue Butterworth caught Jane's eye in the office and the pair coupled up at the work Christmas party. In a burst of liberation and paranoia, Jane realised she was a lesbian. As she writes in her memoir, *A Bookshop of One's Own* (2024): 'It's an explosive thing to move from secure majority privilege to despised outcast in one kiss. Love as overnight radicalization. And yet, nothing could have been better.'

In 1979, she joined the Women in Publishing group, before fleeing Macdonald Educational after it was taken over by Robert Maxwell.* He spat bits of fried chicken in meetings while hungrily stripping the company of all joy. Jane knew she had to get out. Freedom allowed her to complete an MA in women's studies, but then Sue was made redundant, trying her best to cover the financial hole with a quirky mix of copywriting for The Women's Press and a gig at a military publisher, giving her an exhaustive knowledge of feminist literature and aircraft carriers. Still, it wasn't enough to get by; Sue and Jane had two cats, a dog and themselves to feed.

It was a wintry day in Llandudno in 1981 when they made their fateful decision. They were walking along the beach discussing their future when the notion of setting up a publisher was raised. It seemed like a good idea, considering their qualifications, but it would be far too expensive. They walked on in the bluster as their dog bounded about their legs. Perhaps a bookshop was more affordable than a publisher? They looked at each other and smiled. 'Ignorance makes you brave', writes Jane. 'If I'd known then the hurdles and problems that lay ahead, I would never, never have dared.'

First things first, they had to find the right location. For the first time in UK queer bookselling, a new bookshop was having to consider the thorny question of territorial boundaries. They stuck pink stickers on the locations of Gay's the Word and Sisterwrite, as

---

* Robert Maxwell, the bombastic newspaper baron, MP and self-made tycoon with a knack for inflating his business empire, acumen and waistline. Famous for buying *The Mirror* newspaper, suing anyone who crossed him and holding court in a style somewhere between Bond villain and pub landlord, Maxwell was also infamous for his elastic relationship with the truth, a tendency towards creative accounting and a personal life whispered about in Fleet Street with a mixture of awe and disbelief. His mysterious death in 1991 – falling, jumping or being pushed from his yacht, the *Lady Ghislaine* – only cemented his reputation as a man who exited life as dramatically as he lived it.

well as other radical bookshops like Housmans and Compendium. North London wasn't an option. Jane was particularly keen to avoid displeasing Sisterwrite, because it played such a powerful part in her own journey. When she'd first discovered feminism, she'd gone there to learn about the women's movement, it being the only bookshop offering her a literary home. She'd sit in the café upstairs – Sisterbite – and absorb the radical spirit of the other women there, awed by their fearlessness, realising who she was and what she wanted to become.

For a year, Jane and Sue trekked across London having very little luck, but then they saw an advertisement in the trade magazine, *The Bookseller*. The Greater London Council was offering two vacant shop units on the Charing Cross Road. They were available for bookshop use only, giving a rent discount that worked out at ten per cent. This was exactly the opportunity Jane and Sue had been searching for, but they needed some help.

Jane Anger was working with Women in Publishing at the time. She was slight, androgynous, fiercely feminist, vegetarian and a lesbian. As recounted in *A Bookshop of One's Own*, Jane and Sue wrote to her:

> We can promise you at least two years of extremely hard work and near total penury to be followed, hopefully, by a totally rewarding achievement and minor mega star status within the women's movement.

A week later the trio were marching off to Charing Cross Road to view the empty shops. No. 70 was big, square and a little more expensive, but while no. 68 next door was just eleven feet wide and very long with a pokey entrance from the street, it suited their requirements perfectly. The narrowness and depth of the space would allow customers some privacy towards the back. It felt like a thrilling adventure, though the actual shop was in a dilapidated state with grimy windows and discarded syringes in the back alleys. Nevertheless, 'We loved it at first sight', says Jane. The shop would need a name.

They considered 'Swallows and Amazons', but friends assumed they were planning to sell children's books rather than feminist literature, so they thought about 'Dyke and Doughnut' which was funny but a bit blunt and, besides, not all lesbians used that word anymore.* Apparently out of nowhere and at the very last minute, Jane slammed her pencil down (surely a pencil was slammed) and suggested 'Silver Moon', drawing on the relationship in art and culture between the moon (an ancient symbol of womanhood, influencing tides and cycles), silver (an ancient symbol of feminine energy) and – to quote Jane – 'women's things'. It wasn't until a few weeks later they realised that the ancient Greek lyrical poet Sappho had actually written a fragment of poetry commonly referred to as 'Silver Moon'.†

On 22 June 1983, the Greater London Council called to say they'd been successful in their application, which caught them by surprise; they hadn't even met with Sisterwrite yet. The meeting was due two days later. The council offer certainly altered things. An urgent conversation was held and the two shops decided London was big enough for them both. Everything was falling into place. And then.

Jane and Sue had been talking openly with the feminist publisher Virago Press about their plans. They'd seemed supportive, but completely out of the blue it transpired they were opening a bookshop of their own in Covent Garden, just a five-minute walk

---

* 'Dyke' not 'doughnut'.
† The silver moon is set;
The Pleiades are gone;
Half the long night is spent, and yet
I lie alone.
(Translation by J. H. Merivale, *Collections from the Greek Anthology*, 1813)

from Charing Cross Road. After taking such pains to engage in amicable talks with Sisterwrite, this felt like betrayal.

Jane wrote in her diary that night: 'Returned home, got drunk. Haven't felt that way since my father died ... crushed, nearly broken, so angry I hardly know where to begin ... incredibly bitter.'

A summit with Virago was considered, with allegations of unfeminist conduct. It was an uncomfortable confrontation for Silver Moon; they couldn't run a feminist bookshop while refusing to deal with a respected feminist publisher. Jane, Sue and Jane would have to take the high shelf, praying their business wasn't destroyed before it'd even begun. As it turned out a meeting did take place. It was a tense summit, with the Silver Moon team expressing their pain and anger. As Jane recounts, Virago founder Harriet Spicer said she had 'never done anything of which she felt so ashamed'. 'With hard work we laid our bitterness aside,' Jane recalls, 'and Virago responded by helping us enormously with our opening publicity, including Sisterwrite. Three feminist bookshops – the more the merrier.'

The shop itself was a money pit, requiring a serious refit. They only had £5,385 to spend so they asked for donations from friends and family and managed to raise almost £15,000. Still, it was barely thirty per cent of what they needed, so a grant application was made to the Greater London Council and after a nail-biting five months, the money came through. Reading the grant application, it's striking that the words 'lesbian', 'gay' and 'homosexual' make no appearance in the text. The only slight hint that the bookshop might serve the needs of gay women was in relation to the proposed art gallery:

> We wish particularly to have this space used by disabled women, women of colour and *women regularly disadvantaged by the traditional art world*. [emphasis added]

Necessary obfuscation, perhaps belying the fact that while feminism was viewed sympathetically by left-wing politics, homosexuality often wasn't. Would the bookshop have been refused funding if it had stated a clear intention to cater for lesbian women? Either way, Silver Moon knew it had to open by May 1984. There were more unexpected boobytraps with rocketing refurbishment costs and despotic demands from the council, but ultimately, thanks to a deep reservoir of patience and determination, the three women managed to open their bookshop as planned.

The premises had been transformed from a gloomy hole into a bright and pleasant space with cornflower blue doors and woodwork and a new speckled carpet to hide any marks (unfortunately, this would prove necessary in ways they did not expect).

Silver Moon opened at no. 68 Charing Cross Road on 31 May 1984 to the cheering of a female crowd and the hammering of builders in the basement below.

The decision on what books to stock – now a fully established test for any queer bookshop's mettle – had been handled by establishing an advisory group with feminists from different ethnic and cultural backgrounds, while a set of specific rules had been written up. All Silver Moon books were evaluated using four key principles:

1. Fiction: all books had to be written by women.
2. Non-fiction: the books could be written by a woman or a man, but had to be about the condition of women.
3. Comprehensiveness in specialisation was their strength.
4. The shop had a duty to survive.

For a brief period, they had fun with a 'Men's Section', enjoying the irony of treating male writers as a minority group in publishing (imagine such a thing), but the humour was lost on Silver Moon customers and nobody bought the books, so it was mothballed.

One tricky question was how to *label* gay books for women. 'Lesbian', 'Queer', 'Women loving women'? Would putting those markers above certain shelves act as a signpost, exposing customers to risk of abuse? Also, were lesbian books defined by their content or the sexuality of the author? If a straight woman wrote a lesbian romance, for instance – and they did – where would that be shelved? Then there were the different factions of the feminist movement. In Silver Moon, disgruntled sex-positive feminists started hiding Andrea Dworkin's *Pornography: Men Possessing Women* down the back of a shelf, while disgruntled anti-pornography feminists were hiding *Macho Sluts* by Pat Califia.

Meanwhile, the International Feminist Book Fair was coming to London and Silver Moon was hopeful it could sell books as central London's lesbian-feminist bookshop. Unfortunately, organisers had chosen Sisterwrite and given them sole book-selling rights. The Silver Moon team were beginning to feel like they were getting rough treatment from their fellow feminists. Sue Butterworth drafted the write-up for their shop in the Book Fair catalogue with a glancing slap: 'Wearied by Waterstones? Frustrated by Foyles? Are your dungarees too naff for Sisterwrite?' Alas, it didn't make it to print.

Queer and feminist bookshops hadn't been in competition – literal or perceived – in one city like this before, and the territorial tension was palpable. Jane and Sue took a magnanimous approach, supporting their fellow queer bookshops as best they could, none more so than Gay's the Word which was struggling to fight back following the raid by Customs. The swoop had taken place a month before Silver Moon's opening and as soon as the shop was up and running they wrote a letter in solidarity – 'After all, your struggle is ours too' – and held a fundraising party and auction for the Defend Gay's the Word campaign.

A pretty daring move, putting Silver Moon on the government's radar like that. After all, they were ordering stock from

Giovanni's Room, risking raids of their own. As things turned out, Customs left them alone, perhaps suffering burned fingers from all the negative press they were getting, perhaps because of the shop's cryptic name. That's not to say Silver Moon was spared interference. Customs worked hand in hand with the Post Office and it soon became clear that someone at Mount Pleasant Sorting Office was playing silly buggers. Boxes of stock would regularly arrive battered, half opened and covered in boot marks, implying they'd been used as a football. Hundreds of pounds worth of stock was lost, so Jane wrote a stiff letter to the sorting office chief, demanding he pay them a visit. To Jane's surprise, he accepted and whoever was responsible, parcels arrived in mint condition from that point on.

By now, the Silver Moon team were getting used to their customers. 'Some came in with a swagger', writes Jane Cholmeley. 'Others were at the beginning of that scary, liberating journey. If the only lesbian book you knew was *The Well of Loneliness* – pioneering, brave, but oh so depressing – we said, "Come in, we've got stories of love, lust and relationships, beach reads, literature, politics and fun."'

One Christmas Eve, a very drunk gentleman asked whether they had any books about cats. Books about cats? In a lesbian-feminist bookshop? Yes. Jane was adamant that, if Silver Moon and the feminist movement were going to affect social change, men should be welcome. As the shop hit its stride, around thirty per cent of Silver Moon's customers were male, mostly well behaved, occasionally disgusting. On one occasion a man stood by the shelves and masturbated, ejaculating onto the speckled carpet. Another enjoyed throwing books at staff, while dirty phone calls became part of daily life. Hate mail arrived in abundance. Once, a man attacked a female customer with a knife, slashing her dress – fortunately nothing else – while a lunatic with a grey beard liked to shout abuse at staff for not stocking men's books.

He was banned but remained undeterred, standing outside the shop bellowing away like a blowhorn. After being moved on by community police, he took to shouting from the opposite side of the road, scaring nobody but the pigeons.

It was an established requirement by this stage for a queer bookshop to operate as a trusted signposting service for customers seeking support or recreation, and Silver Moon was no different. There was a free noticeboard containing information on accommodation, bike repairs, requests for women plumbers and women electricians, notices for lesbian social groups, 'hiking dykes', HIV information, details about the London lesbian and gay switchboard, lesbian sports groups and gay-friendly lawyers. It was a chore to keep so many flyers and notices in order, but it was an important resource.

After her frosty Pride badge experience at Sisterwrite, aspiring novelist Sarah Waters found Silver Moon more welcoming. 'In the days before the internet, it was one of the only ways to find other like-minded lesbians looking for somewhere to stay,' she says. 'It's incredible now to think we used to put our advertisement up along with our telephone numbers. So trusting.'

A little too trusting perhaps. On one occasion Sarah and her flatmates placed a separate notice in the small ads section of *City Limits* magazine. 'A guy called up', says Sarah, 'pretending to be conducting some sort of survey, then started asking intimate questions – he didn't mention the house share.'

A new era of openness and agency in the lesbian community was exposing women to heightened risk as well as opportunity. Silver Moon called a meeting, at which a warning sign was agreed for the noticeboard:

> We would prefer male customers not to browse in the lesbian section or at the notice board. If you require a specific title, please ask a member of staff.

Sarah Waters remembers going into Silver Moon on one occasion, searching for a book she'd heard about.

> I didn't know what the title was, I only knew it was a book about a lesbian nun in Renaissance Italy. Jane Cholmeley was behind the till and she knew instantly what I meant. It was *Immodest Acts*, by Judith C. Brown. She was very knowledgeable. I wouldn't have asked in a mainstream bookshop, where even saying the word *lesbian* might have made me feel awkward.

Jane and Sue had more than realised the dream they'd cooked up on Llandudno beach. They had beaten the odds with the local authority, supported their fellow bookstores, built a community, batted away perverts and avoided division and potential rancour with a laudable generosity of spirit. They would need to stick together, because the Thatcher government was about to usher in legislation that heralded an even darker era for queer people in the United Kingdom.

This new age of state-sponsored oppression would begin with a seemingly innocent box of books. That box would go off like a bomb.

Section 28:
Pride and Prejudice
1988–2003

GAY'S THE WORD, MARCHMONT STREET, LONDON, 1985. It was just another day in the basement stockroom for deputy manager Amanda Russell. Having replaced the illicit cat litter confiscated by Customs, she was back at work, enjoying sorting through books for an interesting order from Haringey Council. They were looking for reading material to help staff who were responding to the needs of young gay students.

Amanda searched through the stock, picking out titles she thought might fit the bill. A recent translation of a Danish children's book had just come in, published by Gay Men's Press. She picked it up and turned it over. A cheerful cover in bright yellow and blue with black-and-white pictures of two sensible-looking men and a happy girl with scruffy blonde hair. It went straight into the box. She couldn't have guessed at the time, but her choices would lead – through no fault of her own – to an absolute cataclysm for queer people in Britain, lasting well over a decade.

Amanda was born in 1954 and grew up in Essex. She'd always known she was attracted to girls and – like many young lesbians – moved to London after her parents reacted badly to her coming out. She moved into a London flat share with several other women and felt an instant sense of liberation. After a couple of terrible jobs in factories, she worked in the Harrods pet department before entering the book trade with a job in the Scottish bookshop chain John Menzies (gobbled up by WHSmith in 1998) and then at Claude Gill, once a vast 8,000-square-foot bookshop near the Selfridges department store. 'It was hard being a woman, let alone a lesbian', Amanda recalls in her 2018 interview with Janet Jones. 'There was a certain dress code for women, you had to look a certain way ... I remember one manager at John Menzies who was called Mister Sall telling me that I had to wear a skirt to work the next day because he liked to see his girls' legs.' Needless to say, it caused a row and the young bookseller was labelled a troublemaker. From there she got a job as a book-buyer at Whole Foods before landing a job at Gay's the Word – their first woman bookseller.

The male team wanted to make sure the shop was offering an inclusive space for lesbians, stocking the right books for their female customers. It was also her job to supply books to local authorities for libraries and schools, hence that fateful order from Haringey Council. This nascent interest from progressive Labour councils signalled a certain amount of acceptance, and it was a boon for the shop financially. 'They wanted positive images for young people about young people,' Amanda recalls, 'and left it up to us really to decide ... but there was quite a lot of fiction for young teenagers from America and it was around this time that I put into a box for Haringey [Council] a book called *Jenny Lives with Eric and Martin*.'

This brief illustrated book, by the Danish author Susanne Bösche, offered gay couples and their children an innocent family story that felt both familiar and reassuring. It depicted a gay male couple and their five-year-old daughter going on adventures including a trip to the park and planning a birthday party. But one wholesome picture of the family enjoying breakfast in bed (fruit juice and buttered crackers, nipple count: 1) would cause a quintessentially British eruption. In 1986, the copy was 'discovered' in the library of the Inner London Education Authority – not a school library as has often been misreported.

'A lot of people were very pro,' Amanda remembers, 'but the parents who opposed it were the "outraged of Islington" set, and that's what started the ball rolling for Clause 28.'

David Fernbach, co-founder of Gay Men's Press which published the book in translation, looks back on the response with incredulity.

> It was picked up by some *Sun* newspaper journalist with the headline: 'Vile Book in Schools, Pupils see pictures of gay lovers!' The media campaign percolated up through to the Government and Margaret Thatcher* used it as propaganda against Labour councils in two successive general elections, 1987 and 1991. It was the spark that kindled a homophobic blaze.

The outrage around Jenny and her gay dads followed a similar storm a couple of years earlier relating to an American children's book, *The Playbook for Kids about Sex* (Down There Press, 1981). In 1983, the evangelical Christian rights campaigner Mary Whitehouse pressured the Department of Public Prosecutions (DPP) to consider taking the UK publishers, Sheba Feminist Press,† to court under the Children and Young Persons (Harmful Publications) Act 1955 and Obscene Publications Act 1959. A medical adviser judged the text 'inappropriate' and stated he would not recommend it, but ultimately concluded that it would not 'corrupt or deprave'. In the end, the DPP was unable to do anything under the existing legislation and the case was dismissed, but the stage was set for future legislation.

---

* Thatcher was making the most of a growing backlash against gay rights, reflected in the British Social Attitudes surveys from the time. In 1983, fifty per cent of people surveyed agreed that 'sexual relations between two adults of the same sex' were 'always wrong'. By 1987, that figure had jumped to sixty-four per cent.

† Sheba Feminist Press was a UK publishing co-operative formed in 1980 by a collective involved in the Women's Liberation Movement.

SECTION 28

The press had a field day with the story, inaccurately describing the book as a 'sex manual', while MP Jill Knight* declared in Parliament that the book's 'brightly coloured pictures of little stick men showed all about homosexuality and how it was done.' Quite what she meant by 'how it was done' is best left to her own febrile imagination and, on inspection, Marcia Quackenbush's illustrations (she was not the author) are neither brightly coloured, nor stick men, the most singular thing about them being the illustrator's name. Suffice it to say, the characters weren't depicted having sex, but there are cartoon drawings of boys and girls in the nude to show different body types. Did Knight have any grounds for her allegation? It really depends on the reader's attitude towards sex education, nakedness, children's development, boundaries and tone.

On studying the book, it's immediately obvious that it would leave anyone seeking instructions on how to 'do' homosexing completely perplexed. However, the book might prove concerning to the modern eye, more alert as we are to issues around safeguarding.

It instructs the juvenile reader to 'Go into a room where there is a big mirror and close the door. Take off all your clothes and look in the mirror. Then draw a picture of your whole body here:' (blank page for the child's sketch). The book goes on to instruct readers to draw pictures of their private parts. At one point, they are asked to describe the parts they 'like other people to touch'. The prepubescent reader is told:

> ... you can ask the person who gave you the book or someone else for help ...

---

* A member of the Conservative Party's far-right Monday Club pressure group, Knight also campaigned against abortion and non-white immigration and lobbied for the return of the death penalty.

> If you read and write very well, maybe you can help a younger girl or boy with the book, like your brother or sister or cousin or friends ...
>
> If you want to, you can show this book to your mom or dad or some other grown-up.

We gain a better understanding of its approach to sex when we realise that the author, the late Joani Blank, was one of the foremost liberal academic voices in sex education in the 1970s. A radical campaigner for sexual liberation for women, she believed that talking about sex should be as casual as talking about the weather and that sexual information was a birthright. A much-beloved crusader for women's sexual freedom, she was also the founder in 1975 of Down There Press, a publisher of feminist sex-positive books, *The Playbook for Kids* included. Curiously enough, the furore in Britain – and its subsequent impact on millions of lives – never made it onto Joani's radar. Such was the world, pre-internet. Leigh Davidson was managing editor of Down There Press from 1987 to 2004:

> I don't recall Joani ever mentioning a controversy in the UK about *Playbook for Kids about Sex*. I feel fairly sure we would have incorporated it into some kind of publicity ... Had Joani known of the controversy, I think she would have been more than happy to talk about it with anyone who would listen – and those who didn't care to, as well.

Unbeknownst to Joani, her book – along with *Jenny Lives with Eric and Martin* – had helped to whip British Conservatives and the press into a storm of vitriolic horror. 'Sex should be a private thing', went the general refrain, 'and what goes on in the bedroom is not a matter for Town Hall bureaucrats.' Gay sex, however, was a matter for the very highest levels of government, because politicians and journalists couldn't prevent themselves from thinking about it and so Section 28 of the Local Government Bill passed through Parliament on 24 May 1988, stating that a local authority shall not:

(a) intentionally promote homosexuality or publish material with the intention of promoting homosexuality;
(b) promote the teaching in any maintained school of the acceptability of homosexuality as a pretended family relationship.

The clause then added, with a chilling glimpse of the prejudice feeding the roots of this pernicious legislation:

(2) Nothing in subsection (1) above shall be taken to prohibit the doing of anything for the purpose of treating or preventing the spread of disease.

In other words, educators presenting gay people as positive members of society could face draconian sanctions, but they were quite welcome to present homosexuals as akin to disease-spreading vermin.

Customers rushed to Gay's the Word for their copy of *Capital Gay*, which called Section 28 'The challenge of the century ... the most serious legal attack on our rights since male homosexuality was outlawed more than 100 years ago.' The newspaper's office was targeted in an arson attack, which it narrowly survived thanks to the Lesbian and Gay Switchboard which raised the alarm, prompting editor Graham McKerrow to sprint to the office, finding the computers melted. The newspaper was, quite literally, in ashes.

Section 28 was a dreadful and transparently bigoted act of oppression. It utterly failed as a piece of legislation; there were no prosecutions at all in England, Wales or Northern Ireland, and only one in Scotland, when the Christian Institute brought a case against Glasgow City Council for the crime of funding an AIDS charity in 2000. It was also a complete nonsense in an educational sense. If a student was bold enough to come out of the closet, was a teacher supposed to stuff them back in again? And how would they talk about *Twelfth Night* without mentioning queerness? Or Virginia Woolf, Oscar Wilde, or the poetry of Wilfred Owen and Siegfried Sassoon for that matter?

Still, Section 28 was successful in its true purpose. Bullied children were left unprotected by cowed teachers. Staff hid their sexuality. Gay young people grew up in shame. Homophobic adults and their indoctrinated children were empowered to abuse. Meanwhile, the impact of Section 28 on lesbian mothers is too little acknowledged. As noted earlier, they risked losing custody of their children because fathers or relatives were able to present them as a danger to the family. Some nurseries even turned lesbian parents away, fearing that management might be accused of advocating for gay families. At least, that was the excuse given.

This legislation quietly, subtly and persistently encouraged grown-ups to collude in the emotional, physical and psychological neglect and outright abuse of queer young people.

Section 28 was repealed in Scotland in 2000 and in England and Wales in 2003, but its effects lingered for many years after, with schools and local authorities avoiding LGBTQ topics out of habit, fear or preference. An entire generation of children grew up under the chilling message that queer lives and families were something shameful or unspeakable.

Lesley Jones worked at Gay's the Word as a volunteer in the 1980s, having been introduced to the shop by Amanda Russell, her friend then lover. Lesley had been working at *Gay News*, so she was well qualified and Amanda didn't want to be the only woman in the bookshop. 'What Section 28 did was provide a

SECTION 28

focus for men and women to fight together,' she says. 'It provided a focus for us to demand change, a common enemy we could unite against.'

A silver lining perhaps, if excrement can be plated, but it's true that Section 28 galvanised solidarity within the LGBT community, with Gay's the Word, Silver Moon, Lavender Menace and Sisterwrite at the vanguard of the resistance. Women organised self-insemination groups for lesbians looking to have children, quite often with gay men as donors, while groups met at the Sisterwrite bookshop to organise political protests, demanding equal rights. Jane and Sue at Silver Moon were visited by police when they put a copy of *Jenny Lives with Eric and Martin* in their window. Someone had complained and they were told it wasn't allowed, specifically because of Section 28. Complete nonsense; Silver Moon was a bookshop, not a school or a public body. They put up a window display, using the legislation's earlier name: 'STOP CLAUSE 27', warning customers and passers-by that books including *Orlando* by Virginia Woolf, *The Color Purple* by Alice Walker and *The Handmaid's Tale* by Margaret Atwood would disappear from children's libraries.

And so, as the 1980s came to a close, our intrepid bookshops were left breathless, battered, but bolder than ever – there were still so many fights ongoing and battles not yet begun. By now, lesbian and gay bookshops like Gay's the Word, Vrolijk, Buchladen Männerschwarm, the Oscar Wilde Memorial Bookshop, Womanbooks, Giovanni's Room, Prinz Eisenherz, Silver Moon, Lavender Menace, Glad Day and so many more were out and proud, having weathered vandalism, crises, grief, raids and political storms, and in many cases – not necessarily financially – they were thriving.

What, then, would the 1990s bring? And how would queer bookshops play their part in a new decade?

Part Six

PRIDE BEFORE A FALL

O Canada:
The Trials of Glad Day Bookshop and Little Sister's
1982–still open

'DO NOT TOUCH THE CAT!'

CUSTOMER NOTICE,
LITTLE SISTER'S BOOKSTORE

IN 1982, THE BOSTON BRANCH OF JEARLD MOLDENHAUER'S Glad Day Bookshop was destroyed in an arson attack, the flames having ripped through the offices of the *Gay Community News* and *Fag Rag* across the hall. Jearld was away in Paris at the time, enjoying a coffee in the LGBTQ+ bookshop Les Mots à la Bouche, when a bookseller alerted him to an urgent phone call. Shell-shocked and in complete denial, Jearld returned to find his beloved store every bit as gutted as he was. An incendiary device had been ignited on the second floor and while no one was hurt, the entire stock of books was turned to ashes. He was forced to lay off his manager and try to rebuild, but landlords were unsympathetic until, in desperation, he found space at 43 Winter Street. Jearld writes in his website memoir: 'I distinctly remember finding myself alone on my hands & knees, on my 36th birthday scrubbing the floor – and having a good cry.'

The shop reopened three months after the fire with new wooden shelving units and new stock, but three years later, rising rents forced Jearld to move again, this time to a spacious second-floor home overlooking the Boston Public Library.

Glad Day *Toronto* meanwhile had moved to 648A Yonge Street in 1981. That same year, Toronto police raided four gay bathhouses, arresting almost three hundred men. Named Operation Soap, the raids sparked widespread protests and rallies, with a largescale protest march. The mobilisation of the community led to most of the charges against the men being dropped, and it was Glad Day Bookshop that served as the resistance's headquarters, providing a meeting space for activists who were drawing together a legal response while disseminating information via posters and pamphlets. The backlash was akin to Stonewall in some respects, providing a turning point where the authorities began to accept that queer people would no longer take their oppression in cowed silence.

The next April, 1982, Toronto police seized two magazines at the shop: *The Leatherman* and the ingeniously titled *Come Watch* (emphasis frontloaded), charging assistant manager Kevin Orr with possession of obscene material for the purpose of resale. He was found guilty, but spared jail when the conviction was overturned on appeal. A new trial never took place because police couldn't find Orr to serve his subpoena.

In 1985, the Toronto shop inched its way further down the block to 598A Yonge Street where it stayed for many successful but tumultuous years. Things really kicked off in March 1985 when a federal court ruled that the terminology 'immoral and indecent' used by Customs as criteria for seizing books was far too vague. Within months, Brian Mulroney's government reacted with the infamous Memorandum D9-1-1, itemising exactly what kind of material should be seized at the border. It equated depictions of incest and bestiality with consensual anal sex. As with Tudor England's buggery laws some four centuries earlier, straight people engaging in anal sex were unlikely to arouse interest; it was gay men – or books about gay men having sex in this case – who were likely to get fingered. It took no time at all for Glad Day to feel the brunt of the changes,* and, almost immediately, Customs seizures accelerated. Between 1985 and 1991, Glad Day received between 400 and 500 seizure notices, ranging from *The Joy of Gay Sex* to the nineteenth-century French classic *Les Fleurs du Mal* by Charles Baudelaire.

Mulroney's memorandum was designed to appease moral panic around gay liberation by preventing gay and lesbian literature from entering Canada. When Glad Day brought the banning of *The Joy of Gay Sex* before the courts in March 1986, Mr Serge Lavoie, who was then executive director of the Canadian Booksellers Association, decided not to support them. Still, there was a small win for the bookstore. In 1987, Judge Bruce Hawkins of the District Court of Ontario made a melodious pronouncement: 'To write about homosexual practices without dealing with anal intercourse would be equivalent to writing a history of music and omitting Mozart.' With a flick of his baton, Hawkins forced the memorandum to change its tune, or at least its tempo, by adding room for books featuring anal intercourse, provided they weren't 'prurient in nature'.

The intervention came just too late to save Christmas for a second Canadian queer bookstore. Little Sister's had more than 500 of its books and magazines seized by Customs in December 1986, decimating their festive inventory.

The reader should not be fooled by its cute name; Little Sister's bookstore had claws and would go on to change queer rights in Canada forever. It all began when Jim Deva and Bruce Smyth met in the grocery department of the Hudson's Bay Northern Stores in Fort Simpson, a small village in Canada's Northwest Territories. It was 1972, and twenty-two-year-old Deva was working a summer job while training to be a teacher. The two grew

---

* The memorandum wasn't legislation as such; it was a sort of official advisory notice. Changing the law on the matter would have risked contravening the Canadian Charter of Rights and Freedoms.

close, quickly moving in together and falling in love. Theirs would be a forty-two-year relationship, battling together as inseparable queer warriors. Deva soon decided he didn't want to be a closeted teacher and after a few unsatisfactory jobs, the Little Sister's Book and Art Emporium was born. Jim and Bruce had been driven crazy trying to find gay and lesbian books in Vancouver. There was just one store, owned by a lesbian, but her queer books were hidden at the back, forcing customers to get down on their hands and knees to find them. Little Sister's would do things differently.

Located in the living room of a converted house in Vancouver's then-emerging gay village on 1221 Thurlow St, they celebrated their official opening on 3 May 1983. The couple slept in a tiny room out back, using the small shop as their living quarters. Was it luxury? No. Was it easy? No. Was it named after their cat? Absolutely.

One of Jim's earlier jobs was in a game store in Gastown, which had a resident feline. She had kittens, one of which fell from a shelf one night, snagging her head between a pair of planks. When Jim found her the following morning, he thought she was dead, her body dangling like a sock. But he soon realised this particular ball of fluff was made of lightning and though he cared for her, she turned out to have – as Jim put it – 'a real shitty attitude about life'. The new bookstore's mascot turned out to be 'a bitch', lurking on the shelves then pouncing on customers as they browsed. Any attempt to pet her would risk multiple lacerations, while dopey dogs were ridden around the store, pincered by needle-sharp claws. Jim and Bruce kept bandages behind the counter and put up a sign imploring people: 'DO NOT TOUCH THE CAT!' Still, the puss – who was called Little Sister – gave her name to the shop, so she holds an important place in our history, if not the hearts of Jim and Bruce.

She wasn't the only challenge they faced in the early days. Sales in the art gallery were slow from the start, though attendance was strong, but thankfully the bookstore was thriving and it quickly took over. There was one sticking point. With so few lesbian and gay books being published in Canada, a full ninety per cent of their stock had to be ordered in from the United States. They were at the mercy of Customs, which brings us back to Christmas 1986 when Jim and Bruce decided to risk the rest of their meagre savings on a big festive blow-out order. Every single imported shipment was detained. To make things worse, it was the importer's responsibility to prove the stock was legal, and within ninety days. Two days later, officials seized another nineteen titles, including seventy-five copies of the upcoming 3 January 1987 issue of *The Advocate* magazine.* Strangely enough, the titles seized were getting through to mainstream bookstores and many were freely available at the Vancouver Public Library. By the end of the month, Customs had seized more than 600 books and magazines, amounting to at least $4,000 of merchandise. Jim and Bruce decided to fight the decision in court, sending out a press release declaring: 'Canada Customs Declares War on Little Sister's', adding with a daring swipe: 'The agent responsible for the present seizures has threatened to continue with the stringent examinations and long delays until the store is no longer a viable entity.'

Their court case was still pending when, in June 1987, Customs detained another shipment of books, including *Dzelarhons* by Anne Cameron, a popular retelling of First Nations folklore, apparently deemed obscene because a short story depicted a woman marrying a bear. Then in December that year, a bomb was thrown into the Little Sister's stairwell leading from the store's

---

* Through the 1970s and 1980s, *The Advocate* became a vital platform for reporting on gay liberation, lesbian visibility, trans rights and the AIDS crisis – often covering stories ignored or misrepresented by mainstream media. It mixed hard news with interviews, arts coverage and opinion pieces, and it provided early national visibility for queer celebrities and activists.

Thurlow Street entrance, burying shrapnel in the walls. No one was hurt, but it caused $2,000 worth of damage. Two months later, a second bomb was thrown into the restaurant downstairs, exploding just three feet from Jim's table. It was a crowded Saturday night but miraculously, he escaped unhurt.

In April 1988, after two years of waiting and costs of $5,000 – merely weeks before their court case against Customs was due to begin – the federal government admitted that *The Advocate* was not obscene after all. The case was closed, but Little Sister's stock had already been burned, while seizures of other gay and lesbian material continued. The remainder of the Christmas shipments taken in December 1986 were unceremoniously dumped on the store's Thurlow Street steps, stuffed into a mailbag. Jim and Bruce would fight on, but their cat was done with it. Little Sister launched one final unprovoked attack on a customer, then slunk down the stairs and out the door, never to be seen again. She'd given her name to a pillar of queer history, but Jim and Bruce did not follow her into the Vancouver night, whistling and calling her name. They'd lost a cantankerous pet but were about to gain a dream employee.

Janine Fuller was already an author, playwright and performance artist before moving to Vancouver from Toronto in 1989, having starred in her own comedic one-woman show, *Big Women Make Their Own Clothes*. She'd been working at the Toronto Women's Bookstore when it too was firebombed in 1983. There she remained until her move north with the love of her life, Julie Stines. The couple took a sleeper train climbing through forests, the Prairies and the Rocky Mountains, promptly falling in love with the west coast as soon as they stepped from the carriage. Soon after arriving in Vancouver, Janine approached Jim and Bruce at Little Sister's with a ten-page handwritten résumé and was employed on the spot. Her calmness and courage became a core that powered them all through their subsequent struggles.

She barely spent an evening at home, fundraising hundreds of thousands of dollars to pay legal fees, printing posters, attending and hosting galas, talks and cultural events.

In June 1990, after further Customs seizures, Jim, Bruce and Janine decided enough was enough. With help from the British Columbia Civil Liberties Association, they launched a legal challenge, arguing that Customs was enforcing a clandestine form of unconstitutional censorship, discriminating against gay men, bisexuals and lesbians while violating the Charter of Rights and Freedoms. The four-year process of getting to court would cost the store and its supporters a quarter of a million dollars and the trial date was set for September 1991... only to be postponed three times. Hold on to that thread.

Back in Toronto, Jearld sold his original Glad Day store to his friend and former commune roommate, John Scythes. The next year, the so-called 'Butler decision' at the Supreme Court of Canada shifted the onus in obscenity cases away from morality, placing the emphasis on 'social harm' instead. The new edict singled out lesbian, gay and feminist books and magazines which spoke against the tenets of conservative Christian society. In April 1992, Toronto police charged Glad Day with the alleged crime of selling a sexy lesbian magazine named *Bad Attitude*, which had previously been seized on its way to Little Sister's. A judge decided the magazine, as part of five shipments also including gay men's magazines, *Advocate Men*, *In Touch* and *Play Gay*, met the new criteria for social harm and were therefore obscene.

Back in Vancouver, Little Sister's was reeling after a third direct bomb attack, this time a Polish percussion grenade,* thrown into the stairwell. It exploded at around ten o'clock at night while the store was still open. Smoke choked the store and the

---

* A percussion grenade is a non-lethal but potentially dangerous incendiary device designed to disorientate the target with a blinding flash of light and an extremely loud *bang*.

entrance was damaged. No one claimed responsibility. No one was arrested. The store opened the next day in a show of courage but a number of staff resigned. Not Janine Fuller. She stuck with Jim and Bruce, determined to stand her ground against Customs while simultaneously managing a growing business.

The Little Sister's case arrived at the Supreme Court of British Columbia in October 1994. The trial lumbered on for forty days, with star testimony given in support of the store by straight historian, broadcaster and author Pierre Berton, and lesbian icon Jane Rule.* The media attention given to the trial put the store and its staff at increased risk and in February 1995, a man rang the store warning Janine that a bomb had been planted in the building. Police rushed to investigate but found nothing. Next month, a handwritten letter arrived in the post, threatening staff with 'a day of reckoning', warning them to stay away from work the next day. They carried on as usual, relieved no doubt to be intact by closing time. On went the court case.

It wasn't until January 1996 that Justice Kenneth Smith ruled in favour of Little Sister's. Canadian Customs had applied the law in a discriminatory manner. It was a pyrrhic victory though, because he also stated that the law itself remained constitutional. Partially vindicated, Customs went straight back to making seizures. With a degree of tenacity now typical of queer bookstores, Little Sister's took a deep breath and launched an appeal.

That July, the store moved to 1238 Davie Street, not because of the bombings and threats, but because they'd become too famous and too busy to stay squashed in their old location.

---

* Rule's sapphic novel *Desert of the Heart* came out in 1964, five years before the Criminal Law Amendment Act, which decriminalised 'same-sex sexual activity, in private between consenting adults'. Her novel had been rejected by twenty-two publishers. She was flooded with letters from women who'd 'discovered' their sexuality thanks to her writing and she became – in her own words – 'the only lesbian in Canada': the go-to voice on the subject in the Canadian media.

It would be another four years – a full decade since they launched their original legal challenge – before their case reached the Supreme Court of Canada. In December 2000, the highest judges in the land decreed that Customs had, to paraphrase, behaved improperly towards this small LGBT bookstore, picking on it solely for its homosexual focus. Unfortunately, they also stopped short of accepting the unconstitutional nature of Customs' censorship, ruling instead that officers could carry on screening and burning books and magazines at the border, so long as it wasn't simply because they were queer. One positive: Customs would now have to *prove* that any confiscated shipments were obscene; it couldn't just be a matter of subjective opinion.

The State was less than bothered. That same year, Glad Day in Toronto was charged with selling a gay porn video, *Descent*. Minus the 'S', it might have made it through. Glad Day launched its own appeal. A court case in 2001 found they were not entitled to challenge the Ontario Film Review Board (OFRB). So Glad Day appealed that decision too.

Little Sister's troubles had not abated. In July 2001, just seven months after their landmark Supreme Court win, Customs seized another shipment destined for the store: two volumes of an anthology of gay adult comics called *Meatmen*. Back to court they went, but Customs carried on, seizing gay erotic novels, *Of Slaves and Ropes and Lovers* and *Of Men, Ropes and Remembrance*. All men, slaves, lovers and their various ropes were added to the court case, and under the weight of so many trials over so many years, the Little Sister's team reached a point of exhaustion. It was a tough time to stay positive, not least with the state of gay rights in Vancouver.

Forty-two-year-old Aaron Webster was cruising in a wooded area of Stanley Park near Second Beach in November 2001. A gang of youths set upon him, chasing him to a parking lot and beating him with baseball bats. He was discovered by his friend Tim Chisholm, who cradled him as he died. The following day two thousand people held a silent march in Aaron's memory. It was organised by Little Sister's bookstore, from where the procession started.

Glad Day's struggle continued in 2004 when the Ontario Superior Court of Justice ruled in favour of the store. With the OFRB's censorship of a single gay porn movie, the government had violated the store's right to freedom of expression under Canada's Charter of Rights and Freedoms. In August 2005, Ontario's new Film Classification Act came into effect, stating that the OFRB wasn't allowed to censor scenes, but it could ban films likely to be considered obscene by the courts or the law.

In January 2007, the Supreme Court of Canada ruled that Little Sister's case against Customs was, effectively, not special enough to warrant the taxpayers' support and denied the store's request for funding to continue its fight. The ruling was a blow to Little Sister's ability to take Customs back to court and without advance costs, the bookstore was unable to pursue its complaint. A year later, in January 2008, while making plans to celebrate their twenty-fifth anniversary, an understandably exhausted Jim Deva and Bruce Smyth announced the store would be sold. They'd set out to run a queer bookshop; they hadn't expected to spend more than two decades in the trenches, fighting the government at the vanguard of gay rights. Ever loyal, always principled to the point of potential ruin, they rejected all offers for their business, none of the buyers meeting their requirements to maintain all the staff and protect Little Sister's role in the community. Jim Deva died in 2014, leaving behind his companion of four decades, Bruce Smyth, who died five years later. Janine Fuller continued as manager until 2015, when she stepped from behind the counter for the last time, twenty-five years after she'd first walked in with her résumé. In an interview shortly before his death, when asked what Janine Fuller had done for Little Sister's bookstore, Bruce Smyth answered without hesitation, 'Everything.'

Throughout decades of conflict, unfathomable worry, millions of dollars of public funds, all over a few books, magazines and videos, in spite of the wins and losses and the public embarrassment, the federal government has never once apologised or conceded responsibility for its behaviour. For shame, but how fortunate that Glad Day, Little Sister's and so many other queer bookstores around the world had the courage to stand up and fight in court.

Time now for a trip to South Philadelphia, where a frightened little boy is about to find a mysterious friend who will change his life forever. With a book, of course.

A Different Light
SAN FRANCISCO
1987–2011

'The Lord won't mind.'

SAPPHIRE

TOMMI AVICOLLI MECCA WAS BORN IN SOUTH PHILADELPHIA in 1951, the grandson of an immigrant family from southern Italy. His was a diverse neighbourhood, a rich stew of Italian, Jewish, Hungarian and African American families united by their poverty. Tommi attended Catholic school where he suffered physical and verbal bullying. It was hell, until a mysterious guardian took him under his wing. Vinnie (not his real name) wasn't a meathead or a jock; he was of average build, wiry and effeminate, but tough and scrappy with it. When one of the boys threatened to give Tommi a beating after school, it was Vinnie who stepped in and gave the bully a lashing he wouldn't forget, walking away covered in dust and scrapes but unfazed.

Around this time, Tommi was writing poetry about his feelings of loneliness, his family unable to understand why he was so sad. He wanted to talk about it, but he couldn't. It was the fear of never being loved. The feeling that he could never exist in his home as himself. His writing gave him an outlet as he grew, while Vinnie kept him safe. Sadly, the friendship couldn't last.

One day, the boys were hanging out at Vinnie's house when Vinnie announced that he was moving away. 'He seemed unusually awkward', remembers Tommi. 'He held out this package for me from behind his back. He said it was a goodbye gift; I should open it later.' Confused and hurt, Tommi carried the gift home, going straight to his bedroom to open it up. He lifted the package to the light. It was a book with a pair of golden-haired men on the cover, their fingers touching. Tommi read the title. *The Lord Won't Mind.* He opened the first page and began reading. It was the story of two boys named Peter and Charlie who began a love affair at their Ivy League college. Set in the 1960s, it was filled with explicit oral and anal sex scenes but, more than that, it was a tenderly written love affair, riven with tension, longing and regret. One of the characters' friends – an up-and-coming black singer named Sapphire – soothes their religious guilt, saying: 'The Lord won't mind.' Gordon Merrick's* 1970 novel was pulp fiction, but it stayed in the *New York Times* bestseller list for no fewer than sixteen weeks.

It was the first gay story Tommi had ever read, and it had an electrifying effect. He wasn't alone and, though the boys would never meet again, Vinnie's knowing gift had given him something he would carry for the rest of his life: an appreciation for the consoling and affirming power of books.

Tommi went on to study at Temple University, joining the Gay Liberation Front and battling with homophobia on a sports-mad campus. He edited the *Philadelphia Gay News* from 1981 to 1991 – often frequenting Giovanni's Room bookshop – before leaving Philly for San Francisco. It was time to start a new chapter. His parents had died, and the AIDS pandemic had claimed the lives of many of his friends.

The early 90s Castro district was San Francisco's golden-tanned epicentre of LGBTQ+ life, activism and culture. Known

---

* Merrick was studiously apolitical in his writing, preferring to focus on love rather than activism, though he did write with a moral purpose. In an interview for the former queer culture guide *Michael's Thing*, he said: 'It was important that straight people know exactly what gay men did. Otherwise, straight people would fill in the gaps with their own distorted, horrifying, stereotypical fantasies.'

for its colourful streets and equally colourful residents, as well as a cocktail of lively bars, and community centres. On arrival, a friend told Tommi to seek out a guy named Richard Labonté at a bookstore named A Different Light, so he found a place to crash just round the corner with a lesbian friend he knew from Philly and headed over first thing.

The manager of the bookshop was the same Richard Labonté who'd helped Norman Laurila open the first A Different Light bookstore in Los Angeles way back in '79. By the early 90s, the chain had grown to four stores with eighty staff, turning over $2 million a year. Queer bookstores had become, at least relatively, big business. The second branch opened in New York City's Greenwich Village in '83 with San Francisco next at 489 Castro Street in '85, then a second Los Angeles store in 1990, popping up at 8853 Santa Monica Boulevard.

The first manager of the San Francisco store was Terry (Tez) Anderson – the partner of novelist Armistead Maupin at the time – but Richard Labonté had taken over in 1987 and managed the branch ever since, effectively sculpting it in his own image while becoming something of a local legend. Many customers assumed the bookshop was his; an impression he cultivated, when in fact his former boyfriend Norman Laurila remained the owner of the chain and therefore his employer and boss. Not an easy professional relationship at times, as Norman recalls, especially with Richard's disregard for turning a profit. 'I used to joke that he'd give the books away for free,' says Norman, 'and he would have!'

Instantly recognisable with his too-large trousers and steely beard, Richard was known for his superhuman ability to tear through towering piles of books faster than any man alive. He was also loved for his tireless work supporting countless LGBTQ+ poets and writers. Tommi Avicolli Mecca was one of them. It turned out Richard had already read and enjoyed his articles in the

Philadelphia Gay News and his published poems, so he offered the young man a job on the spot. He was in dire need of assistance.

At the time, the shop was offering refuge to people displaced by the 1989 earthquake which claimed sixty-three lives, injuring nearly four thousand. But it was a refuge, first and foremost, for vulnerable lesbian and gay people. There was no community centre at that time, so Richard, along with his new bookseller Tommi, offered their first floor and yard, refusing to accept any money for bookings. Activist groups and support groups needing places to meet were also welcomed.

By the mid-90s the store started seeing a lot of young homeless people in the area, many of them thrown out by their families for being queer, and while other merchants reacted by calling the cops to chase them away, Richard and Tommi did what they could to help. 'It became the norm to arrive in the morning and find someone using the doorway as a safe place to sleep', says Tommi. 'I would shake them on the shoulder and offer to buy them some soup, allowing them to hang out in the garden if they needed to.' Some of the other shopkeepers accused them of encouraging vagrants into the Castro, but Tommi and Richard took no notice and redoubled their efforts to support the community, homeless or otherwise, making unexpected connections along the way.

They got word that the pastor of the local gay church was giving free marijuana to people with AIDS in defiance of the law. 'Marijuana helps people suffering the pain of the HIV virus, mental and emotional', explains Tommi. 'We decided to join forces with the pastor, Jim Mitulski, and the church's meals programme, which served dinner three nights a week.' The Friday evening meal was soon staffed by A Different Light, with booksellers and even Richard himself cooking and serving the food. Then the church, with the help of local out gay supervisor Tom Ammiano, got the high school a few blocks from the bookstore to open up its showers so homeless folks could scrub up at weekends. That was also controversial in the neighbourhood, but Tommi learned from his boss that queer bookstores were different to other businesses. 'With Richard, compassion came first, business second.'

With the AIDS crisis continuing to rage through the early 90s, and thanks to the joint work of the store and the church and supervisors Ammiano and Mark Leno, more and more homeless gay men sought a safe place to put their heads down for the night. The first shelter was at the Eureka Valley Recreation Center, the second at Metropolitan Community Church, the third at an old gym at Castro and Market. It was an extraordinary sight for everyone to see these young people, homeless and frightened, sometimes men who'd travelled thousands of miles to San Francisco from all over the country, finding sanctuary as well as friendship, dignity and safety. All thanks, in no small part, to a queer bookshop.

Foreign tourists visited from far-flung countries including Japan and Australia, searching for information about AIDS, and Richard responded by ordering books in foreign languages on the subject, setting up a specific section in the shop. 'Many times, someone would come in and be so grateful because they couldn't access what they needed in their own country', says Tommi. 'Things weren't great in the US, but some countries were even worse, censoring books on the subject and banning anything explaining what the disease was.'

The bookstore's legend grew to such an extent they started opening late into the night. It was often Tommi's job to close the store. 'Sometimes you would have to almost throw people out at midnight. We were a library as well as a bookstore really and people would stand there for hours reading. They couldn't afford to buy the book, but Richard didn't mind.'

Richard's custodianship of A Different Light in San Francisco offers perhaps the most complete example of what a queer bookstore could be at that time (Norman's considerable business concerns notwithstanding). All of the bookstores were refuges, but none took that role quite so literally as Richard. When he died in 2022 aged seventy-two, there was an outpouring of tributes from writers the world over who owed him thanks for supporting them when they needed it most. He was not a businessman. Left to his own devices, the shop would never have survived. But boy was he a queer bookseller, and for that he will always be remembered.

The Bookshop Darlinghurst
SYDNEY
1982–2025

&

Hares & Hyenas
MELBOURNE
1991–still open

> *'The mid- to late 90s were a golden time
> before the big chains arrived…'*
>
> GRAEME AITKEN

IN 1982, WAYNE HARRISON AND LES MCDONALD BECAME the first gay booksellers in Australia. Wayne was then the editor of *Campaign*, Australia's national gay magazine/newspaper, with an office in York Street, Sydney. His book editor repeatedly complained about the lack of newly released gay and lesbian books and suggested something should be done about it. So, Wayne got in touch with Michael Denneny, who was establishing St Martin's Press in New York as the biggest name in gay and lesbian publishing. They were flying to the States on holiday anyway, so a meeting was set up. It went well and Michael opened an account for Les and Wayne on the spot, sending them fifty copies of a recently released St Martin's Press hardback, *Aphrodisiac – Fiction from Christopher Street*; along with fifty copies of *Le Gay Ghetto – Gay Cartoons from Christopher Street*. The books arrived in Sydney before Les and Wayne had touched down and the second they got home they set up a mail-order business and sold out in a month. So they ordered more, and expanded their list, and eventually added more publishers too. Business boomed, with piles of books taking over their house. They needed a shop.

'We decided to place our excess books on the shelves of established bookshops,' says Wayne, 'but mainly in the Link Bookshop, in the old butcher's shop on Crown Street, and Exiles Bookshop on Oxford Street near Taylor Square.' Sales went so well that David Beschi, who owned the Link, asked them to create a full-scale bookshop at the rear of his Leather Emporium on the other side of Crown Street (in a former funeral parlour). That thrived too, so Les and Wayne decided to strike out on their own. Right on cue, Exiles Bookshop on Oxford Street went bust, to be replaced by a charity shop that folded soon after opening. 'Les did the deal,' says Wayne, 'and stage designer Michael Scott-Mitchell did the interior design ... I came up with the inspired name: The Bookshop Darlinghurst. It opened in 1982 and the rest, as they say, is history.'

The Sydney gay scene at the time was a dynamic blend of underground parties, lively pubs and burgeoning political activism, with venues like the Albury Hotel and the Midnight Shift offering spaces where primarily gay men could gather. Homosexuality in New South Wales was only partially decriminalised in 1984,[*] so activism gained momentum alongside the nightlife, with groups like the Campaign Against Moral Persecution (get it?) fighting police harassment and advocating for decriminalisation and anti-discrimination laws. Known simply as 'The Bookshop Darlo' by locals, Wayne and Les's store remained at the epicentre of Sydney's queer scene until Christmas 2025.

---

[*] Gay sex was partially decriminalised in New South Wales in 1984. The amendment initially set an unequal age of consent (eighteen for homosexual acts, sixteen for heterosexuals and lesbians), with equalisation not arriving for gay men until 2003.

They also sold tickets to gay dance parties including the two major Mardi Gras parties, the post-parade party and Sleaze Ball. The queues often stretched right down the street.

By 1990, Wayne and Les had opened a second shop in Newtown (The Bookshop Newtown, naturally) and that same year, it gained a new buyer/manager. Graeme Aitken quickly graduated to the much busier and more successful Darlinghurst branch, the Newtown shop closing its doors in 1998. As with Janine Fuller at Little Sister's bookstore in Vancouver, or Jim MacSweeney at Gay's the Word, Graeme would become one of the world's longest-established LGBTQ+ booksellers, and in 1995, partly thanks to his work with the bookshop, he became a published novelist in his own right. Graeme had come out as gay in the mid-1980s, after moving to Sydney from New Zealand. Like many others, he bought *A Boy's Own Story* by Edmund White, finding affirmation in its semi-autobiographical coming-of-age story. 'Books helped gay people in Australia affirm their identity', he says, 'because even by the 90s, there wasn't really any representation in TV or film here.' A sense of Aussie isolation was made even starker when he started travelling abroad for The Bookshop to source new stock.

In fact, Graeme gave his interview for this book on his lunch break in the shop's final year of trading, asking what the latest LGBTQ+ books were in the UK and ordering them in real time. He explained:

> When I first started you didn't have the internet, so it was very difficult researching titles. I would fly overseas to the American Book Fair where the forthcoming books were showcased. It might be in Anaheim, Chicago, sometimes New York, sometimes Miami. It was also a time to visit American gay bookshops such as the three A Different Light shops in Castro, West Hollywood and Chelsea, or the Oscar Wilde Memorial Bookshop in Greenwich Village.

Graeme's counterparts were generous in sharing their knowledge, as was Jim MacSweeney from London's Gay's the Word.

Meanwhile, Les and Wayne founded a book distribution company, Bulldog Books, which posted lesbian and gay literature from presses including Gay Sunshine Press, Alyson Books, Naiad Press, Cleis Press, Onlywomen Press and Gay Men's Press. While their own bookshops were the main customers, they also supplied other bookshops Australia-wide, feeding queer literature to the entire country when before, the queer lit scene Down Under had been a virtual wasteland.

By the mid-90s there was a massive upswing in foreign books Graeme wanted to order. 'Suddenly, the big publishers in America realised that gay men had quite a lot of disposable income, so they started publishing books targeting a lucrative market, then lesbian fiction became more established too, it was a heady, exciting time.' Small presses were set up, including Firebrand Books, which was particularly important as a source of black lesbian writers such as Audre Lorde and Jewelle Gomez. Graeme was equally amazed on his travels by the sheer number of queer *bookstores* in the United States in the early to mid-90s. 'There were maybe 150 specialist gay and lesbian-feminist bookshops in America', he estimates. 'It was a golden time before Amazon, before e-books, and before bookshop chains took an interest in LGBT+ titles.'

Just as the Oscar Wilde Memorial Bookshop had inspired new stores in 1970s America, so Australia's first gay bookshop in Sydney went on to inspire a quirky new arrival in Victoria State.

The Hares & Hyenas bookshop was opened in Melbourne by Rowland Thomson and Crusader Hillis, who'd met at university in 1975. Crusader was working for Les and Wayne's distribution company, Bulldog Books, in fact, and they'd visited the Bookshop Darlinghurst in Sydney, liking what they saw. A bookstore wasn't their first venture, however. First, they opened an art-house video store and then a record shop before deciding to embark on a new chapter as bookshop owners.

They started out on Commercial Road, Melbourne, a few doors up from the Beat Bookshop which sold a small selection of gay adult books. The locals didn't bat an eyelid on opening day, apart from one drag queen who poked her head through the door and told them the shop wouldn't work unless they covered up their windows. No. Hares & Hyenas wasn't going to be the world's first queer bookshop to hide behind covered windows; the advice was politely ignored and the window display and signage were duly unveiled. Rowland and Crusader had no premonition then that the name 'Hares & Hyenas' would live on for decades.

Surely, theirs was the oddest name yet on the queer bookstore scene. From the reverent but somewhat schematic Oscar Wilde Memorial Bookshop, queer booksellers had allowed their imaginations to take flight. There was the literary provenance of Giovanni's Room and Gay's the Word, the lyrical resonance of Silver Moon, the politically defiant Lavender Menace, the reassuring declaration of A Woman's Place, the slap-bang simplicity of Vrolijk; all of them proving every bit as revealing as their stock. In the case of Hares & Hyenas, the attention-grabbing but somewhat elusive name heralds from medieval folklore. Along with weasels and stoats, such animals were associated in the Dark Ages with outsiders and sexual deviance. Hyenas were synonymous with the Devil, prowling graveyards at night and devouring the dead, while hares were believed to have multiple vaginas and were therefore symbolic of female avarice.* Female hyenas happen to boast a seven-inch clitoris, referred to by zoologists, somewhat chauvinistically, as a 'pseudo penis'.† All in all, these fascinating and much-maligned

---

* For those wishing to venture down this particular rabbit hole, our long-eared friends have a single vagina but two cervixes with a double uterine horn.
† Could hyena penises not be pseudo clitorises? The patriarchy is real.

animals held a peculiar place in queer history and were now being celebrated by a proud and punchy new bookshop in Melbourne.

In some ways, things in the early 1990s hadn't changed since Craig Rodwell opened his doors in 1967, a generation earlier. Customers often lingered outside, nervously waiting for a quiet moment to duck in while many perused the shelves in dark glasses, afraid they might be spotted. Co-owner Rowland quickly realised he couldn't make any assumptions. One day a buttoned-up elderly lady walked into the shop with all the demeanour of a Christian missionary, sure to breathe fire, only to leave with a bag full of bondage gear. From the start, the shop was determined to cater for all queer people, young and old. They were ahead of their time, becoming part of the new wave of bookshops by giving equal space to gender-diverse customers and people of all ages, including a section of children's books.

Melbourne now had a safe space for gender-diverse people to read, mingle, explore and relax. The books on the shelves reflected a noticeable shift in culture. Increased acceptance and understanding of trans identities was leading to frank discussion in the queer community, reflected in some of the books being published at the time. It posed a difficult question for booksellers like Rowland and Crusader. They tried to tiptoe around things and present different sides but in the 90s pretty well all the fiction with transgender characters seemed to present trans folk as an aberration or a threat.

Fortunately, there were positive books starting to appear, reflecting trans lives. *Transgender Warriors: Making History from Joan of Arc to Dennis Rodman* (1996) was born of a pamphlet published by the Marxist-Leninist Workers World Party in 1992, authored by the butch lesbian and activist for transgender acceptance, Leslie Feinberg. She had previously won the Lambda Literary Award for her debut novel *Stone Butch Blues* (1993). Her trans umbrella was perhaps a little broad for radical feminists and trans activists today, including anyone who crossed the cultural boundaries of gender including 'butch dykes' and drag queens, but still, it was one of the first books to articulate trans identities through history, and acknowledge their activism during important historical moments like Stonewall.

This was an early sign of what most established queer bookshops would come to embrace if they were to stay relevant and thrive in the coming years. The term 'lesbian and gay bookshop' was fast feeling outdated.

Genderqueer

*'They came in 'cos their kid just came
out, and we had books ready to go.'*

DOMINIQUE JOHNSON

DOMINIQUE JOHNSON IS A REPRESENTATIVE IN THE Connecticut legislature and is happy to use she/her pronouns for the purposes of this book. She identifies as genderqueer and nonconforming, making her the first genderqueer person to join the state legislature in Connecticut. She first visited Giovanni's Room in Philadelphia back in 1995 when she was eighteen. 'I started to hear about this bookstore. Friends talked about how fabulous it was, so one day I secretly went on the train to visit.' She had never been inside a queer bookstore before. After graduating, she went back and got a job in the store as a bookseller, watching as others plucked up the courage to enter. 'I have so many memories of being at the front of Giovanni's Room and seeing people hovering outside looking nervous and we'd wave and say: "we're open, come in!"'

For Dominique, the store offered more than a job, it was her chosen family. That was no mere happenstance; Ed and Arleen's view of their shop had grown from being a lesbian and gay movement to being more overtly trans inclusive, moulding and mixing with new ideas and identities as the years rolled by. In the 90s, the notion of a 'genderqueer identity' was in its infancy and still somewhat obscure.

As early as 1987, the 'gender binary' was being challenged by the scholar Sandy Stone with her book *The 'Empire' Strikes Back:*

A Posttransexual Manifesto (1978). In the essay, Stone writes that trans folk needed to 'speak from outside the boundaries of gender'. Today, the essay is considered a founding text of transgender studies. At the time, it was a rebuttal.

This new language and sense of identity was looked on with curiosity in Europe. Joachim Bartholomae took an interest from his bookstore in Hamburg, Buchladen Männerschwarm:

> One could see with envy that a new queer subculture had emerged in the USA. In Europe, instead of solidarity, there is a constant guerrilla war between dogmatic positions that reached frightening proportions within the queer movement. We tried very hard to take a neutral position, but it wasn't that easy: even someone who actively doesn't take sides can be attributed to this or that position through external perception.

Some gay customers left when genderqueer stock was brought in, but for Joachim it was a natural progression. 'The reason we presented ourselves as a "gay bookstore" was because we only had gay people working there', he explains. 'However, the range went far beyond "purely gay" and included everything that had anything to do with sexual emancipation. So we found it completely natural that when the "transsexual" movement came through in the 90s, the bookstore became a meeting place and contact point for trans people.'

In 1990, the hitherto gay, lesbian and bisexual publisher, Alyson Publications, released Lou Sullivan's *From Female to Male: The Life of Jack Bee Garland*, a relatively early title about a transsexual man, and in 1992, around the time Dominique first paid her visit to Giovanni's Room, the store was carrying a Leslie Feinberg pamphlet, *Transgender Liberation: A Movement Whose Time Has Come*, which expanded the term 'transgender' from a primarily male-to-female focus, using it as a term for all gender variations. Giovanni's Room sold author and activist Kate Bornstein's hit book *Gender Outlaw* (1994), making it clear to customers where it stood as a queer business.

By the time Dominique joined in 1995, the term 'genderqueer' was beginning to appear in print. The activist Riki Anne Wilchins was quoted in the *Washington Times*: 'It's high time "genderqueers" came out of the closets, out of the shadows and out of the margins.'

The term was soon appearing in Giovanni's stock of zines and activist flyers. Queer Nation and other radical groups were coming through. Dominique identified as a 'butch' woman back then, organising the lesbian booklist for the store, assuming she was a lesbian herself. *Female Masculinity* by Jack Halberstam was published in 1998, the author visiting the store for a reading. The event, and others, cemented the store's reputation as a safe space for young people exploring their gender identity, often in fear of rejection.

For years, gay men and women had been coming to the shop seeking sanctuary; now young genderqueer people were doing the same. There were trans book groups and queer community groups gathering beneath a chandelier on the first floor, with young people congregating on comfy chairs. Teenagers would buy a slice of pizza across the street, then run across to the store to do their homework somewhere safe and peaceful. These were the dying days of in-person forums, right before the advent of Yahoo Groups and MySpace.

Dominique got used to seeing high school students arriving in their school uniforms, making a dash to the bathrooms to change before reappearing like butterflies, sometimes furtive, sometimes outrageous, as their chosen identities. It wasn't just their physical appearance that had gone through a metamorphosis; it was their whole demeanour. 'It was the liberation on people's faces,' she says, 'the way they'd change, how they would rush in and then return with that moment of "this is me", putting makeup on, clothes they feel comfortable in, hairstyles that were more them, it was totally transformative and for that moment they could be who they really were.'

Only for a moment, mind you. They would change before leaving, dressing in their school uniforms again, wiping off makeup and smiles. At least they could buy a rainbow pin or genderqueer badge at the counter: a subtle hint to themselves and others as to their true identity. 'They'd leave with a button or a book', says Dominique, 'or something less physical like a conversation or even just a feeling that nobody could take away from them.'

While the shop was open to every gender expression, much of Philadelphia wasn't. The Giovanni's Room staff offered advice on safety, making sure customers knew how to protect themselves from verbal or physical abuse. Just walking to the bus stop nearby wasn't safe for people openly presenting their genderqueer identity.

A more hopeful sign of the times arrived when parents started turning up at the shop seeking help because their kid had come out as trans. Giovanni's Room had a shelf specially arranged for them with books written for moms and dads wanting to understand. 'It was for parents of gay or genderqueer young people', explains Dominique, who curated the selection. 'They came *in* 'cos their kid just came *out*, and we had books ready to go. There was a book by the LGBTQ+ awareness charity PFLAG, as well as pamphlets and books on gender and sexuality science, mixed in with memoirs by famous queer people so they felt more reassured.'

For those families, young customers seeking refuge and young staff members, Ed and Arleen's store gave them space to explore their own identities and it was there that the first genderqueer person to join the state legislature in Connecticut came to understand who she was, taking 'hardcore academic' essays to the beach along with 'fluff' that was fun to read. Being from the Midwest, Dominique hadn't had access to queer books in her local library.

Now it was her job to read those books and talk to customers about what they might like. She would spend hours hunting through the stacks, finding herself amongst the pages, old and ancient, coming to realise she wasn't a lesbian, she was genderqueer.

Giovanni's Room was, by the late 90s, a landmark destination, where young staff and visitors entered a sacred space, imbued with decades of rebellion and self-discovery. Unlike bars and clubs, unlike the internet for that matter, those queer bookstores strong – or lucky – enough to be open at the close of the twentieth century were a communal space for people of all generations. Here, older gay men and women perused the shelves – surprised and a little affronted perhaps, after a lifetime of discrimination, to be told they were 'privileged' and 'mainstream' – but mixing together all the same in a small and cosy bookshop, and by doing so, continuing a sense of communal belonging mature enough to be called a queer bookstore 'tradition'. But that tradition might not last.

As the early 90s arrived, queer booksellers would face the greatest threat in their history. Greater than government raids, arson attacks and vandalism, greater even than the law. Many, in fact *most*, would be wiped out within a decade.

Requiem

THE MILLENNIUM ARRIVES. A NEW ERA OF ACCEPTANCE and legal rights for queer people in many parts of the Western world. Yet, for queer bookstores, the new century might as well be dusk as dawn. According to the American Booksellers Association, independent bookshops in the US – queer and mainstream – plummeted from an estimated 7,000 in 1995 to just 1,401 in 2009. In the UK, there were 1,894 independent bookshops registered with the government in 1995, but that number would halve over the following fifteen years and in 2003 alone, some 400 independent shops were registered as 'incorporated but now dissolved'.

The competition from chain stores was a considerable part of the problem, customers drawn away from indies by discounts and snazzy branding, but there was something more innate to queer and feminist bookshops that made them particularly vulnerable. In the cruellest of ironies, it was their authenticity that proved a significant part of their downfall. It's a strange notion for any other retail sector, but bookshops are able to return books for a full refund if they don't sell. The bookseller must cover the cost of postage and packaging, but that's all. It gives them the opportunity to refresh their stock with confidence, jettisoning less popular titles and replacing them with the latest releases. This suits larger retailers and mainstream bookshops but, as the author and journalist June Thomas writes in her book *A Place of Our Own*, resolute lesbian and feminist booksellers are less likely to take advantage. Her point here tracks across queer booksellers more generally:

Feminist Booksellers were much less likely than other stores to reduce their debt by returning books. Many bookwomen considered their true vocation to be compiling lists of essential titles in key subject areas, which naturally affected how they curated the selection of books on offer in the store. Every section, from lesbian romance novels to titles on recovery or spirituality, feminist theory or poetry, disability rights or international fiction, was stocked with books they felt women in their community needed. They wanted to have those titles on hand at all times, even if they only sold one or two copies per year.

Aside from their stalwart loyalty to their books, there were many other factors that cut queer booksellers off at the knees, as we shall discover in what promises to be a sorrowful lament.

Sisterwrite closed in 1993 and **West & Wilde** (formerly **Lavender Menace**) closed in 1997. **A Woman's Place** in Oakland had already closed in 1989, while **Vrolijk** closed in 2017, now operating online as Vrolijk.nu. **The Bookshop Darlinghurst**, Australia's first queer bookshop, closed in December 2025 after 43 years of trading. Big financial losses and delays surrounding a move to new premises forced owner Charles to close it down. Heartbroken customers and staff called for fundraisers to save it, but a reprieve didn't materialise. A huge loss and another reminder that historic queer bookstores are as vulnerable as ever.

SILVER MOON

The new century heralded 'squawks of alarm' on Charing Cross Road as the accounts showed a drop in revenue for the first time since opening. In her diary, Jane Cholmeley wrote: 'Am I depressed – or what! This is horrible.' Customers had thinned out and the shelves had grown sparse. 'So many bookshops closed at that time', remembers Jane. 'With the breaking of the Net Book Agreement* and aggressive discounting, the rents, and then the arrival of Amazon.com. All those things were killing bookshops. I do feel angry a bit.'

Silver Moon's revenue topped £805,000 in 1999 and profits were £57,815 in 1997 – impressive – but alas, due to market pressures and other external issues, things began to slide, and Silver Moon went into the red in 2000. Sales were stagnating, salaries were meagre, career opportunities non-existent. The ceiling at Silver Moon wasn't made of glass; it was papered over with bills and bank statements. They started their own website in 2001, but it didn't fly and that same year, on 18 November, Jane and Sue locked up their beloved shop at 68 Charing Cross Road for the last time. It had been a destination for lesbian readers for seventeen years. For writers too, including Sarah Waters – today a multi-award-winning international bestselling novelist whose books have helped redefine mainstream society's understanding of lesbian history. Silver Moon changed her perspective as an aspiring young author. 'It was really empowering to realise that I could write for my own community,' she says, 'that I didn't have to be, say, Angela Carter or any other writer. And there was no need to pander to the mainstream; I could write freely as myself. It's true, without Silver Moon I might not have ended up a novelist.'

Sue Butterworth died of cancer in 2004, aged fifty-three, and Jane looks back on their venture with fond memories. 'I was walking home from the theatre the other night. I passed our old shop doorway and caught sight of the most beautiful crescent moon. I looked up at it and thought... Sue, we did it.'

---

* The Net Book Agreement in the UK had existed since 1900, where publishers set a fixed retail price for books, preventing booksellers from discounting them. The NBA came to an end in 1997, thanks to publishers wanting to support big chains which were seeking the freedom to provide discounts and multi-buy offers.

LAMBDA RISING

That same year, Deacon Maccubbin's last two remaining stores closed in Washington and Rehoboth, Massachusetts. Sales had been sliding for a while and Deacon Maccubbin could see the writing on the noticeboard. 'I didn't want to see the store get to the point that it could no longer sustain the service and stock we had been known for.' His health was also beginning to decline after decades of long hours. He considered selling the flagship Washington branch to a new bookseller, but he couldn't stomach the thought of walking down Connecticut Avenue and seeing his baby run by someone else. Anyway, hadn't he succeeded? The press release he sent out to announce his sad news was headlined: *MISSION ACCOMPLISHED*. 'The original idea was to put ourselves out of business,' says Deacon, 'because everyone would be stocking gay books, and that's what we did.' He closed the satellite store in Norfolk first, then the Oscar Wilde Memorial Bookshop was sold, then Lambda Rising in Baltimore, before the last two were shuttered. It took an emotional toll, but Deacon sold the Washington store for a healthy price, paying for his retirement, along with his partner, Jim. That last day, he thought about multiple Christmases with his famous window displays with little gay figures sharing festive same-sex kisses, two sitting on a sleigh, two on a snowy bench. It was an institution and a childhood memory for citizens of Washington, queer and straight alike. He could think about the thousands of events they'd put on and the store he'd opened in the hometown where he'd once worried about coming out to his best friend. Ultimately, it's the lives Lambda Rising touched that serve as Deacon's legacy. He still receives 'thank you' letters and emails, and he keeps some precious letters too; letters which reflect the extraordinary reach and diversity of a business that grew out of a single shelf in a tiny pipe shop. Today, the Lambda Literary Awards stand as a world-renowned beacon for the best in queer fiction, poetry and non-fiction; a legacy that promises to live on for generations to come.

THE OSCAR WILDE MEMORIAL BOOKSHOP

The Oscar Wilde Memorial Bookshop closed on 29 March 2009, the end of the beginning for queer bookshops the world over. It had fought and stumbled, then fought and stumbled again before finally giving in. Having been diagnosed with stomach cancer, Craig Rodwell had sold the shop to its manager, Bill Offenbaker, in 1993, dying soon after on 18 June the same year. The shop was then bought by a bookseller named Larry Lingle in 1996. After seven years of valiant struggle, Larry said he could no longer afford to keep the store open so, in 2003, Deacon Maccubbin of Lambda Rising stepped in to rescue the treasured institution. 'We felt strongly that it was too important historically to let it fail', explains Deacon. 'We managed to buy it and turn it into a profitable operation for three years.' At the 1993 Lambda Literary Awards, Deacon acknowledged Craig's place as the founding father of the movement.

> Craig's vision and courage in 1967 gave birth to a whole network of lesbian and gay bookstores across the country. He showed many of us that such stores were viable and could serve a useful purpose in our communities. He gave publishers an outlet, and authors a home.

The Oscar Wilde was then bought by the store's manager, Kim Brinster, and nobody can say she didn't do her level best to keep it alive. But ultimately, her efforts proved hopeless and with dwindling tourists in the city, the financial crash of 2008, the weak euro, competition from online as well as the chains and – perhaps – a store that never stopped mourning its creator, the Oscar Wilde Memorial Bookshop finally closed on 29 March 2009. The landlord had capped the rent at $3,000, well below market value, but the storefront was by then a woefully neglected landmark, a largely forgotten shrine to the Stonewall era. On the last Tuesday it was open, Kim welcomed only two paying customers. Another couple of years and the advent of social media might have saved the day, as it would for Gay's the Word, but it was too late; the shop was gone forever. Speaking to Betsy Kalin for the Outwords Archive in 2018, Kay Tobin Lahusen shared a treasured vision of the shop and its owner when they were young.

> He would sit there on the cold winter nights with his little dog by his side, his Schnauzer, and he would have the coffee pot on and some donuts ... And he would talk to the people who wandered in. Many of them were gay people who just desperately needed somebody to talk to and needed to see a book that was halfway positive, at least. He was doing, I think, a very good service in the movement.

A DIFFERENT LIGHT

Not long after the loss of the Oscar Wilde, the last A Different Light store entered into history, heralding the toppling of the world's biggest queer bookstore chain. Norman Laurila owned stores in West Hollywood and New York City, as well as San Francisco. 'Running the stores for twenty-one years was a delight and my life's mission,' says Norman Laurila, 'but it was incredibly stressful keeping things going in three cities.' His co-founder and money man George Leigh died in 1996, so when an offer came in to buy the store, Norman took it. He knew his stores intimately and could tell they were in trouble. 'I'd seen the writing on the wall with the big stores, then Amazon. The buyers assumed we were bad businesspeople, and they'd struck gold, but they were shocked maybe by how narrow the profit margins were.' Narrow hardly covers it. Norman estimates they were as tight as one per cent net profit. He sold his business in 2000, performing a dignified and profitable getaway. He made $1. Still, he was debt-free. Under new ownership the stock lost its depth and was replaced with rainbow keyrings and porn, and in 2001, the New York store was shuttered, citing Manhattan's high rental costs, followed by the West Hollywood store in 2009 and the Castro store in San Francisco in 2011.

TO AFRICA AND ASIA

In spite of a growing queer literary scene, the African diaspora awaits its first LGBT+ bookshop, though Cape Town in South Africa has **Clarke's Bookshop**, opened in 1956, which offers a small but significant section on gender and queer studies. With powerful African voices increasingly finding international acclaim at home and abroad, perhaps the continent's first queer bookshop is at last on the horizon, though considerable cultural obstacles would have to be overcome. It is also likely there are individuals running proto-queer bookshops in African nations at the time of writing, distributing books from discreet locations and knapsacks – just like the early booksellers in this chronicle – but let's just say, if one of them happened to share their dream with the author, they likely asked him to protect their identity and keep their ambition a secret for now.

To Asia, and Tokyo's gay district in upscale Shinjuku Ni-Chome, where a second-hand queer bookstore called **Okamalt** was – or is – run by Toh Ogura, a former writer and magazine editor known as Margarette in drag queen circles. There, customers could – or can – peruse some 400 books with tea and biscuits. The Okamalt bookstore seems to have closed at some point but is rumoured to have reopened in a new location behind a locked entrance. Whatever's going on with Okamalt, it's clear Toh Ogura, Japan's first queer bookstore owner, cares very deeply for his book collection. 'One day,' he says in a Facebook video posted in 2020, 'if I can pass this on to someone who will protect and archive it all then I think I can die in peace.'

Over the East China Sea to Taipei, the sprawling capital of Taiwan, we discover a strikingly familiar story. The GinGin (晶晶書庫) bookstore was opened in a small lane off Roosevelt Road, Taipei on 1 January 1999, making it the first LGBTQ+ bookstore in Asia. 'GinGin' means 'sparkling', with the characters symbolising six suns, a nod to the six colours of the rainbow flag. It was created by gay rights campaigner J. J. Lai and though its window was smashed with bricks in 2001, he pressed on, establishing a 'Rainbow Community' in the Kungkuan district, with neighbouring businesses displaying rainbow stickers to show they were LGBTQ+ allies. Then, in March 2003, Customs officers seized 400 gay magazines imported from Hong Kong, while another 500 were seized from the shop by police in co-ordinated raids. J. J. Lai was prosecuted under Taiwan's Article 235 obscenity laws even though the magazines were wrapped in opaque plastic so kids couldn't see them and they had warning labels. After two failed appeals, J. J. Lai narrowly avoided jail, but was forced to pay a fine of NT$45,000. GinGin battled on and that same year in 2003 the intrepid bookstore owner co-founded his city's first ever Pride parade. Taipei was the first Chinese-speaking city to march for queer rights, with around 1,000 people – mostly wearing masks for their own safety – marching through the capital to protest against a ban on gay people in the military. Taiwan lifted the ban that year, becoming the first Asian country to do so. Today, thanks to GinGin, Taipei Pride gathers almost 200,000 people for a huge city-wide celebration of queer rights. Alas, it appears GinGin closed following the Covid pandemic.

India does not appear to have a queer bookshop at the time of writing, though it did once have a feminist bookshop that became a hub for a secret community of lesbian women. In 1985, a feminist bookshop was opened in Bangalore named **Streelekha**. Feminist campaigner Donna Fernandes is in her seventies now, still pressing for women's rights after fifty years of activism. She's a happily married mother and grandmother, but she saw first-hand what the shop meant to lesbian women.

> Lesbian women were often hounded, forced into hiding and living in fear of harassment, not only from their families but even within the women's movement itself, where their relationships were rarely recognised or respected. Most complaints against them came from parents and family members, especially when women refused marriage. Families would approach the police, demanding action against their daughters. Many young women were locked up at home, beaten, and denied the opportunity to continue their studies. Access to safe spaces, including feminist bookstores, was not only limited but also fraught with fear of exposure and repercussions.

Streelekha stocked fiction and poetry as well as books on the feminist movement. 'I'm not sure if the bookstore really changed anything for lesbian women,' says Donna, 'but it surely did give lesbian women a safe space to meet, smoke, read and maybe have a cup of coffee without hassles.' On a personal level then, if not political, it surely changed much.

REQUIEM

AMAZON BOOKSTORE COOPERATIVE VS. AMAZON.COM

So, we return to the Amazons of Minneapolis who were blissfully unaware they were standing on the brink of a bookselling tsunami that would sweep so many independent bookstores away. They were doing very nicely at the time, with $600,000 turnover in 1995 and fourteen staff, including part-timers. Customer loyalty and an assertive campaign for ongoing support had largely bolstered the Amazons from the impact of the chain stores. A new Starbucks was bringing in more customers, though exacerbating a woeful lack of parking. They had just set up a video rental scheme as well as a membership programme and were hosting more author events and open mic nights than ever before.

Then, one morning in the mid-1990s, a young tech entrepreneur called Jeff Bezos was flicking through the 'A' section of his dictionary searching for a name to call his new venture. He'd been working on Wall Street for a few years, researching new business opportunities for a hedge fund and he'd had an idea. A Silicon Valley company called Computer Literacy was selling books online, but the website was clunky and it was hard to make a purchase. Jeff knew he could do better, but he needed the right *name*. He'd been advised by friends that 'Relentless.com' was a tad aggressive. According to tech folklore, he had a sudden epiphany and marched out to the garage where the new company was being constructed, declaring:

> This is not only the largest river in the world, it's many times larger than the next biggest river. It blows all other rivers away.*

---

* Not to be a size queen, but the Nile is generally considered longer than its South American cousin by some 150 kilometres. Mind you, as all guys know, it ultimately depends where you put the ruler, and, as with the male member, the Amazon is a little longer if measured from Peru.

If you're competitive about rivers, you're probably the right guy to set up an internet company, and Amazon.com was born.

It was around Christmas 1998 when strange things started happening at the Amazon Bookstore Cooperative. 'We'd get these weird orders', says bookseller Mev Miller, 'for some technology book that cost $400. I was like, "what the heck?"' Customers started coming in and congratulating the women on their amazing website. They didn't *have* a website. More persistent calls started coming in. Amazon.com had no customer support line, so disgruntled customers were mistakenly calling a lesbian collective with complaints about missing books. It began as one or two calls a week, then one or two a day, then a flood.

Help arrived in the unlikely form of a young man who came jogging past the store one day. He stopped and looked up at their sign with a thoughtful expression. Matt Samuels was a plucky patent and trademark lawyer with a taste for adventure and buckets of ambition. 'I think of him as like this puppy that was bouncing around us at the time', says Jo den Boer, who was working at the shop when he first appeared.

He had a habit of asking clumsy questions, attempting to guess which staff were straight and which were 'dykes'. Still, he was naive, not malicious, and the lesbian collective grew to like him for his positivity, optimism and enthusiasm, and together, this plucky band of feminists and their young D'Artagnan filed a lawsuit against Bezos's company for trademark infringement.

Unsurprisingly, Amazon.com kicked back. They had millions in equity funding secured on Wall Street, plus the ability to run at a loss while the brand established itself.* The lesbian Amazons

---

* In its first two months of business, Amazon sold books to all fifty US states plus forty-five foreign territories, with sales reaching $20,000 per week. The company quickly expanded to include music, DVDs and other merchandise, and by 1999 it had become the largest online sales platform in the world. It didn't achieve consistent profitability until 2003.

in Minneapolis were a mere raindrop in comparison, but nothing prepared them for pre-trial.

The suit was contested on the website's behalf with a line of questioning that proved controversial. In deposition, their attorney repeatedly asked one member of the Cooperative to reveal her sexual orientation and that of her colleagues, going on to ask: 'Have you had any interest in promoting lesbian ideals in the community?' and 'I'll ask you this, are you gay?' and 'Are any of the employees of the bookstore gay?'

All the while, Mev was distracted because she'd been persuaded to shave to make a 'better' impression in court.

> Yeah, appalling and shocking and it like, you know, really got my dyke spine up. And that was the first time I felt – I didn't really feel *betrayed* – but I felt like, wait a minute, why don't you guys stick up [for me]? Like, why are you getting into this patriarchal bullshit, you know.

In 1999, the lawsuit was settled with the feminist-lesbian bookstore effectively conceding full rights to the 'Amazon' name. It was a true whiplash for the bookstore that had brought the original claim, but lawyers' fees had become too much and they found themselves under strict orders to refer to themselves *only* as the Amazon Bookstore Cooperative. For this humiliation, they received a still undisclosed fee.* The 'small cash settlement' helped keep the store open a little longer, moving twice until 2008/9 when it was sold to a new owner, Ruta Skujins, who later told the press she sank her entire $250,000 retirement savings into the store. Omens were not good from the start,

---

* A further request was made for the precise sum in the writing of this chronicle, but it seems after more than a quarter of a century, the collective are determined to keep the exact figure a secret.

and Ruta was forced by contractual terms with Amazon.com to change the store's legendary name. In spite of attempts to reach a younger audience via the new platforms Facebook and MySpace, the store closed for the last time in February 2012. Poor Ruta had lost everything and, after forty-two years, the Amazon Bookstore was back selling from boxes. An extraordinary and world-changing run for the oldest feminist-lesbian bookstore in the United States.

'This is going to sound really strange,' says former bookseller Mev, 'but I took one of those ugly bookshelves [from the old store]. I still have that thing. It's in my basement and I have tons of books on it and it's like, I still… I still have a piece of the bookstore with me. I'm going to have to write on the side: *This bookshelf came from the Amazon Bookstore back in the day. Some dyke built this thing.*'

Revival

BY THE END OF THE NOUGHTIES, THE OBITUARY FOR THE independent bookstore – queer and straight – had been written so many times it was practically boilerplate, but in the 2010s something strange happened. Against all odds, small, independent bookstores began to reappear. The American Booksellers Association reported a forty-nine per cent jump in the number of US indies, from 1,651 in 2009 to 2,470 in 2018. In the UK, numbers rose steadily from just 867 in 2016 to 1,052 by the end of 2024.

We'll mention many of them in our final chapter and pay one last visit to some old friends.

GIOVANNI'S ROOM, PHILADELPHIA

Ed Hermance realised in the early 1990s that he had to do something quickly if he was to save the store. The year 1992 had proved the most profitable year of sales in the bookstore's history and Ed thought he'd make at least a million dollars over the next twelve months, but then a chain store opened nearby. 'They would open a store across the street from an indie', says Ed, 'and promote books at a steep discount until the competition was closed.' One of the most crushing disappointments was seeing big-name queer authors – who'd been championed at Giovanni's Room when they were in the wilderness – holding signing events with the same chains that snubbed them before mainstream approval. To add insult to injury, trusted customers were sneakily copying down book titles, then scurrying home to order them online. 'The internet turned our stores into display rooms', says Ed. Things continued to slide and, though Ed never lost his drive, he announced his retirement in 2013 after more than thirty-seven years as the world's no. 1 queer book distributor and bookseller. 'I need to sell the store because we are now losing money and I can't afford to lose money', Ed told a reporter for the *Temple News* at the time. 'I'm hoping we can find a buyer who has the resources to change the store in ways that will make it profitable again.' But no buyer was found, and on 17 May 2014 America's oldest surviving queer bookstore closed its doors. Lifelong customer, novelist and columnist for *Philadelphia Gay News* Victoria A. Brownworth wrote at the time:

> When Ed shuts the doors that last time, he will close them on a major chapter in our literary history. Giovanni's Room was a great story, a compelling, engaging, provocative story. It deserved a sequel, however. And we are far, far the less for not getting that next part of its tale.
>
> *Lambda Literary Review*, 30 April 2014

Not so fast. Giovanni's Room was not finished yet. Snatched from the jaws of extinction, Ed leased the store to the non-profit organisation Philly AIDS Thrift in 2014. And it's still going strong at the time of writing, selling donated items and new books to support HIV/AIDS patients.

'We're in the business of preserving precious things,' Ed told reporters, 'and what can be more precious than Giovanni's Room?'

Katharine Milon now co-manages the store with Christopher Cirillo, preserving and rejuvenating Giovanni's Room for customers young and old. Some have known it since the beginning in the 1970s; others are discovering it for the first time. The store even hosted its first queer wedding in 2023. As Christopher touchingly commented at the time: 'What better way to celebrate this wonderfully unique space than to be able to host such a beautiful moment in someone's life?'

That's what Giovanni's Room has been for decades. A truly unique space for countless moments, whether in joy, fear, empowerment, enlightenment or great sorrow, all rendered beautiful, brave or at the very least bearable by a queer bookshop.

GLAD DAY, TORONTO

Jearld Moldenhauer's Boston branch of Glad Day closed in June 2000, the bookshop's founding father packing up his knapsack one more time and leaving the United States for a new life abroad. Meanwhile, with the closure of the Oscar Wilde Memorial Bookshop, Glad Day in Toronto had become the oldest operating queer bookstore in the world, a title it maintains at the time of writing. By the dawn of the 2010s they were also witnessing a sea change in behaviour. With the availability of online shopping and porn, queer-positive shows on TV and streaming sites, plus the popularity of hook-up apps,* the store's traditional clientele – gay men – were connecting with gay culture and each other elsewhere. By early 2012, sales had dropped to around eight books a day, so owner John Scythes put the store up for sale. It looked like it was the end of the road, but a collective of twenty-three supporters banded together and purchased the shop. Still, sales still weren't enough to cover staff costs and rent and it was time for another move. From Jearld's backpack in the 60s, to the annex at no. 65 Kendal Avenue in 1970, to 4 Kensington Avenue a year after that,

---

* Netflix moved from home-delivering DVDs to online streaming in 2007; Grindr came out in 2009.

to 139 Seaton Street, to 4 Collier Street in 1974, then 648A Yonge Street in 1982, hopping down the block in 1985 to 598A Yonge Street, now, after an uncharacteristically long stay of thirty-one years, and thanks to a $50,000 crowdfunder, the store moved to a ground-floor coffee shop and bar at 499 Church Street. For the first time, the shelves were stocked with queer books reflecting the full sweep of the 2SLGBTQ+ spectrum. The oldest queer bookstore in the world had also become a bar pioneering the concept of drag brunches. In May 2024 another crowdfunder was posted, raising an impressive $192,000, but the shop was still forced to move to its eighth location: a low-cost temporary home, thanks to the City of Toronto, at 32 Lisgar Street. They're currently appealing for a further $150,000 to find home number nine.

GAY'S THE WORD, LONDON

There's no rivalry between the two, but while Glad Day holds the title for the longest-running queer bookshop in the world, Gay's the Word is undoubtedly the most enduring. From its opening in 1979 to this day, it has remained at the same premises on Marchmont Street, a shrine to the sacred values of its pioneers, but with a fresh and all-embracing response to the modern world.

Jim MacSweeney joined Gay's the Word as a bookseller in 1989, then took over from manager Paud Hegarty in 1997, running the shop for twenty-seven years. In that time, he's seen the shop flirt with disaster more than once before shooting back to fame. 'When so many LGBT bookshops closed around the world, we found ourselves an endangered species,' Jim says, 'not just as a bookshop but also as a historical archive. When I first joined, we were incredibly busy but then in the 90s, the chains took over and started stocking a limited selection of queer books.'

The wider availability of queer literature was welcome news beyond London, but it siphoned customers away from the capital's only queer bookshop. Even if Jim and his fellow booksellers could afford to slash prices (they couldn't), they had no intention of doing so. 'Books aren't a commodity to us,' says Jim, 'they're more important than that.'

Then the internet arrived and... we are familiar with the story. By 2007, feeling dusty and forgotten, Gay's the Word faced imminent closure. Determined to go down fighting, they set up a campaign, led by impassioned new arrival Uli Lenart with support from the newspaper journalist Tim Teeman. Supporters were asked to 'sponsor a shelf for £100' and the campaign took off, gaining coverage on the BBC and in national newspapers. Now, as though waking from a daze, the community realised they were about to lose their precious bookshop and, unlike the lamentable neglect of the Oscar Wilde Memorial Bookshop in New York, London's queer community stepped up just in time.

Then, in 2014, the movie *Pride* was released, based on the Lesbians and Gays Support the Miners campaign of the 1980s. It faithfully depicted activists collecting money at the bookshop, cementing Gay's the Word's place in the popular imagination. It was perfect timing: the film was an international hit just when social media was taking off. Paradoxically, while the internet had sounded the death knell for so many indie bookshops, it was now transforming a once-forsaken institution into a global icon. The shop has embraced social media ever since. 'We can put positive stuff out there', says Jim. 'We're able to cut through the traditional media and celebrate our books, our staff, our customers directly with a worldwide audience.'

That customer base has changed since 1979. Women used to be in the minority but are now equal – perhaps a slight majority – and, while most are still gay, there's been a big increase in genderqueer customers. Whereas in the old days, the shop split the shelves between lesbian and gay books with a single shelf for trans titles, now trans fiction and theory claims a whole bank of shelves. The age of customers has shifted too. Greater social acceptance has led to teenagers coming out earlier, and Jim says that's reflected in the shop. 'One of the big changes has been the number of young people visiting, often with their parents, which I find very moving. At a time when we see so much homophobia and transphobia on social media and in the press, it's a joy to see teens being supported and given unconditional love by their mums and dads.'

Uli Lenart stayed with the shop and took over as manager on its forty-sixth birthday, in January 2025. He was well qualified for the role, having been deputy manager for twenty years. 'The plan is simple,' he says, 'treasure our history and respect our role as an archive as well as a bookshop.' He hasn't dragged his heels. In summer 2025 Gay's the Word moved to a temporary pop-up down the road* to allow for some much-needed fireproofing, but even though walls and ceilings had to be stripped and clad, the cellar that acted as operational HQ for the Defend Gay's the Word campaign in the 80s has been preserved. Even the scrubby basement doors with retro glazing were raised from the basement with reverential care. During the final research trip for this book, one of the doors was leaning against a wall in the back office, the other transformed into a makeshift desk. There's a metaphor in there somewhere. Both are to be rehung like treasured relics, much to Jim's befuddlement and Uli's delight. Leaning on the door-desk, looking around the many teetering piles of books in the stockroom, Uli considers the shop's place in people's hearts:

---

* Opposite the childhood home of the famous British comedian Kenneth Williams, whose father owned the barbershop below. It seems he never visited Gay's the Word during his lifetime, conflicted as he was about his homosexuality, but his diary is available to buy from the shelves.

In 2018 when our window was broken in an attempted robbery, we were tearful, picking shards of glass from the floor and clearing out damaged books. It was like a physical attack on us, not just a pane of glass. Then, as I stood back and watched volunteers clearing up the mess, I was overcome by this great wave of warmth, realising we would always be here, because we have *always* been here and no attacks, no bigotry, *nothing* the future has planned can take that institution from us.

Asked to sum up Gay's the Word in one sentence, he ponders for a while, then answers, eyes closed. 'Kind,' he says, 'caring and wise… with inner metal.'

With those words, we can be sure that Gay's the Word is in safe hands.

SOMOS VOCES, MEXICO CITY

The largest and longest-running LGBT bookstore in Latin America, Somos Voces, sits snugly between a taco takeout and a cocktail bar in the middle of a row of ornate colonialist *edificios*. The project started life in around 2001 thanks to founder Bertha de la Maza, an avid reader who'd journeyed across Europe exploring LGBTQ+ literature. She returned with books that weren't available in Mexico, sharing them with eager friends who were hungry for more. She set up an online shop called LesLibros (a word play on Lesbian Books in Spanish).

The website, Voces en Tinta (Voices in Ink), was launched in 2005, with the bricks-and-mortar shop opening its doors in the 'Zona Rosa' queer district on 27 August 2009. In 2016, new management changed the shop's name to Somos Voces (We Are Voices), putting LGBTQ+ titles on full display in the window for the first time. The shop's focus on Latinx publishers makes it an influential champion of South American queer literature and today, like Giovanni's Room of old, it delivers to any part of the Mexican Republic and right across the world.

Unlike so many queer bookshops, Somos Voces has never experienced vandalism or violence, only occasional abuse from the street; and the Mexican government is increasingly reaching out to the shop asking for advice and offering support. The staff report a steady revolution in Mexican attitudes to queer lives. There was a time when people would avoid them at book fairs, loitering until the end of the day when the hall was almost empty; now people throng their stand wherever they go. Staff remember a construction worker in his forties approaching them accompanied by a little girl. They thought he was going to rant about traditional masculine values but instead, he politely asked for materials on feminism because he wanted to protect his young daughter from violence. The shop has helped support its own staff too, including transgender people looking for a place to work in safety and acceptance. North of the Mexico border, society proved less welcoming to one of its newest queer bookstores, at least in the early days.

VIOLET VALLEY, MISSISSIPPI

When word got around Water Valley that a queer bookstore was opening on Main Street, it was the talk of the town. Strange rumours were circulating that a gang of lesbians were launching an invasion, possibly funded by the Democrats, possibly going to sell porn, probably planning workshops to turn kids transgender. It was 2017 and this tight-knit community in the rural South was spooked. An emergency prayer meeting was organised in the park across the street, attracting concerned citizens and Christian nationalist protestors alike. 'They're all going to Hell and they're happy about it!' shouted a preacher. 'We don't need books!'

Jaime Harker, a lesbian English professor, published author and leader of the gender studies programme at the University of Mississippi, realised she was facing way more hostility than she'd anticipated. 'The rural South, it's a complicated place.'

With the help of her wife Dixie, they installed security cameras on the front of the shop and around their home. 'The prayer meeting was streamed online. It was frightening to watch and eerie.'

Jaime's troupe of happy volunteers delivered the first load of stock to the store on a Sunday morning, just when everyone was going to church. Locals stared as they passed by in their cars and Jaime was grateful for the presence of a friendly ex-cop who parked his truck outside and stood guard as they unloaded, his hand resting on his gun.

Meanwhile, an underground campaign was set up to try and get the candidates in the city's ongoing mayoralty race to condemn the store and the owner of the premises was pressured to cancel the lease. Such demands were ignored.

Jaime had dreamed of owning her own bookstore for years. She never made it to the Oscar Wilde Memorial Bookshop – 'The Mothership' – before it closed, but as a grad school student she virtually *lived* in Giovanni's Room. She'd also travelled to London to visit Gay's the Word and was blown away by how encompassing it was. When she heard about a quirky retail space coming up at 303 North Main Street, she *had* to go for it.

The owner agreed instantly. After all, Water Valley was the perfect place for a queer bookstore, it being home to the pioneering gay novelist Hubert Creekmore.*

---

* An attractive green and gold memorial sign in front of Creekmore's former family home at 114 Panola Street describes him as a veteran of the US Navy and mentions his various literary achievements, but fails to mention his status as a pioneering queer writer.

The Violet Valley bookstore opened in February 2017, an adorable mint-green shop, squeezed like a slice of cheesecake between its red-brick neighbours. Non-profit, trans-inclusive, feminist *and* LGTBQ+, this tiny store, only ten feet wide, is a nineteenth-century cigar shop transformed into a magician's library, with teetering piles of books at every angle, shelves stuffed top to bottom with literature, mainstream, feminist and queer. Naturally, there's also a huge papier-mâché fish hanging from the ceiling.*

'There's still people in this town who won't set foot in the bookstore', says Jaime. 'But I think they respected the fact we didn't back down.'

The naysayers are few, compared to the store's many customers who travel from far and wide, not all of them the clientele she originally envisioned. 'There's a guy who comes in wearing camouflage gear', says Jaime. 'I don't know if he clocks that we're a queer-feminist bookstore or not, but it doesn't matter, he likes our mystery section. We're not a women-only space, I've always been clear about that.'

But it's the young, queer visitors Jaime loves to welcome most.

> I see them taking pictures outside, singing and laughing and doing little dances of excitement, it's too cute. We always have the queer section right near the front of the store. I remember a girl once putting her hands to her face in surprise and saying to me, 'I didn't know there was this much queer lit in the world', and I was like *my dear!* This is barely scratching

---

* Water Valley, Mississippi, is known for its annual 'Crappie Drop' New Year's Eve celebration, which features a large, mechanical crappie fish being lowered ceremoniously at midnight like the Times Square ball. This event pays tribute to the town's proudest moment, not the birth of a renowned queer author, but the auspicious day in 1957 when Fred Bright caught the world's largest 'crappie fish' in nearby Enid Lake.

the surface of it! She couldn't believe it when I said we had an entire section on the Queer *South*.

The existence of a queer-feminist bookshop in Mississippi seems – regrettably – more, not less, extraordinary as the years go by. With President Trump's 'war on woke', book banning at schools and public libraries has gained momentum.

Looking at the most recent available statistics, the free speech organisation PEN estimates that more than 10,000 individual books were banned from public (non-private) schools in the 2023/4 academic year. That's more than twice as many as the year before. Forty-four per cent of the banned books featured people and characters of colour; thirty-nine per cent featured LGBTQ+ people and characters.* The anti-queer movement has been supercharged by vitriolic campaign groups like Utah Parents United and Moms for Liberty.

In 2022, Florida governor Ron DeSantis signed into law House Bill 1557 in a chilling echo of Britain's Section 28. Better known as the 'Don't Say Gay' law, the legislation effectively banned discussion around sexual orientation and gender identity in classrooms from kindergarten up. Then in 2023, further 'Don't Say *They*' legislation was introduced, preventing students from being referred to by any pronoun or gender identity that might contradict their biological sex. It also prevents school staff – employees and contractors – from presenting as genderqueer. Nobody is allowed to contradict 'the classification of a person as either female or male based on the organisation of the body of such person for a specific reproductive role, as indicated by the person's sex chromosomes, naturally occurring sex hormones, and internal and external genitalia present

---

* Since 2021, book removals include Republican *and* Democrat districts. The stats likely reflect a mere fraction of the books being removed from the shelves. PEN's figures come from news reports, public records requests and publicly available data, but it's thought the majority of removals go unreported.

at birth'. In sex education, no 'instruction' is permitted around queer sexual orientation or gender identity, and 'All materials used to teach reproductive health or any disease, including HIV/AIDS, its symptoms, development, and treatment … must be approved' by the Department of Education. The legislation also effectively gives any parent the right to read any books in school libraries that they think might be inappropriate and to demand their removal. If the school disagrees with their request to ban specific books, they have to pay for a magistrate to arbitrate with those parents. For good measure, teachers who refuse to comply with book bans can be sacked for 'gross insubordination'.

Meanwhile, conservative outrage around 'Drag Queen Story Hours', where drag artists read stories to children, has led to a flurry of attempted state-wide bans on queer performance artists. In Minnesota, public libraries risked losing state funding if they hosted Drag Queen Story Hour events. However, the bans are considered unconstitutional because they break First Amendment protections of freedom of speech and discriminate against people based on their orientation. In 2023, Tennessee, Texas and Montana all passed laws banning drag artists from performing in public schools and libraries, but judges blocked them after an outcry from civil liberties groups.

Ever capable of finding the silver lining, Jaime at Violet Valley takes strength from her customers. Young readers are actively searching out banned authors and titles and the shop now takes orders from further afield, including Connecticut, Hawaii and Montana.

Jaime asks for a brief pause when asked what the town would be like without Violet Valley. She loses her voice for a moment and wipes her eyes.

> I'm sorry, it makes me cry thinking about my students and young customers. They have to move away from their homes

because they can't be who they are. They say, 'I've got to get out of here, I'm so stifled I can't keep hiding.' I get calls sometimes from trans people asking if they're allowed in because we're a feminist store and they assume they'll be turned out. That makes me so sad. All we're doing in this little shop is trying to imagine a utopia, where everyone can take as much space as they like, how they like, and if they can imagine a happier life for themselves in here, just for a little while, then leave with that feeling close to their hearts, maybe they can take that with them wherever they go and feel safe.

Jaime looks back on their tense opening day. 'The chamber of commerce usually have a ribbon cutting for every new business in town', she says, with a smile. 'They did it for the guy who opened a Trump Store further up the street.' She laughs. 'I get on great with them these days but, back then, they did *not* do it for me.'

Turns out, demand for MAGA hats and Donald Trump cut-outs was lower than anticipated and the Trump Store shut down after a couple of years.

'Trump Stores come and go', says Jaime with a wink, 'but queer bookstores are eternal.'

GAYBERYSTWYTH, ABERYSTWYTH

Pete and Matt walked into the newly opened Gay-on-Wye bookshop in Wales's legendary book town, Hay-on-Wye, in 2023. They were just going to say 'hello' and have a browse, but they got talking with the owner, Tom Owen, who encouraged them to open their own shop, even offering them LGBT+ books so they had some free stock to get started. Tom's now famous generosity was, unbeknownst to him, an echo of Craig Rodwell giving Ed and Arleen books for Giovanni's Room in the 1970s. Aberystwyth on the west coast of Wales was about to get its first queer bookstore, and one particular customer would be thankful for that.

Pete Shea and Matt Townsend imagined most of their customers would be younger people, students probably – and they weren't wrong – but one customer, Gwyn, was different. When Gayberystwyth opened in the old Market Hall on Saturday 30 March 2024, most people poking their noses in were the usual supportive types: solemn but curious teenagers, boisterous children, chatty mums, jolly dads and queer people celebrating the arrival of a bookshop just for them. But Gwyn. Gwyn stood out. At first, Pete and Matt were a little wary of him. It had been a mad week getting the shop open and they'd told each other it would be fine, people would be nice. They'd rushed about all week glamming up the unit – barely ten feet squared – with bright blue paint on the walls and zingy furniture, plus lots of rainbow prints, pride flags and of course a glowing neon flamingo. Pete watched as Gwyn stood in the open doorway, taking in the selection of books about the history of trans people, children's queer comics and greetings cards declaring 'I'm gay, get over it!'

He shifted in his boots and glanced up. Pete took a breath and was about to invite their visitor in when the man turned and left without saying a word.

The following Saturday, Gwyn returned and looked inside, without crossing the threshold. This time, he hung around a little longer, nervously flicking his eyes along the arcade. Pete smiled and Gwyn smiled back and then he was off again, without a word.

The next Saturday came around and Pete and Matt couldn't help but wait for their mysterious customer to appear. They were experiencing what every single queer bookstore owner had experienced since those earliest days in the 1960s: furtive customers walking in circles, plucking up the courage to enter.

Gwyn was in his sixties, a proud Aberystwyth man born and bred. Left school early. Worked in a factory all his life.

Surrounded by men, never had a proper girlfriend, never had anyone apart from his family, never any kids. He lived alone, in a small house, in a small village, tucked into the hills on the outskirts of town.

'I just retired', said Gwyn, after stepping inside the shop properly for the first time. He browsed the selection of books, talking in a gentle voice. 'Almost fifty years in the factory.' He took a book from the shelf. A queer history with a lurid cover. 'What's this then?'

Pete breathed a private sigh of relief and chatted to their new customer about books and then about the shop in general. Thankfully, it was going well, or well enough to cover the rent.

Gwyn was now a regular, taking home books about gay history and gay culture, as well as books about trans lives; 'I want to understand it better', he would say and, over time, Pete and Matt looked forward to his Saturday visits, though he'd only enter if it was quiet, walking past if he saw other people inside. As he grew more comfortable, he shared snippets about his life. He'd always known he was gay, but he couldn't tell anyone. It would have been a problem at the factory and he didn't want to embarrass his parents. Now though, with more time on his hands after his retirement, and with the new bookshop supplying him with reading material to better understand his feelings, he was almost ready to come out and maybe, for the first time in his life, go on a date or two. 'It's been a bit of a lonely life really', he said. 'I'm hopeful I'll find a partner one day. I just need to talk to my family and friends first.'

At the end of December 2024, he popped his head around the door to wish Pete and Matt '*Nadolig Llawen*' (a Merry Christmas) and they waved back, wishing him season's greetings. It was the end of their first year, nine months after opening. It hadn't been easy, sales were ticking over, but it was hard work and the quiet months when the students were away had proved difficult. It didn't matter. 'We've gotten used to being a safe space', says Pete. 'People like to come in when we're quiet so they can take a seat in our comfy chair, which we call the "confessional chair" and talk about their lives and share stories. We didn't realise it when we opened, but we're not just a bookshop, we're a space for people seeking refuge.'

If there is a queer booksellers' heaven, Craig Rodwell, Richard Labonté and friends will be smiling to hear that.

The new year came around and the shop reopened, welcoming back some familiar faces, as people took advantage of the January sales. New customers arrived too, having received LGBTQ+ books as Christmas presents, and Pete and Matt were feeling excited at the start of their first full year of trading. 2025 would be the year they'd really put themselves on the map with a list of exciting author visits and events. Then, some desperately sad news.

Gwyn had died at home over Christmas.

'Nothing prepared me for the shock', says Pete. 'I was waiting to see his smile again. I hoped he'd say he got a bit tipsy and told a member of his family about how he felt. Forgive me, I'm getting tearful now, I do this every time I talk about it. It's just so sad, that he was getting ready for his life to begin. He'd lived with a secret for so many years and then, just when he was ready to find a partner ... I can still hear that gentle voice asking nervous questions about which books to read.'

Matt will always remember Gwyn's words: 'It's been a bit of a lonely life really. I'm hopeful I'll find a partner one day.'

How many stories like Gwyn's are hidden amidst the history of queer bookstores? So much of this chronicle talks about 'overcoming' and 'finding space', but for millions of queer people around the world, they have no queer bookstore to go to, or they're too afraid to step inside. For many, affirmation comes too late or not at all. Which is why we have to treasure the shops we have and tell the owners and booksellers what they mean to us.

Pete and Matt attended Gwyn's funeral, concerned that their books had been found in his house. It wasn't mentioned, and Gwyn was remembered fondly by his co-workers from the factory and by his family. Nothing was said about his personal life, no hint that he might have told someone he was gay. But he *was* gay, by his own testimony, and thanks to Pete and Matt, he didn't pass away a stranger, or a secret; he took a risk and found the courage to open his heart to new friends in a tiny bookstore and to learn about other people's lives so he could better understand his own. Thanks to Gayberystwyth Books, he didn't die in the closet. He was an out gay man, appreciated, valued, seen, remembered.

Just as every queer bookstore should be remembered. Because they have changed lives and, in doing so, changed the world.

Queerly Beloved

'The books that the world calls immoral are books that show the world its own shame.'

OSCAR WILDE,
THE PICTURE OF DORIAN GRAY

THIS STORY ISN'T FINISHED; THERE ARE SIMPLY TOO MANY tales of bravery, defiance and liberation to tell in one book. Perhaps it can be updated in future editions or maybe someone will tell the story from a new perspective, maybe from a different part of the world. I hope that amongst these pages, the reader has gained a sense of the people and places that embody this movement to which we owe so many of our freedoms. Bookshops themselves were not rioting at Stonewall, nor marching against Section 28, nor picketing parliaments – they were selling books. But in almost every case, they were places where those actions were seeded, informed, nurtured and planned. 'Information matters', trailblazing journalist and co-founder of *Capital Gay*, Graham McKerrow, says.

> If you tell people what's going on they can respond and *they* can change the world. If you think what's on the shelves of Gay's the Word today, it's a massive amount of information, an incredible number of ideas, hundreds of thousands of hours of thought all in one room. What's gone into those books on the shelves is just astonishing and every page opens up ideas on how we as queer people can lead our lives. You can't build a community without ideas and information, and we couldn't have built ours without gay bookshops.

The spirit of rebellion; the ability to imagine and manifest a better, safer world for new generations; the chance to harvest the opportunities earned by past heroes; all can be traced back to LGBTQ+ bookshops and the people who ran and supported them. Would the rioters at Stonewall have been less combative without the Oscar Wilde Memorial Bookshop? It is speculation, but not a historian's opportunism, to point out that some of those protesting were Craig's customers – not to mention Craig himself – and that keen sense of injustice was fed by the very pamphlets, papers and books they'd encountered in his bookstore in the months leading up to the uprising. Craig was part of the protest and it was he, and the network reaching out from his bookstore, who planned history's first Pride march the following year. It was Gay's the Word that exposed and defeated homophobic censorship within the British establishment and disseminated lifesaving information when the AIDS crisis hit. It was Glad Day and Little Sister's bookshop that fought the Canadian government's ingrained bigotry and withstood violent attacks. It was Silver Moon, A Woman's Place and Sisterwrite that fed feminist activists with the literature and security they so desperately needed in their ongoing fight for equality. It was Giovanni's Room that distributed revolutionary literature to hundreds of bookshops around the world – and some nuns in the Vatican – and supported Joseph Beam with his pioneering anthology of black, gay lives.

Across the decades, queer bookstores have nourished our lives and proved to the wider world that we are a community built on politics, philosophy and beauty, with stories to tell, love and rage to express and bodies to celebrate. Felice Picano, legendary novelist, member of the pioneering Violet Quill collective, publisher in his own right, gave two interviews for this book on his final trip to London in November 2024. 'People have *never* given lesbian and gay bookshops the credit they deserve', he said. 'Their contribution is beyond doubt, because they established writers who were being ignored by the mainstream and they gave a stage to authors who were out of favour, proving against the tide that gay books could sell. Gay publishing and gay bookshops grew up at the same time, and you couldn't have one without the other.'*

Queer bookshop owners and staff know how significant they are – they see it in their everyday interactions with customers – but they don't shout about it. That wouldn't be their style. 'It never occurred to me why there wasn't a book about LGBTQ+ bookselling', says the former owner of A Different Light, Norman Laurila.

> I never thought to ask the writers and publishers whether they wanted to tell our story. I think we were just seen as part of the apparatus for bookselling but now, looking back, it's clear we were much more than that. We were the heart and soul of LGBTQ+ writing. Glad Day, Giovanni's Room, Gay's the Word, together we all created the vibrant community in publishing for the large and small presses. It's true. Without us, the world would be a very different place.

A different place, with very different outcomes for many lives. Mev Miller from the Amazon Bookstore Cooperative in Minneapolis looks back with pride, knowing the difference they made to lesbian lives.

> I mean, there were a lot of different communities that were impacted, I think, by our presence. And I have to say it's one of the few times in my life where I felt a sense of a belonging, of pride, of accomplishment, of like doing socially important

---

* Felice died four months after this interview, in March 2025, and his wisdom is written throughout this book. Thank you, Felice.

work ... I wasn't a retail bookseller. I was a movement builder. And that's how it really felt ... it fit into my whole political, radical sensibility. We were a part of a movement that really did positively impact our culture, our awareness, our livelihood, our sense of self and worth.

For HIV campaigner Marc Thompson, having access to Gay's the Word and Lambda Rising was profound.

Without gay bookshops, all I had was the mainstream. I wouldn't have had that safe space, I wouldn't have been able to get my weekly papers, or look at the noticeboard to see what groups were meeting up. They provided me with the tools I needed for my lifetime of advocacy, and helped me imagine a world we, as the black queer community, could build for ourselves.

The role of queer bookshops as repositories for our collective history is unique in bookselling, with a sense of purpose as crucibles for LGBTQ+ wisdom. 'Our shops saw themselves as a living bibliography on the subject of homosexuality', says the founder of Buchladen Männerschwarm, Joachim Bartholomae. 'We invested a considerable part of our work in maintaining a catalogue [of queer books] that offered a voluntary service to the community.'

Not every queer person has stepped inside a queer bookshop, but their influence has touched all of our lives in myriad ways; how we were educated and the attitudes born of past generations have roots in these often small and jumbled shops, too many of which are lost. For those still open, their legacy is clear. 'We do get older customers thanking the staff', says Graeme from the Bookshop Darlinghurst. 'Just for helping them accept their sexuality, and for giving them hope.'

Chapters could be written on that word 'just'. Rarely do you find a group of people so influential and yet so modest. Former co-director of Gay's the Word, Charles Brown, saw first-hand how queer bookshops changed the way lesbian and gay people saw themselves in the 1980s.

> The fight against Customs was an early example of gays being attacked by the state but fighting back. I think a lot of people got confidence from how stoic and resilient we were, which led to campaign groups which then led to the lowering of the age of consent, and all sorts of advances that came after that. The bookshop is at the root of the notion that if you fought back you could win.

Lynn Alderson looks back on Sisterwrite's legacy with the knowledge she and her lesbian feminist collaborators affected genuine change.

> Without our shop, we wouldn't have had the sense that we had a voice in the world, and that we had a right to that voice. Women were writing, but they needed somewhere to bring it all together and connect them with the movement; without us that outpouring would have been lost. I know for a fact we saved lives.

Away from the anguish of politics and protest, queer bookstores have had a softer influence on countless people across generations, simply by offering their peculiar blend of rapture, familiarity and calm. 'One woman said that a visit to West & Wilde saved her life', says the legendary Edinburgh bookseller and queer advocate, Sigrid Nielsen. 'She said she had been considering suicide because of her situation at home, and by chance found our shop. She never had any idea there could be an LGBT+ bookshop, and her unexpected delight changed her mind about the rest of her life. Maybe it could turn out differently.'

'We did not change the world alone,' says Peter Hedenström of Prinz Eisenherz, 'but we were part of a movement that brought about changes in consciousness as a whole. We can now determine the extent to which we have contributed as a store when people tell us how they dared to visit for the first time and gained a bit of self-confidence.'

This history is unfinished and, we hope, unfinishable. New shops are opening every month around the world, some destined to close soon thereafter, others embarking on a journey that will endure for generations, all of them beacons for queer people alive and yet to be born. Hopefully, the recognition of their contribution will continue to grow, as will the queer community's support for their treasured books and the people who sell them. The threat of extreme politics threatens to make it ever more difficult for new generations to find facts in the fog, sense amidst the screaming, peace amidst war and we should be thankful that there are still places to go where stories and essays are curated by human beings, not radicalising algorithms and subjective influencers. Marc Thompson puts it best.

> Young people have access to a lot more diverse information than I did but I worry about how much of that information is right because there's going to be a lot of *misinformation*. The books and articles and essays I was reading when I was a young man were few and far between, but they'd been filtered, handled with love, care, and due diligence to make it safe for me. Today, some faceless entity is going to tell me what I want to see and who I am.

The calm and care in a queer bookshop are the opposite of what one gets on social media. It is lifegiving, being in a real place amongst people both younger and older than oneself, to sit in silence away from the madness of the outside world and discover notions that might inspire, enrich and challenge, without judgement. We need to support queer bookshops and enable them to grow and expand and open new spaces for us to be together, all generations, all identities, all queer people, as one. Uli Lenart, manager of Gay's the Word, used to think it was his job to influence the bookshop; he now understands it is also there to influence *him*.

> What I didn't expect was the way the shop would nurture me as a person, so it enriched me, my confidence and my awareness, working alongside Jim with his knowledge and sense of history. I wouldn't be who I am today without this bookshop and we have evolved symbiotically. Together, the bookshop and I have become more sure-footed, more together.

We must never forget our collective past, represented in the books we admire, and with brave and brilliant queer booksellers as our guides we'll continue to write our story for many years to come. Since the beginning, queer bookshops have overcome seemingly insurmountable odds – penury, violence, doubt and derision – to change the world, for individuals and for us all. We close with the words of Craig Rodwell, just before his shop moved to Christopher Street in 1973. He'd been told by friends that a 'legitimate' gay bookshop could never fly. They were wrong. Their legitimacy – not their profitability – was their true power. 'While the past 4½ years haven't been financially spectacular for me,' he wrote, 'the personal satisfaction and joy in seeing our people begin to stir and throw off the chains that have bound us for centuries, is reward enough.'

To every queer bookseller past, present and future: thank you.

Fanfare

THIS CHRONICLE HAS TRAVELLED THROUGH TIME TO bookshops around the globe, but there are many still to visit, and the spotlight shone on certain bookstores within these pages should cast no shadow on those omitted. It is the author's sincere wish that this chronicle will provide a starting point for the study of queer bookshops and their ongoing mission to change the world. At the time of writing, these are just some of the queer and queer-supporting bookshops the reader is encouraged to visit.

AUSTRALIA

Hares & Hyenas opened in 1991, Melbourne's queer bookshop and performance space open to all, friendly, informed and with an unmatched history of being super inclusive to all.

AUSTRIA

Buchhandlung Löwenherz opened in June 1993 in Vienna. Owners Jürgen Ostler and Andreas Brunner are Austria's trailblazing gay booksellers. Today, with well over 12,000 titles in stock, the selection is practically overflowing with books for lesbian, gay, bisexual and transgender readers. A must-visit.

CANADA

Glad Day in Toronto opened in 1970 and has moved around a lot since then! Currently searching for its new long-term home, you have to visit the world's oldest queer bookseller.

Little Sister's Book and Art Emporium in Vancouver opened in 1983, named after a vicious cat and proving to have more than nine lives. Go celebrate their nation-defining history with them. Manager Kesian Smart-Abbey says, 'The 2SLGBTQ+ community exists peacefully here. The store is an institution, signalling that queer people are safe and welcome in Vancouver. We want to continue the fight that Jim, Janine, and Bruce went through for us all those years ago and carry that victory forward with us.'

Spartacus Books, also in Vancouver, opened in 1973, beginning life as a book table run by students at Simon Fraser University the previous year. In 2004, after thirty glorious years on Victoria Square, the building burned to the ground, destroying everything. With nothing left, they started from scratch with thousands of donated books. There are many stores yet to be celebrated by this chronicle, but Spartacus, with its explosively wonderful volunteers, is top of the list.

FRANCE

Les Mots à la Bouche opened in 1980, becoming Paris's famed and much-beloved LGBTQ bookstore. With thanks to bookseller Eva, she says they stock a wide range of books, hoping publishers will translate more queer foreign-language literature into French, because the selection can sometimes be limited by language. They work with many independent (and really small) publishers who work specifically around queer subjects with knowledge and passion. 'It's changing', says Eva, 'but it's still too slow.' Hear hear.

Librairie Vigna opened in 2011 in Nice, selling used and new antique books on gay culture and women's history.

GERMANY

Buchhandlung Erlkönig opened in Stuttgart in 1983. Small it may be, but it is a true bastion of carefully curated literature and this shop is a mainstay for the queer community in Stuttgart, still hosting regular events and stocking a general selection of books on LGBT+ topics. The shop also sources antiquarian gems and out-of-print classics.

Prinz Eisenherz was opened in 1978 in Berlin by a collective within the new gay movement. What began as a meeting place and focal point for gay political activists quickly became a specialist bookstore for homosexuality. Now selling books and paraphernalia as well as hosting author events and photography exhibitions, the Prince is a must-visit for anyone seeking to learn about queer history.

ITALY

Libreria Antigone opened in Milan in 2016 and then in Rome in 2022, co-founded by Mauro Muscio, LGBTQ+ activist, owner of Babele queer bookshop in Rome (now closed) and founder of queer publishing house, Asterisco Edizioni. The shops are an intended bridge between queer culture and feminism, selling accessories and sex toys as well as books on gender studies, feminism, art and queer theory.

MEXICO

El Armario Abierto in Mexico City was opened in 1998 by international sexology experts Rinna Riesenfeld and Luis Perelman. The bookstore specialises in books exploring sexuality.

Somos Voces opened in 2009, then named Voces en Tinta, at the summit of Calle de Niza in Mexico City's bohemian Juárez district. The 'Zona Rosa' boasts more than fifty LGBTQ+ venues and trans inclusive Somos Voces stocks novels, short-story collections, theatre, poetry, memoirs, biographies, essays, dictionaries, recipe books, art books, histories, even colouring books, as many titles as can fit arranged beneath the rainbow swags that adorn the ceiling.

THE NETHERLANDS

Boekwinkel Savannah Bay first opened in 1975 in Utrecht as the first women's bookstore in the Netherlands, but has since expanded its audience to men and gender-diverse folk as well as women, specialising in LGBTQ+ literature. Savannah Bay plays an important role in the city's literary scene by regularly organising activities and stalls. It's also home to Pink Point, the leading information centre for LGBTQ+ people in Utrecht.

Vrolijk.nu was launched when the historic Vrolijk bookstore closed its doors on 30 April 2017. In early 2018, Antoine van den Berg, a former employee of Vrolijk, launched a completely new and independent LGBT+ webshop, Vrolijk Boeken & Films. The bookshop and café might be gone – missed by many of its former clientele – but Antoine emails book recommendations and is hopeful he can maintain the community and, possibly, bring the bricks-and-mortar shop back one day.

PORTUGAL

Livraria Aberta opened in Porto in 2021, offering a wide selection of LGBTQ+ titles in a bright and bijou space.

SPAIN

Acció Perifèrica opened in Barcelona in 2022 as a transfeminist cultural hub on the outskirts of Barcelona, providing queer literature, from graphic novels to poetry.

Antinous opened in 1997 in Barcelona, building a reputation as *the* place to go for queer books, paraphernalia and author events.

Berkana is Madrid's pioneering LGTBIQ+ bookstore with a huge catalogue and regular author events, opened in 1993.

A Different Life opened in Madrid in 2020, selling books as gifts and thrilling toys (not for children *cough*).

La Raposa opened in Barcelona in 2017, a women-owned feminist/queer co-operative with a vegan bar and feminist/queer bookshop.

Mary Read opened in 2020 in Madrid, a transfeminist/LGTBQ+ bookshop.

SWEDEN

PAGE 28 opened in Malmö in 2020, 'a sanctuary for the LGTBQ+ people of the world'.

SWITZERLAND

QueerBooks in Bern is a department opened in 2013 within a general bookshop named **Buchhandlung Weyermann**, selling books, films and magazines, revolving around lesbian, gay, bisexual, pansexual, asexual, transgender, intersex, gender-fluid and feminist topics.

UK

The Bookish Type in Leeds is a community bookshop offering queer tours of the city as well as books for all ages.

BookWyrm opened in Durham's indoor market in 2022, owned by husbands Chris and Miles, specialising in LGBTQ+ books as well as books by small authors and independent presses.

Category Is Books in Glasgow is run by 'trans wusbands' Bug and Fin, who channel their upbringing under Section 28 to promote queer history and culture.

Clock Tower Books in Hay-on-Wye is owned by renowned bookseller Dale Headington, offering general pre-owned literature, also specialising in books with an LGBTQ+ sensibility, not to mention luxury gifts.

The Common Press in London celebrates writing by queer people and people of colour, the first in the UK to platform intersectionality as a core focus. With comfy chairs for reading and an impressive range of titles with a taste for activism, equality and global awareness, they're working to give the capital a permanent space for queer people from under-represented backgrounds.

Dial Lane Books in Ipswich is owned by Andrew Marsh and run alongside his trusty sidekick Karen 'Jonesy' Jones. Hidden down a magical snicket off the high street, they offer general fiction with a curated selection of queer titles.

Five Leaves Bookshop is a radical/general bookshop in Nottingham which opened late October 2013. Owner Ross Bradshaw is also publisher at Five Leaves Publications and worked at Mushroom, a radical bookshop in Nottingham which first opened in the 70s but closed in 2000.

Gayberystwyth was a small but perfectly formed queer bookshop in Aberystwyth Market Hall, but Pete and Matt decided to close in early 2026. Check out their socials to see where they're popping up now.

Gay-on-Wye can be found in the UK's no. 1 'booktown', Hay-on-Wye. Owner Tom Owen curates a hugely popular self-built bookshop packed with a large selection of queer titles, while assisting other queer bookshops with donated stock and business support. His shop also includes pre-owned LGBTQ+ titles curated by fellow Hay bookseller, Dale Headington. Tom is the queer bookshop oracle, compiling the Wikipedia list of the world's queer bookshops.

Gay Pride Shop opened in Manchester's Northern Quarter in 2014, the UK's biggest LGBTQ shop selling books as well as accessories and well … everything under the rainbow.

Gay's the Word opened in 1979, London's iconic LGBT bookshop, a place of pilgrimage for queer people the world over. An inclusive and historic must-visit for books, events, activism and Pride history.

Juno Books is an intersectional feminist and queer community bookshop run by co-owners Rosie and Sarah in Sheffield. First opened in October 2022, they support greater representation of women and marginalised voices.

Lavender Menace in Edinburgh first opened in 1982, and after changing its name to West & Wilde and then sadly closing, it now operates as a reference library and archive.

Lighthouse bookshop in Edinburgh opened in 2017, establishing itself as an 'eclectic, slightly eccentric' queer-owned destination for LGBTQ+ books, offering an antiracist, feminist community space.

News from Nowhere in Liverpool has been run by a women workers' co-operative since 1974. One of the UK's pioneering radical bookshops, they continue to offer a range of books for queer readers.

North Books in Hay-on-Wye champions women's fiction and under-represented voices as well as regular events and launches thanks to owner Jules and her friendly team in a wonderfully warm and inviting shop.

Paned o Gê is an online bookshop opened in 2020 with space in the Queer Emporium in Cardiff. It's a social enterprise designed to highlight, promote and celebrate LGBTQ+ talent and creators.

Paperxclips in Belfast is more than just a queer bookshop for all ages and identities. Co-founder Fern is trained as a hairdresser, so they run a pop-up salon, offering haircuts for trans and gender nonconforming people. Fern and Ren also have a background in support services, so they offer informal support and a friendly welcome to all queer people and their families who are invited to visit for information.

The Portal Bookshop in York is truly a portal to another world, specialising in science fiction and fantasy alongside every type of LGBTQIA book they can squash into their bright and welcoming shop.

Proud Geek run by Tom Buckle takes the concept of the queer bookstore and brings it faithfully to life online. He sells books from home, making sure they're up to standard, and he's digitised the hallowed gay bookshop noticeboard, signposting to everything from gender-neutral hairdressers to sports clubs and neurodivergence in queer fiction.

Queer Lit in Manchester boasts a truly extraordinary range of queer titles, and is the largest LGBTQ+ bookshop in Europe, hosting regular events while supporting schools with free LGBTQ+ books.

Shelf Life in Cardiff is run by former chain store bookseller Rosie, whose cosy shop drew on the grand tradition of queer bookselling by starting life as a pop-up before gaining a bricks-and-mortar home. That shop is now closed, but it continues to sell online and via social media.

Wave of Nostalgia in the heart of historic Haworth is set amidst some rich Brontë heritage, but owner Diane has made her bookshop a destination for booklovers of all sensibilities, championing feminist and queer fiction, plus hosting regular author events.

US

Always Here Books in Portland, Oregon is run by avid readers Rafael and John. It's a queer and neurodivergent-owned bookstore that carries queer books for all ages.

BookWoman opened in Austin, Texas in 1977; the 'oldest, queerest, feminist-est' bookstore in Texas also hosts events and is trans-inclusive.

Charis Books & More in Decatur, Georgia opened in 1974; a feminist bookstore, also selling LGBTQ+ titles, plus cards and more.

Charlie's Queer Books in Seattle is a Hanna-Barbera-style triumph of pink and purple with a tonne of events. The store is beloved as a warm and friendly space where staff know their stuff and have fun sharing their passion for books with customers of all sorts and intersectionalities.

Common Ground Books in Tallahassee, Florida is a friendly neighbourhood bookstore, specialising in LGBTQ+ and radical titles. They also act as a focal point for activism, hosting rallies against book bans and general censorship.

Fabulosa Books in San Francisco's legendary queer Castro district first opened as Dog Eared Books in 1992, changing its name in 2021. They stock bestsellers and 'rare delights you never knew you'd love', with an emphasis on LGBTQ+ titles.

Firestorm Books & Coffee opened in 2008 in Asheville, North Carolina, an anti-authority queer, feminist collective maintaining a welcoming, sober and anti-oppressive space.

Frenchmen Art and Books opened in 1978 as Faubourg Marigny Art and Books in New Orleans, Louisiana. Still going strong in its historic location, the store hosts events and sells a broad range of new and used titles.

Hive Mind Books & Coffee Shop in Bushwick, Brooklyn offers seating for those wishing to watch the world go by and/or enjoy some writing or reading. It offers queer, including trans, books, new and used.

The Lavender Bookshop in Marietta, Georgia opened in 2024, specialising in queer stories and welcoming all readers for books and events.

The Legendarium in Salt Lake City is a trans-owned and -run science fiction and horror bookstore offering 'a safe space for all identities and imaginations'.

Little District Books in the Capitol Hill neighbourhood of Washington, DC opened in 2022. This queer-owned and -operated store celebrates LGBTQ+ authors and stories.

The Little Gay Shop opened in Austin, Texas in 2019, an 'unapologetically queer marketplace and community organizer in the heart of Texas that amplifies the voices and artistry of queer creatives from around the world.'

Philly AIDS Thrift @ Giovanni's Room in Philadelphia originally opened in 1973 and is an essential pilgrimage for anyone passionate about queer books and bookselling. No other location in the United States represents such a rich history.

A Room of One's Own in Madison, Wisconsin opened in 1975, offering an LGBTQ fiction and non-fiction section.

Unabridged Bookstore opened in Chicago, Illinois in 1980 and is still flourishing, with its famous A-board outside adorned with quotes of the day and of course a wide array of queer books.

Under the Umbrella, also in Salt Lake City, Utah, opened in 2021 and prioritises the stories of under-represented people within the queer community, channelling the Sylvia Rivera quote, 'There's no pride for some of us without liberation for all of us.'

Violet Valley in Water Valley, Mississippi is a destination for queer people from far and wide. Go visit Jaime and request an informal tour from one of the friendliest and most knowledgeable booksellers in the United States, heck, the world. The history of the shop itself is fascinating – it used to be an alleyway, you know – catch a crappie fish and make a pilgrimage to the Hubert Creekmore sign nearby.

Acknowledgements

MY THANKS TO DALE HEADINGTON AND STANTON Stephens for their friendship and wisdom. To my husband Nicholas Robinson for his quiet support, Victoria Hyde for being patient and funny and William Hollinshead for the sea and the swimming. To my mother for turning me gay.

To Ed Hermance of Giovanni's Room, still the queer bookselling wizard, this chronicle could not have been written without you. No less, Jim MacSweeney of Gay's the Word, who has shown such warmth and generosity during the writing of this book, as has Uli Lenart, all power to you. Thank you Tom Owen of Gay-on-Wye, you are the true embodiment of queer bookselling. Jane Cholmeley, thank you for taking the time to share your knowledge with me and for your faith in this project. Lynn Alderson, you suffered an earnest fool with great kindness. So too Graeme Aitken, Charles Gregory, Charles Brown, Piet van der Waal, Sigrid Nilsen, Deacon Maccubbin, Joachim Bartholomae, Norman Laurila, Tommi Avicolli Mecca, Colin Clews, Reggie Blennerhassett, Ray Aller, Pete Shea, Fern, Tom Buckle, Dominique Johnson, Mev Miller, Dr Jamie Harker, Marc Thompson, Peter Parker, Lesley Jones, Janet Jones – friend and champion of the late, great Amanda Russell – and so many more.

My thanks to Sarah Waters, to whom I owe a great deal as a novelist and now, also, as an author of non-fiction. Thanks to Christopher Stephens for his nobility and munificence. To Jake Arnott for his contribution to the early draft and encouragement at the beginning of this voluminous project. My thanks to Adrian

Hindle-Briscall for his previously untapped memories of Pip. Marius Kociejowski for his candid and generous correspondence; I shall treasure our spat. Tim D'Arch Smith for his recollections of Cecil Court, vast knowledge as one of London's very first openly gay booksellers and cups of tea. Likewise, Tim Bryars and Angus O'Neill, antiquarian book dealers of renown, for their advice, maps, tips, introductions, editorial nudging and, most of all, wine.

Publishers and journalists David Fernbach, co-founder of Gay Men's Press, Sasha Alyson, founder of Alyson Publications, Leigh Davidson, former managing editor of Down There Press, and Graham McKerrow, journalist and co-founder of *Capital Gay*, we owe you more than words can express but also... words!

For their guidance, friendship and expertise, Dr Claire O'Callaghan, literary scholar and cultural historian; Peppermint, activist, broadcaster and performer; Vanessa Heron, Michael Seeney, Simon Wilson, Devon Cox, esteemed experts on Oscar Wilde; fellow queer author Layla McCay; translator Luis Alberto Ramirez Garcia. My thanks to all.

To Andrew Roff, who can claim credit for this chronicle's original concept and for engaging the author, and to David Headley, who set me on this adventure.

To my copyeditor Kathleen McCully and head of production at Oneworld, Paul Nash, you have done a brilliant job, thank you. Finally, my heartfelt gratitude to my editor, Cecilia Stein. Great editors are much like queer bookshops. Elevating, determined, often unsung and deftly persuasive. You have made this book sing.